BUILDING
EFFECTIVE
DECISION
SUPPORT
SYSTEMS

BUILDING EFFECTIVE DECISION SUPPORT SYSTEMS

Ralph H. Sprague, Jr.
University of Hawaii

Eric D. Carlson
IBM Research Laboratory, San Jose

PRENTICE-HALL, INC., *Englewood Cliffs, New Jersey 07632*

Library of Congress Cataloging in Publication Data

Sprague, Ralph H.
  Building effective decision support systems.

  Includes bibliographies and index.   ·
    1. Decision-making—Data processing.   2. Management
information systems.   I. Carlson, Eric D.   II. Title.
III. Title: Decision support systems.
HD30.23.S7   658.4′03′02854   81-20963
ISBN 0-13-086215-0   AACR2

Editorial/production supervision by Margaret Rizzi
Manufacturing buyer: Ed O'Dougherty

Printed in the United States of America

10   9   8   7   6

ISBN 0-13-086215-0

Prentice-Hall International, Inc., *London*
Prentice-Hall of Australia Pty. Limited, *Sydney*
Prentice-Hall of Canada, Ltd., *Toronto*
Prentice-Hall of India Private Limited, *New Delhi*
Prentice-Hall of Japan, Inc., *Tokyo*
Prentice-Hall of Southeast Asia Pte. Ltd., *Singapore*
Whitehall Books Limited, *Wellington, New Zealand*

CONTENTS

WHAT IS AVAILABLE?

*Specific DSS   /   DSS
Generators   /   DSS Tools*

WHAT IS IN THE FUTURE?

*Organizational Change   /   Technology
Change   /   Decision Change*

CONCLUSION

QUESTIONS AND PROBLEMS

*Review Questions   /   Discussion
Questions   /   Exercises*

PREFACE

Personal computers, computer networks, large data bases, color graphics and computer-based models are among the technological developments which are stimulating interest in the use of computers to support decision making. Such uses are being called *Decision Support Systems* (DSS). DSS differ from the traditional recordkeeping and transaction processing uses of computers primarily because they require a symbiosis between the users (i.e., the problem solvers and decision makers) and the system in order to be effective. For this symbiosis to occur, the decision maker must understand what the DSS can do, and systems developers must understand how to integrate the DSS technologies into the decision making process. The interests of both the potential users and developers of DSS in acquiring this understanding is evidenced by the increasing number of journal articles, professional development seminars, academic courses, conference sessions, and working groups on the topic of DSS.

Responding to the increased interest in DSS, a few textbooks have appeared. These books focus on describing DSS, either from a general organizational point-of-view or by way of case studies. In addition, a number of computer science and business administration texts deal with topics relevant to DSS. In contrast to the descriptive texts on DSS and the texts on related topics, this book focuses on *how to develop a DSS*. The book describes how DSS development differs from developing traditional computer-based systems, and describes the steps and components necessary to develop effective DSS. The book therefore is intended for those who are, or may need to be, involved in developing a DSS, whether from the perspective of a user, an analyst, an implementor, or an information systems manager.

The Intended Readers

This book is written with two "classes" of readers in mind. One class consists of potential DSS users. These readers are assumed to be familiar with decision-making processes and existing decision support techniques, such as operations research or financial analysis. The book does not attempt to instruct these readers on how to make decisions or to describe new decision making processes or models. For these readers we provide guidelines on how DSS can be used, on the users' roles in developing DSS, and how and what they should communicate to those that are building the DSS. The second class of reader for whom we intend this book is the analysts or technicians who need to build a DSS. We assume that these readers are familiar with computer software and hardware. For the technical reader we explain how technical knowledge and skills should be applied to build usable, effective DSS.

The Use of the Book

We expect the book to be useful both for the practicing professional and for the student in a professional degree program (e.g., business administration, industrial management, data processing). For the practicing professional, the book can be used as a guide for participating in or managing a DSS project, or it can serve as a practical reference or self introduction to the topic of DSS. The book also could be used for professional development seminars and other "technical vitality" courses.

As a text, the book is organized to be used in courses on DSS. It is expected that these courses will replace or augment existing courses on MIS in the next five years. Because it covers the development process and the major components for DSS, the book provides a framework for course organization and for supplemental readings on topics related to DSS (e.g., decision making or computerized data bases). Thus the book can be used whether the course is focused on DSS applications or DSS implementations. The book provides knowledge on how to use fundamental techniques and technologies to develop DSS. It is therefore not a "basic" text but an "applied" text, for use in professional masters degree programs (e.g., MBA) or upper level undergraduate courses in business administration or data processing. The book will be particularly useful in courses which include class projects or "hands-on" exercises. The book also could serve as a supplemental text in traditional MIS courses, because it covers a set of material usually included in such courses by journal reprints or selected readings from other texts.

The Format and Contents

The book, divided into four major parts, describes the framework, processes, and technical components for building DSS, and illustrates each with substantive and real case examples. Part One is a *conceptual framework* which has proven helpful in organizing the evolving "field" of DSS. Part Two deals with the *processes* of building a DSS capability in an organization in terms of the activities that will be required and the issues (technical and organizational) that must be dealt with. These first two parts should be read by anyone who will participate in the development of DSS in any role.

Part Three deals with the *technology components* of DSS and is aimed at the systems analyst who will work directly with the hardware and software to develop the DSS capability. It assumes computer familiarity but not necessarily extensive programming skills or experience. The final chapter constitutes Part Four. It contains a summary of the framework, process, and technology components for building effective DSS. We also suggest a set of criteria for the technology to support DSS development, and indicate where we think significant progress will be needed in the near future.

We have attempted to make the book specific through the use of examples, both within the text and in case illustrations at the end of the chapters. To illustrate technical concepts we use GADS (the Geodata Analysis and Display System), developed as a research vehicle at the IBM San Jose Research Laboratory from 1970–1976. We have chosen to use GADS because we have personal knowledge of its history and content, because many details of the GADS experience are available in the open literature, and because it was developed specifically to explore the technology required to support the DSS philosophy. It is also an "objective" example because it is not a product or service of any vendor in the marketplace.

To illustrate the organizational issues and concepts, we have developed the Pacific Diversified Industries, Inc., case which is a composite of several real companies with which the authors have dealt. We have used different aspects of the GADS and PDI cases throughout the book in order to provide a comprehensive and cohesive context to integrate different topics in the book.

At the end of each chapter are three types of questions and exercises. A set of review questions enables the reader to assess comprehension of the key principles, topics and issues in the chapter. Discussion questions deal with one or two issues on which there is probably a legitimate difference of opinion; they serve to focus discussion on the issues when the book is used in a seminar or classroom setting. The exercises provide an opportunity for the reader to internalize some of the concepts and processes by putting them into practice on a small scale. Taken as a whole, the result is a structured guide to the procedures and key issues in building of DSS, reinforced by a set of integrated examples and exercises.

How the Book Came About

The authors first discussed the need for a book of this type while both were working at the IBM San Jose Research Laboratory in 1978. A major project on DSS had just been completed in the Laboratory. Because of the widespread interest in DSS but the apparent difficulty in developing these systems, we had investigated tools and techniques that could be used to develop effective DSS. Over the next two years, the authors independently pursued further research on DSS, some of it technical (better software architecture for dialog handling), some empirical (a survey of 150 organizations to discover DSS efforts) and some conceptual (a series of interviews and lectures on DSS and its relationships to other information systems activity).

In late 1980, many of these threads began to merge and gel. It became apparent that the technical developments, the information needs of managers and professionals, the organizational mechanisms, and marketplace products and services, were converging to create a viable environment for the development of effective DSS. This book is our attempt to articulate these trends and forces in an integrated way, and to provide guidelines and principles for building DSS.

In mid-1981 we actually began writing the book. With the DSS field developing so rapidly, it was important to develop a process for production of the book in time for its contents to have an impact on the field. In a case of "practice what you preach," we sought a way to apply technology to speed the production process. Through the hard work and expertise of the editorial and production staff at Prentice-Hall, the manuscript was prepared initially on a word processing system and the machine-readable tape was used as direct input to a typesetting machine or compositor. The resulting six-month production time is a credit to all those who made it work, especially Margaret Rizzi and David Hetherington who went beyond the usual call of duty to produce a high quality book under great time pressure.

Acknowledgments

Although the authors are solely responsible for the contents of this book, it represents a synthesis of ideas and experiences of many others. Many of the ideas in this book were developed as direct results of the GADS and DSS projects at the IBM San Jose Research Laboratory. Over 20 researchers participated at one time or another in this work. In addition, over 200 users from IBM and other organizations (primarily the County of Santa Clara, the City of San Jose, and several school districts) participated in studies of GADS use. We thank all of these people who directly or indirectly contributed to the book. We would particularly like to thank John Bennett, Gary Giddings, Barbara Grace, Jean-Paul Jacob, Jimmy Sutton, and Steve Zilles whose research contributed greatly to the book, and to thank Pat Mantey for his managerial support of the DSS research at IBM. Much of the insight into the organizational issues and processes of building DSS came from creative people on the firing line of DSS development who were willing to share their thoughts and experiences with the authors. Special thanks go to Robert Vierck, Frank Trevor, John Skelly, and Jim Todt of Dillingham Corporation, Laurance Burden of Northwest Industries, Richard Klaas of American Airlines, and Jim Scott of Procter and Gamble. For support in the form of hardware and software for illustration and comparison, we also thank Dr. G. R. Wagner of Execucom Systems, Park Thoreson and Ron Koval of Boeing Computer Services, and Alan Paty of TYMSHARE.

Once again our thanks to the editorial and production team at Prentice-Hall and to our "friendly neighborhood PH representative," Joe Murray, whose cheerful and gentle nudging launched us on the project. Special thanks goes to Gail Masaki and Karen Martin at the University of Hawaii College of Business who courageously bore the responsibility for typing the manuscript.

Both the College of Business at the University of Hawaii and the IBM Research Division provided time and some production support for the book, for which we are grateful. However, the views expressed herein are ours and not those of the University of Hawaii or the IBM Research Division.

Ralph H. Sprague, Jr.

Eric D. Carlson

ACKNOWLEDGMENTS

Portions of the material in this book were previously published elsewhere, and have been used by the permission of the original publishers. They are listed and acknowledged as follows:

1. The majority of the text for Chapters 1 and 2 have been reprinted by special permission from the *MIS Quarterly*, from "A Framework for the Development of Decision Support Systems," by Ralph H. Sprague, Jr., in Volume 4, Number 4, published December 1980. Copyright 1980 by the Society for Management Information Systems and the Management Information Systems Research Center.

2. The decision-making scenario in the GADS Case Example of Chapter 2 was taken from J. A. Sutton, "Evaluation of a Decision Support System: A Case Study with the Office Products Division of IBM," IBM Research Report RJ2214, IBM Research Laboratory, San Jose, California, 1978.

3. The majority of Chapter 4 was adapted from Eric D. Carlson, "An Approach for Designing Decision Support Systems," *Proceedings, Eleventh Hawaii International Conference on System Sciences*, Western Periodicals, North Hollywood, California, 1978.

4. The section on evaluation in Chapter 6 was adapted from Eric D. Carlson, "Evaluating the Impact of Information Systems," *Management Informatics*, Volume 3, Number 2, Norddhoff International Publishers, Leyden, Netherlands, 1974, pp. 57–67.

5. The GADS cost-benefit analysis in the Case Example of Chapter 6 as taken from J. A. Sutton, "Evaluation of a Decision Support System: A Case Study with the Office Products Division of IBM," IBM Research Report RJ2214, IBM Research Laboratory, San Jose, California, 1978.

6. Chapter 7 was adapted and extended from Eric D. Carlson, "Developing the User Interface for Decision Support Systems," IBM Research Report RJ3112, IBM Research Laboratory, San Jose, California, April 1981.

7. The example in Chapter 9 of the modeling system for a commercial bank was taken from R. H. Sprague and H. Watson, "A Decision Support System for Banks," *Omega — The International Journal of Management Science*, Volume 4, Number 6, 1976, pp. 657–71.

BUILDING
EFFECTIVE
DECISION
SUPPORT
SYSTEMS

PART ONE
THE FRAMEWORK FOR BUILDING DSS

Part One of the book presents the first prerequisite for building DSS in an organization over a period of time. It is a conceptual framework to act as a communication mechanism for all the people who must work together in building DSS. Interest in DSS, and the development of early systems, have evolved from a variety of sources. Each source of heritage contributed a separate set of terms, definitions, and perspectives to the DSS movement. The purpose of Part One is to suggest a common framework and a set of terms on which DSS development efforts can be based.

Nearly all the ideas, concepts, and approaches contained in the entire book are included in the two chapters of Part One. Subsequent chapters in the book extend, expand, and expound on these ideas. We do not claim to possess the absolute truth, or an ultimate theory of DSS. Obviously, there is no such thing with a field evolving as rapidly as this one. Neither are these ideas merely the personal opinions of the authors or a miscellaneous assortment of thoughts from our previous work. They have resulted from a careful synthesis of the "threads" mentioned above, some dating from as early as 1970, extensively field tested in discussions and presentations with users, managers, systems analysts, toolsmiths and vendors over the past two years. This process generated several insights on the levels of technology, the types of DSS, the different roles of persons involved in DSS, the different tools/techniques for building DSS, and how the components of DSS fit together.

As the basis for integrating DSS development efforts, Part One should be read by all those who will participate in that effort.

CHAPTER ONE

AN INTRODUCTION TO DSS

OUTLINE

INTRODUCTION

We seem to be on the verge of another "era" in the relentless advancement of computer-based information systems in organizations. Designated by the term *decision support systems* (DSS), these systems are receiving reactions ranging from "a major breakthrough" to "just another buzz word."

One view is that the natural evolutionary advancement of information technology and its use in the organizational context has led from electronic data processing (EDP) to management information systems (MIS) to the current DSS thrust. In this view, DSS pick up where MIS leave off. An alternative view portrays DSS as an important subset of what MIS have been and will continue to be. Still another view recognizes a type of system that has been developing for several years and "now we have a name for it." Meanwhile, the skeptics suspect that DSS is just another buzz word to justify the next round of visits from the vendors.

The purpose of this chapter is to briefly examine these alternative views of DSS and present a framework that has proven valuable in reconciling them. The framework articulates and integrates major concerns of several "stakeholders" in the development of DSS: executives and professionals who use them, the MIS managers who manage the process of developing and installing them, the information specialists who build and develop them, the system designers who create and assemble the technology on which they are based, and the researchers who study the DSS subjects and process. It also serves as the superstructure on which the remainder of the book is built.

Definition, Examples, and Characteristics

The concepts involved in DSS were first articulated in the early 1970's by Michael S. Scott Morton under the term "management decision systems" [9]. A few firms and a few scholars began to develop and research DSS, which became characterized as *interactive* computer-based systems that *help* decision makers utilize *data* and *models* to solve *unstructured* problems. The unique contribution of DSS resulted from the key italicized words. That definition proved sufficiently restrictive that few actual systems completely satisfied it. Recently extended by some authors to include any system that makes some contribution to decision making, the term can be applied to all but transaction processing. A serious definitional problem is that the words have a certain "intuitive validity." Any system that supports a decision (in any way) is a decision support system—obviously!

Unfortunately, neither the restrictive nor the broad definition helps much, because neither provides guidance for understanding the value, the technical requirements, or the approach for developing DSS. A complicating factor is that people from different backgrounds and contexts view DSS quite differently. For example, a manager and a computer scientist seldom see things in the same light. The model we develop later recognizes this divergence of perspectives, and utilizes it to suggest alternative ways to organize our thinking about DSS.

Another way to get a feeling for a complex subject like DSS is to examine some examples. Consider a few specific systems that were a part of the early days of the DSS "movement."

1. Getty Oil developed a Plan Analysis and Modeling System (PAMS) for use in supporting capital investment decision making. It allowed managers to interrogate and analyze historical data with an English-like language, displaying the result in tabular or graphic form. The system also provided access to a large repertoire of financial routines and models for generating future plans which were analyzed and displayed to aid in the decision-making process [4].

2. American Airlines developed An Analytical Information Management System (AAIMS) to support planning, finance, marketing, and operating functions. The system manages a large amount of historical data on the entire airline industry, and provides managers with the ability to interactively access, analyze, compute, and display historical and future data. AAIMS is used to facilitate studies and forecasts of load factors, market share, aircraft utilization, productivity measurement, and revenue/yield, among others [8].

3. A large paper company developed an interactive CRT-based system for capacity planning and production scheduling. It is used almost exclusively by the chief analyst for the vice-president of production to create and evaluate alternative plans and schedules for all production facilities nationwide. It draws on detailed historical data and utilizes forecasting and scheduling models to simulate overall performance under a variety of planning assumptions.

4. Northwest Industries modified and interfaced a data query language and a modeling language to create an Executive Data Base System. It is used by financial analysts, corporate development staff, and top management to interrogate, analyze, and evaluate the performance of the conglomerate's many operating divisions.

The examples above are just a few of the systems for decision support that have begun to spring up in the literature. Evidence suggests that many firms are moving to develop systems such as these which have as their main focus the support of managerial decision making. In a 1976 survey, 12 percent of the responding organizations reported the use of advanced systems which could be characterized as decision support systems [12]. A 1977 conference in California devoted to the presentation of implemented DSS drew an audience of over 200 to discuss 11 existing systems [3]. Alter examined 56 systems that might have some claim to the DSS label, and used this sample to develop a set of abstractions describing their characteristics [1]. More recently, Keen identified several examples of what he feels are DSS and compared their characteristics [7]. The First International Conference on Decision Support Systems in June 1981 drew 300 users, developers, researchers, and vendors to assess the nature and potential of DSS [13].

The "characteristics" approach seems to hold more promise for an understanding of DSS and their potential than either definitions or collections of examples. More specifically, a decision support system may be defined by its capabilities in several critical areas, capabilities which are required to accomplish the objectives that DSS are designed to accomplish. Observed characteristics of DSS which have evolved from the work of Alter, Keen, and others include the following:

- They tend to be aimed at the less well structured, underspecified problems that upper-level managers typically face.
- They attempt to combine the use of models or analytic techniques with traditional data access and retrieval functions.
- They specifically focus on features that make them easy to use by noncomputer people in an interactive mode.
- They emphasize flexibility and adaptability to accommodate changes in the environment and decision-making approach of the user.

A serious question remains. Are the definitions, examples, and characteristics of DSS sufficiently different to justify the use of a new term? Do DSS herald the arrival of a new era in information systems for organizations? Or are the skeptics right? Is DSS just another buzz word to replace the fading appeal of MIS?

DSS versus MIS

Much of the difficulty and controversy with terms such as DSS and MIS can be traced to the difference between an academic or theoretical definition and a "connotational" definition. The former is carefully articulated by people who write textbooks and articles in respectable journals. The latter evolves from what actually is developed and used in practice, and is heavily influenced by the personal experiences that the user of the term has had with the subject. It is the *connotational* definition of EDP–MIS–DSS that is used in justifying the assertion that DSS is an evolutionary advancement beyond MIS.

The Connotational View.   This view can be articulated using Figure 1-1, a simple organizational chart, as a model of an organization. EDP was first applied to the lower operational levels of the organization to automate the paperwork. Its basic characteristics include:

- A focus on data, storage, processing, and flows at the operational level
- Efficient transaction processing
- Scheduled and optimized computer runs
- Integrated files for related jobs
- Summary reports for management

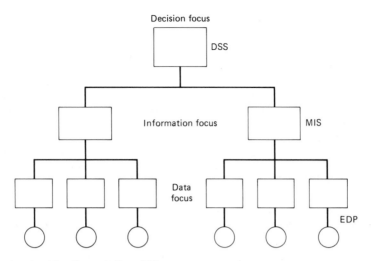

FIGURE 1-1   The Connotational View

In recent years, increased hardware capacity and speed, on-line operating systems, enhanced data communication options, and powerful terminals have made the EDP level of activity in many firms a well-oiled and efficient production facility for transactions processing.

The MIS approach elevated the focus of information systems activities, with additional emphasis on integration and planning of the information systems function. In *practice*, the characteristics of MIS include:

- An information focus, aimed at middle managers
- Structured information flows
- Integration of EDP jobs by business function (production MIS, marketing MIS, personnel MIS, etc.)
- Inquiry and report generation (usually with a data base)

The MIS era contributed a new level of information to serve management needs, but was still very much oriented to, and built upon, information flows and data files.

According to this connotational view, DSS are focused still higher in the organization, with an emphasis on the following characteristics:

- Decision focused, aimed at top managers and executive decision makers
- Emphasis on flexibility, adaptability, and quick response
- User initiated and controlled
- Support for the personal decision-making styles of individual managers

This connotational and evolutionary view has some credence because it corresponds roughly to developments in practice over the past few years. It has some serious deficiencies, however, and is definitely misleading in the future development of DSS.

- It implies that decision support is needed only at the top levels. In fact, decision support is required at all levels of management in the organization.
- The decision making which occurs at several levels must often be coordinated. Therefore, an important dimension of decision support is the communication and coordination between decision makers across organizational levels as well as at the same level.
- It implies that decision support is the only thing that top managers need from the information system. In fact, decision making is only one of the activities of managers that benefit from information systems support.

There is also the problem that many information systems professionals are not willing to accept the narrow connotational view of the term MIS. To us, MIS refers to the entire set of systems and activities required to manage, process, and use information as a resource in the organization.

The Theoretical View. To consider the appropriate role of DSS in this overall context of information systems, let us characterize the broad charter and objectives of the information systems function in the organization as:

Dedicated to improving the performance of knowledge workers in organizations through the application of information technology.

1. *Improving performance* is the ultimate objective of information systems—not the storage of data, the production of reports, or even "getting the right information to the right person at the right time." The ultimate objective must be viewed in terms of the ability of information systems to support the improved performance of people in organizations.
2. *Knowledge workers* are the clientele. This group includes managers, professionals, staff analysts, and clerical workers, whose primary job responsibility is the handling of information in some form.
3. *Organizations* are the context. The focus is on information handling in goal-seeking organizations of all kinds.
4. The *application of information technology* is the challenge and opportunity facing the information systems professional for the purposes and in the contexts given above.

A triangle was used by Robert Head in the late 1960's as a visual model to characterize MIS in this broad comprehensive sense [5]. It has become a classic way to view the dimensions of an information system. The vertical dimension represented the levels of management and the horizontal dimension represented the main functional areas of the business organization. Later authors added transactional processing as a base on which the entire system rested. The result was a two-dimensional model of a management information system in the broad sense—as the total of all activities that

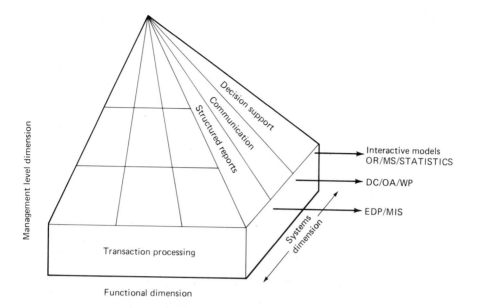

FIGURE 1-2   The Theoretical View

comprise the information system in an organization. Figure 1-2 is a further extension of the basic triangle to help conceptualize the potential role of DSS. The depth dimension shows the major technology "subsystems" which provide support for the activities of managers and other knowledge workers.

Three major thrusts are shown here, but there could be more. The structured reporting system includes the reports required for the management and control of the organization, and for satisfying the information needs of external parties. It has been evolving from efforts in EDP and MIS (in the narrow sense) for several years. Systems to support the communication needs of the organization are evolving rapidly from advances in telecommunications with a strong impetus from office automation and word processing. The DSS concept seems to be evolving from the coalescence of information technology and operations research/management science approaches in the form of interactive modeling.

To summarize this introductory section, DSS represent not merely an evolutionary advancement of EDP and MIS, and certainly will not replace either. Nor are they merely a type of information system aimed exclusively at top management, where other information systems seem to have failed. Rather, DSS comprise a class of information system that draws on transaction processing systems and interacts with the other parts of the overall information system to support the decision-making activities of managers and other knowledge workers in organizations. There are, however, some subtle but significant differences between DSS and traditional EDP or so-called MIS approaches. Moreover, these systems require a new combination of information systems technology to satisfy a set of heretofore unmet needs. It is now becoming clearer how these technologies fit together, which important problems need to be solved, and what steps are required for the development of DSS. Indeed, that is what this book is all about. It is also becoming apparent that DSS have the potential to become another powerful weapon in the arsenal of the information systems professional to help improve the effectiveness of the people in organizations.

THE FRAMEWORK

The remainder of this chapter sets the stage for exploring these technologies, problems, and steps in subsequent chapters. The mechanism for this exploration is another of the oft-maligned but repeatedly used "frameworks."

A framework, in the absence of theory, is helpful in organizing a complex subject, identifying the relationships between the parts, and revealing the areas in which further developments will be required. The framework presented here has evolved over the past two years in discussions with many different groups of people.* In this chapter we consider (1) three levels of technology, all of which have been designated DSS (with considerable confusion), (2) the development approach that is evolving for the creation of DSS, and (3) the roles of several key types of people in the building and use of DSS.

Three Technology Levels

It is helpful to identify three levels of hardware/software which have been included in the label DSS. They are used by people with different levels of technical capability, and vary in the nature and scope of task to which they can be applied.

Specific DSS.   Systems that actually accomplish the work might be called *Specific DSS*. These involve an information systems "application," but with characteristics that are significantly different from those of a typical data processing application. Specific DSS are the hardware/software that allow a specific decision maker or group of them to deal with specific sets of related problems. An early example is a portfolio management system

*This chapter grew out of the workshop on DSS at the 1979 Annual Meeting of SMIS in Minneapolis [11]. Portions of the material were subsequently published as an article in the *MIS Quarterly* (December 1980).

described, together with several other examples, in the first major DSS book, by Keen and Scott Morton [6]. Another example is a police-beat allocation system used on an experimental basis by the city of San Jose, California. This system allowed a police officer to display a map outline and call up data by geographical zone, showing police calls for service, activity levels, service time, and so on. The interactive graphic capability of the system enabled the officer to manipulate the maps, zones, and data to try a variety of police-beat alternatives quickly and easily. In effect, the system provided tools to *amplify* the officer's judgment. Incidentally, a later experiment attempted to apply a traditional linear programming model to the problem; the solution was less satisfactory than the one designed by the police officer.

DSS Generators. The second technology level might be called a *DSS Generator.* This is a "package" of related hardware and software which provides a set of capabilities to build specific DSS quickly and easily. For example, the police beat system described above was built from the Geodata Analysis and Display System (GADS), an experimental system developed at the IBM Research Laboratory in San Jose and described in detail in this book. By loading different maps, data, data dictionary, and statements for sample procedures (command strings), GADS was later used to build a Specific DSS to support the planning of territories for IBM customer engineers. The development of this Specific DSS from the GADS Generator required less than one month.

Another example of an embryonic DSS generator is the Executive Information System (EIS) marketed by Boeing Computer Services. EIS is an integrated set of capabilities, including report preparation, inquiry capability, a modeling language, graphic display commands, and a set of financial and statistical analysis subroutines. These capabilities have all been available individually for some time; the unique contribution of EIS is that the capabilities are now available through a common command language which acts on a common set of data. The result is that EIS can be used as a DSS generator, especially for specific DSS that aid financial decision-making situations.

Although there are no "full-service" DSS generators as we visualize them here, evolutionary growth toward DSS generators has come from special-purpose languages. In fact, most of the software systems that might be used as generators are evolving from enhanced planning languages or modeling languages, perhaps with report preparation and graphic display capabilities added. The Interactive Financial Planning System (IFPS), marketed by Execucom Systems of Austin, Texas, and EXPRESS, available from TYMSHARE, are good examples.

DSS Tools. The third and most fundamental level of technology applied to the development of DSS might be called *DSS Tools.* These are hardware or software elements which facilitate the development of specific

DSS *or* DSS Generators. This category of technology has seen the greatest amount of recent development, including new special-purpose languages, improvements in operating systems to support conversational approaches, and color graphic hardware and supporting software. For example, the GADS system described above was written in FORTRAN using an experimental graphics subroutine package as the primary dialog-handling software, and a laboratory-enhanced raster-scan color monitor.

Relationships.   The relationships between these three levels of technology and types of DSS are illustrated in Figure 1-3. The DSS tools can be used to develop a Specific DSS application directly, as shown on the left half of the diagram. This is obviously the same approach that has been used to develop most traditional applications with tools such as general-purpose languages, data access software, and subroutine packages. The difficulty with this approach for developing DSS is the constant change and flexibility that characterize them. The nature of a Specific DSS depends on the characteristics of the task or problem, the user's approach to the problem, and the organizational environment in which the user faces the problem. All these things are subject to frequent change, and a major value of DSS is their ability to accommodate change. The DSS Generator promises to facilitate change more effectively than the development of Specific DSS directly from tools.

Because DSS must respond to changes in the way managers want to approach the problem, a serious complicating factor in the use of basic tools is the need to involve the user directly in the change and modification of a Specific DSS. APL has been heavily used in the development of Specific

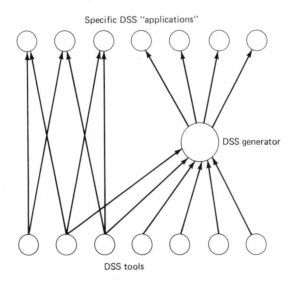

FIGURE 1-3   Three Levels of DSS Technology

DSS because it is cheap and easy for APL programmers (especially APL enthusiasts) to produce "throwaway" code which can easily be revised or discarded as the nature of the application changes. Except for the few users who become members of the APL fan club, however, that language *does not* help capture the involvement of users in the building and modification of DSS.

In summary, Specific DSS can be developed directly from tools, and in some cases that will continue to be the best approach. However, the development and use of DSS Generators promises to create a "platform" or staging area from which Specific DSS can be constantly developed and modified with the cooperation of the user, and without heavy consumption of time and effort.

Evolving Roles in DSS

All three levels of technology will probably be used over time in the development and operation of DSS. Some interesting developments are occurring, however, in the roles that managers and technicians will play.

Figure 1-4 repeats part of Figure 1-3 with a spectrum of five roles spread across the three levels.

1. The *manager or user* is the person faced with the problems decision—the one who must take action and be responsible for the consequences.
2. The *intermediary* is the person who helps the user, perhaps merely as a clerical assistant, to push the buttons of the terminal, or perhaps as a more substantial staff assistant, to interact and make suggestions.
3. The *DSS builder* or facilitator assembles the necessary capabilities from the DSS generator to configure the specific DSS with which the user/intermediary interacts directly. This person must have some familiarity with the problem area and also be comfortable with the information system technology components and capabilities.
4. The *technical supporter* develops additional information system capabilities or components when they are needed as part of the generator. New data bases, new analysis models, and additional data display formats will be developed by the person filling this role. The role requires a strong familiarity with technology and a minor acquaintance with the problem or application area.
5. The *toolsmith* develops new technology, new languages, new hardware and software, and improves the efficiency of linkage between subsystems.

Two observations about this spectrum of roles are appropriate. First, it is clear that the roles do not necessarily align with individuals on a one-to-one basis. One person may assume several roles, or it may require more than one person to fill a role. The appropriate role assignment generally depends on the following factors:

- The nature of the problem, particularly how narrow or broad
- The nature of the person, particularly how comfortable he or she is with the computer equipment, language, and concepts
- The strength of the technology, particularly how user oriented it is

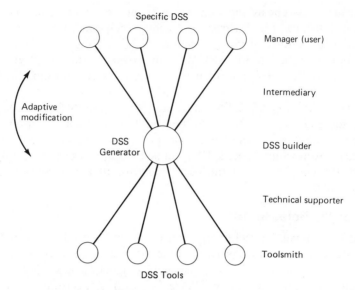

FIGURE 1-4   Framework for DSS Development

Some managers do not need or want an intermediary. There are even a few chief executives who take the terminal home on weekends to write programs, thereby assuming the upper three or four roles. Decisions that require group consensus or systems design (builder) teams are examples of multiple persons per role.

Second, these roles appear similar to those present in traditional system development, but there are subtle differences. The top two are familiar even in name for the development of many interactive or on-line systems. It is common practice in some systems to combine them into one "virtual" user for convenience. Users of DSS, however, will play a much more active and controlling role in design and development of the system than has been true in the past. The builder/technical supporter dichotomy is relatively close to the information specialist/system designer dichotomy, which has become a common distinction as a result of the ACM curriculum recommendations [2]. Increasingly, however, the DSS builder resides in the functional area and not in the MIS department. The toolsmith is similar to a systems programmer, software designer, or computer scientist, but is increasingly in the employ of a hardware or software vendor, not the user's organization. The net result is less direct involvement in the DSS process by the information system professional in the EDP/MIS department. (Some implications of this trend are discussed in Chapter 3.) Moreover, the interplay between these roles is evolving into a unique development approach for DSS.

The Development Approach for DSS

The very nature of DSS requires a different design technique from traditional transaction processing systems. Because there is no comprehensive theory of decision making, and because of the rapidity of change in the conditions that decision makers face, the traditional approaches for analysis and design have proven inadequate. Designers literally "cannot get to first base" because no one, least of all the decision maker or user, can define in advance what the functional requirements of the system should be. As a result, DSS require a unique approach to systems analysis and design.

Systems Analysis. Most systems analysis tools and approaches are based on the assumption that the computer system will have a well defined process (i.e., system and flow program flow charts). By their very nature, DSS need to be independent of any imposed process because different decision makers approach problem solving in different ways. In Chapter 4, we present a process-independent approach based on Representations that decision makers use to conceptualize problems, Operations on those representations, Memory Aids, and Control mechanisms. The ROMC approach to systems analysis for DSS is thus the user-oriented paradigm for articulating system performance requirements.

Iterative Design. DSS need to be built with short, rapid feedback from users to ensure that development is proceeding correctly. They must be developed to permit change quickly and easily. The result is that the most important four steps in the typical systems development process (analysis, design, construction, implementation) are combined into a single step which is iteratively repeated. The essence of the approach is that the manager and builder agree on a small but significant subproblem, then design and develop an initial system to support the decision making that it requires. After a short period of use (a few weeks), the system is evaluated, modified, and incrementally expanded. This cycle is repeated three to six times over the course of a few months until a *relatively* stable system is evolved which supports decision making for a cluster of tasks. The word "relatively" is important, because although the frequency and extent of change will decrease, it will never be stable. The system will always be changing, not as a necessary evil, but as a conscious strategy on the part of the user and builder.

In terms of the three-level model presented earlier, this process can be viewed as the iterative cycling between the DSS Generator and the Specific DSS (Figure 1-4). With each cycle, capabilities are added to or deleted from the Specific DSS from those available in the DSS Generator. In Chapter 5 we deal extensively with this interactive cycle and the mechanisms for implementing it.

Note that this approach requires an unusual level of user involvement and participation in the design. The user is actually the iterative designer of the system; the systems analyst is merely the catalyst between the user and the system, implementing the required changes and modifications. Note also that this is different from the concept of "prototyping"; the initial system is real, live, and usable, not just a pilot test. The iterative process does not *merely* lead to a good understanding of the systems performance requirements, which are then frozen. The iterative change ability is actually *built in* to the DSS as it is used over time. In fact, the development approach *becomes the system*. Rather than developing a system which is then "run" as a traditional EDP system, the DSS development approach results in the installation of an adaptive process in which a decision maker and a set of information system capabilities interact to confront problems while responding to changes from a variety of sources.

The Adaptive System. In the broad sense, DSS are adaptive systems which consist of all three levels of technology in place, operated by the participants (roles), with the technology adapting to changes over time. Thus the development of full-function, broad-based DSS is actually the development and installation of such an adaptive system. Simon describes such a system as one that adapts to changes of several kinds over three time horizons [10]. In the short run, the system allows *search* for answers within a relatively narrow scope. In the intermediate time horizon, the system *learns* by modifying its capabilities and activities (the scope or domain changes). In the long run, the system *evolves* to accommodate much different behavior styles and capabilities.

The three-level model of DSS is analogous to Simon's adaptive system. Specific DSS give the decision maker the capabilities and flexibility to *search*, explore, and experiment with problem areas (within certain boundaries). Over time, as changes occur in a task, the environment, and the users' behavior, specific DSS must *learn* to accommodate these changes through the reconfiguration of elements in the DSS generator (with the aid of the DSS builder). Over a longer period of time, the basic tools *evolve* to provide the technology for changing the capabilities of the generators out of which the specific DSS are constructed (through the efforts of the toolsmith).

The ideas expressed above are not particularly new. Rapid feedback between the systems analyst and the system user has been pursued for years. In the long run, most computer systems *are* adaptive systems; they are changed and modified during the normal system life cycle, and they evolve through major enhancements and extensions as the life cycle is repeated. However, when the length of that life cycle is shortened from three to five years to three to five months or even weeks, there are significant implications. The resulting changes in the development approach and the traditional view of the systems life cycle promises to be one of the important impacts of the growing use of DSS.

PURPOSE OF THIS BOOK

The purpose of this book is to provide a guide for the key people who must work together in the process of building Decision Support Systems.

- For DSS users: what they should expect from DSS and what they will have to do to get the benefits DSS have to offer.
- For DSS builders: what capabilities they will need from a DSS Generator or DSS Tools to build the Specific DSS required by a variety of users, and how to obtain or develop those capabilities.
- For managers under whose responsibility the development of DSS will take place: what organizational mechanisms, strategies, and procedures are appropriate and necessary.
- For the toolsmith: what capabilities are needed but not yet available in DSS? How can these be provided with DSS Tools and efficiently integrated in a DSS Generator?

Perhaps the primary focus of the book is, as the title suggests, on the Builder of DSS. It is our feeling that the long-run strength and viability of DSS in organizations rests on the extent to which DSS Generators and Tools are developed and managed by a group of DSS builders. We thus aim the book at the group of information specialists who will develop the necessary skills and understanding to work closely with DSS users using the adaptive design approach with a DSS Generator to build and evolve a wide variety of Specific DSS.

At this time, there are many DSS tools available, but DSS generators do not exist "off the shelf" in the software market. As we mentioned earlier, many vendors are enhancing their products (data base systems, planning languages, modeling languages, report generators) to give them the capabilities that a DSS Generator must have. In the short run, builders must assess the necessary capabilities for DSS Generators and Tools, identify and evaluate those that are available in the marketplace, and implement those that must be developed in-house. This book provides guidelines for those activities.

Summary of the Chapters

Chapter 2 develops a design framework which looks at each of the three levels of DSS from the viewpoint of its primary "stakeholder." The *user* is concerned with what benefits he or she can derive from the Specific

DSS, the *builder* is concerned with what capabilities DSS Generators must have to build Specific DSS, and the *toolsmith* is looking at the DSS tools that must be "architected" to build efficient Generators. Part Two deals with the *process* of Building DSS. Chapter 3 deals with the organizational issues and strategies for creating the environment within which DSS development and use can take place. Chapters 4 and 5 deal with the new systems analysis and design procedures that will be needed for DSS. Chapter 6 summarizes alternative implementation strategies and deals with two key issues—user education and DSS evaluation.

Part Three deals with the technology components of DSS. Dialog, data, and model management are each treated separately, and then integrated through the examination of several alternative DSS architectures. These chapters guide builders and toolsmiths in selecting, modifying, and evolving the technology required for DSS. Pulling the details together, the final chapter summarizes the entire book and provides specific steps for getting started on the road to building effective DSS.

QUESTIONS AND PROBLEMS

REVIEW QUESTIONS

1. What is the narrow definition of DSS?
2. What are the general characteristics of
   a. EDP?
   b. MIS?
   c. DSS?
3. What is a connotational view?
4. What is the difference between the connotational view and the theoretical view of DSS?
5. What is the difference between Specific DSS, DSS Generators, and DSS Tools?
6. Who are the key "players" in DSS development?
7. Explain how the players align with the three levels of technology (Specific DSS, DSS Generators, DSS Tools).
8. What is the adaptive system concept, and how does it relate to DSS?

DISCUSSION QUESTIONS

1. Are the differences between DSS and MIS great enough to herald a new era in information systems? Or are DSS just doing under a new buzz word what we always intended for MIS to do?
2. If we make it possible for managers to use Specific DSS directly, they are certain to use them incorrectly, with potentially damaging results.

They just do not understand data, files, and analysis models well enough. Discuss and comment.

3. The DSS Generator is unnecessary. Toolsmiths should build tools that the user can access and manipulate directly without the need for intermediaries or DSS Builders. Discuss and comment.

4. All computer systems are "adaptive systems," so there is no need to make any distinctions for DSS. Discuss and comment.

EXERCISES

1. From recent journal articles or books, find two examples each of what you think are DSS Tools, DSS Generators (perhaps partial but potential), and specific DSS. Explain why you think each example qualifies for the category you assigned to it.

2. Contact someone in your business community or organization who has helped develop a Specific DSS.
   a. Briefly describe the nature and purpose of the Specific DSS.
   b. What tools or Generators did the person use?
   c. What were the advantages and disadvantages of using these tools to develop the Specific DSS?

REFERENCES

1. ALTER, S. "A Taxonomy of Decision Support Systems," *Sloan Management Review*, Vol. 19, No. 1, Fall 1977, pp. 39–56.

2. ASHENHURST, R. L. "Curriculum Recommendations for Graduate Professional Programs in Information Systems," *ACM Communications*, Vol. 15, No. 5, May 1972, pp. 363–98.

3. CARLSON, E. (ed). Proceedings of a Conference on Decision Support Systems, *Data Base,* Vol. 8, No. 1, Winter 1977.

4. COOPER, D. O., L. B. DAVIDSON, and W. K. DENISON. "A Tool for More Effective Financial Analysis," *Interfaces*, February 1975, pp. 91–103.

5. HEAD, R. "Management Information Systems: A Critical Appraisal," *Datamation*, Vol. 13, No. 5, May 1967, pp. 22–28.

6. KEEN, P. G. W., and M. S. Scott Morton. *Decision Support Systems: An Organizational Perspective*, Addison-Wesley Publishing Company, Inc., Reading, Mass. 1978.

7. KEEN, P. G. W. "Adaptive Design for DSS," *Data Base*, Vol. 12, Nos. 1–2, Fall 1980, pp. 15–25.

8. KLAAS, R. L. "A DSS for Airline Management," *Data Base*, Winter 1977, pp. 3–8.

9. SCOTT MORTON, M. S. *Management Decision Systems: Computer Based Support for Decision Making*, Division of Research, Harvard University, Cambridge, Mass., 1971.

10. SIMON, H. "Cognitive Science: The Newest Science of the Artificial," *Cognitive Science*, Vol. 4, 1980, pp. 33–46.

11. SOCIETY FOR MANAGEMENT INFORMATION SYSTEMS. *Proceedings of the Eleventh Annual Conference*, Chicago, September 10–13, 1979, pp. 45–56.

12. WATSON, H. J., R. H. SPRAGUE, and D. W. KROEBER. "An Empirical Study of Information Systems Evolution," *Proceedings, Tenth Hawaii Interna-*

tional Conference on Systems Sciences, Western Periodicals, North Hollywood, Calif., 1977.

13. YOUNG, D., and P. KEEN (eds.). *Transactions of the First International Conference on Decision Support Systems*, Execucom Systems Corp., Austin, Tex., 1981.

CASE EXAMPLES

PDI, INC.

Pacific Diversified Industries, Incorporated (PDI, Inc.) is a large conglomerate based in San Francisco, with major operating divisions all over the world (see Figure 1-5). The Information Services Department (ISD) located in the headquarters staff has three major functions.

1. It serves as the coordination and standard-setting authority for data processing departments in several of the larger operating divisions.
2. It provides data processing services for the corporate headquarters.
3. It acts as a type of internal service bureau to do processing for some of the divisions that are too small to have their own data processing operation.

The Information Services Division is organized as shown in Figure 1-6.

After attending a seminar on DSS, the manager of ISD realized that he had approved several projects recently that had some characteristics of specific DSS. Included were:

1. A request from the planning staff at headquarters for a flexible financial planning language to assist in the development of alternative plans in the annual planning process. The manager had approved the purchase of a commercially available planning language to be run on the machine under ISD control at headquarters.
2. A request for a set of statistical and financial analysis packages to assist all divisions in the preparation of requests for capital expenditure authorizations. The manager had approved subscription to a commercial time-sharing service which had a large variety of these analysis packages. Since the time-sharing service was available in all major cities, all divisions could use it directly.
3. A request from the president to compare the return on investment for each of their major divisions with a selected set of similar companies. The manager had approved the purchase of the COMPUSTAT tapes and assigned an analyst to assist in comparing the data from about 29 companies.
4. A request from the controller and treasurer to provide up-to-the-minute information *and analysis capability* on financial and economic data. The manager had approved temporary use of a news wire service but was currently looking for a service that would also provide analysis, tracking, computation of trends, and so on, for these data.

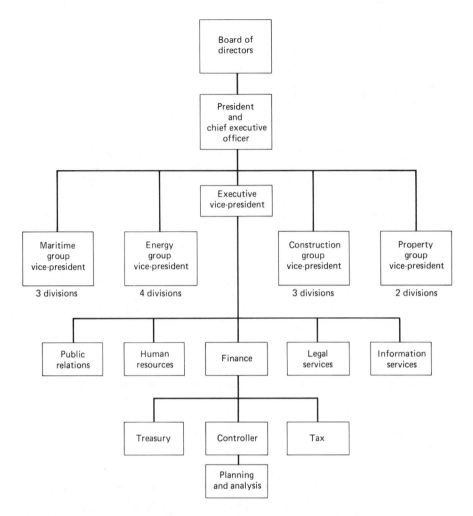

FIGURE 1-5 Organization Chart: Pacific Diversified Industries, Inc.

These requests, all from headquarters personnel, had been handled in the typical way, by assigning an analyst to do a study, select or define a computer system to meet the needs, and implement. The manager began to sense, however, that requests of this type would become more and more frequent. Preliminary conversations with key people at headquarters and in the divisions confirmed this feeling.

At the next meeting of the ISD staff (headquarters group heads and DP managers from all division installations), the members decided to investigate the development of a general DSS capability so that requests of this type could be accommodated quickly and efficiently in the future. In the chapters that follow, we will return to PDI, Inc. to illustrate how the company dealt with the concepts and issues presented in each chapter.

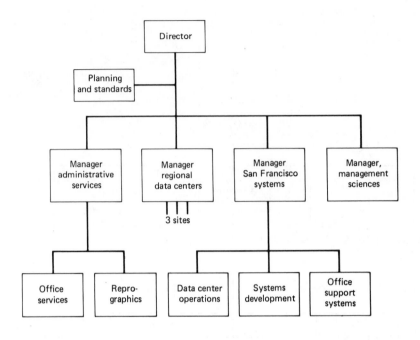

FIGURE 1-6   Organization Chart: Information Services Department

GADS

In the early 1970s, the IBM Research Lab in San Jose, California, developed an interactive system called the Geodata Analysis and Display System (GADS) as a vehicle for studying interactive problem solving. The research goal was to develop a system to enable nonprogrammers to solve unstructured problems more effectively by applying their job-specific experience and their own heuristics. It is an interactive system with strong graphic display and "user-friendly" characteristics to enable non-computer people to access, display, and analyze data that have geographic content and meaning. Problem-solving applications using data that can be related to a geographic location were chosen because they include underdeveloped applications in both business and government. The system was used initially by police officers to analyze data on "calls for service" by type, geographic zone, time of day, day of week, and so on. The rapid interactive feedback and graphic display (sometimes superimposed on a closed-circuit TV picture of a real map) enabled the police officer to amplify his or her judgment in designing more efficient allocation of personnel (police beats).

In a series of case studies testing the use of the system, the IBM personnel were able to load different maps, data files, and analysis routines to support different problems and different decision makers. In fact, over a six-year period, 17 specific DSS were developed using GADS (as a DSS generator). These specific DSS, involving over 200 users, can be divided into eight groups.

1. Police
    a. Personnel allocation   (1 application)
    b. Burglary analysis   (1)
    c. Calls for service analysis   (2)
2. School
    a. Attendance boundary formation   (4)
    b. School closing   (1)
3. Urban planning
    a. Urban growth policy evaluation   (1)
    b. Urban growth modeling   (1)
4. Fire
    a. Inspection planning   (1)
    b. Fire equipment planning   (1)
5. Human service delivery evaluation   (1)
6. Commuter bus route planning   (1)
7. Shopping center location   (1)
8. Customer engineer territory planning   (1)

In the police personnel allocation application, it appears that GADS enabled the police department to develop a solution that provided the same level of service for several hundred thousand dollars less than solutions developed with a manual approach. Perhaps more important, the GADS-developed solution had much wider support among police personnel, because of increased participation, than did previous methods of solving the problem. In several school districts' uses of GADS, the users stated that they could not have solved the problem in time without GADS. Two very significant indications of the value of the system are that users were willing to pay for the system, and that in almost all applications the system was used on weekends, days off, or evenings in addition to use during normal working hours.

These studies demonstrated that GADS could be used to generate a series of Specific DSS for a variety of nonprogrammer users, which they believe is valuable. Although GADS was expensive to develop (partly because of the experimental nature of some of the technology), these additional applications of GADS were developed at a cost of $5000 to 10,000 each. GADS is certainly not an ideal or full-service DSS Generator, but it is clearly an example of the Generator concept at work. In subsequent chapters we will use the GADS system to illustrate the concepts and capabilities described in each chapter.

CHAPTER TWO

DESIGN FRAMEWORK FOR DSS

OUTLINE

Chapter 1 dealt with some aspects of the technological and organizational contexts within which DSS will be built and operated. This chapter deals with what DSS must accomplish and what capabilities or characteristics they must have. The three levels of hardware/software technology and the corresponding three major "stakeholders" in the development and use of DSS can be used to identify the characteristics and attributes of DSS. The attributes, defined in terms of the three stakeholders complete the framework for building DSS introduced in Chapter 1.

THE VIEW FROM THREE LEVELS

At the top level are the *managers or users* who are primarily concerned with what the Specific DSS can do for them. Their focus is on the problem-solving or decision-making tasks they face and the organizational environment in which they operate. Users will assess the DSS in terms of the assistance they receive in pursuing these tasks. At the level of the DSS Generator, *builders* or designers must use the capabilities of the generator to configure Specific DSS to meet managers' needs. Builders will be concerned with the capabilities the Generator offers and how these capabilities can be assembled to create the Specific DSS. At the DSS tool level, the *toolsmiths* are concerned with the development of basic technology components and how they can be integrated to form a DSS Generator that has the necessary capabilities.

Let us now look more closely at the attributes and characteristics of the DSS as viewed from each level. From the user's view, we can identify six general performance objectives for Specific DSS. These objectives are not the only six that could be identified, but as a group they represent the overall performance of DSS that seems to be expected and desirable from a decision maker's viewpoint. The characteristics of the DSS Generator from the viewpoint of the builder are described by a conceptual model that identifies performance characteristics in three categories: dialog handling (the user-DSS interface), data base and data base management capability, and modeling and analytic capability. The same three-part model is used to depict the viewpoint of the toolsmith but from the aspect of the technology, tactics, and architecture required to produce those capabilities required by builders.

The User's View: Performance Objectives

The following performance requirements are phrased using the normative word "should." It is likely that no specific DSS will be required to satisfy all six of the performance requirements given here. In fact, it is important to recall that the performance criteria for any Specific DSS will be entirely dependent on the task, the organizational environment, and the decision maker(s) involved. Thus it is impossible to identify a typical Specific DSS; each needs only the attributes required to support a decision maker facing a task in a given environment. *As a group*, however, the following objectives represent a set of capabilities that characterize the full value of the DSS concept from the manager/user point of view. The first three pertain to the type of decision-making task that managers and professionals face for which DSS should provide support. The latter three relate to the type of support that is needed.

1. A DSS should provide support for decision making, but with emphasis on semistructured and unstructured decisions. These are the types of decisions that have had little or no support from EDP, MIS, or management science/operations research (MS/OR) in the past. It might be better to refer to *hard* or *underspecified* problems because the concept of "structure" in decision making is heavily dependent on the cognitive style and approach to problem solving of the decision maker.

2. A DSS should provide decision-making support for users at all levels, assisting in integration between the levels whenever appropriate. This requirement evolves from the realization that people at *all* organizational levels face "tough" problems. Moreover, a major need articulated by decision makers is the need for integration and coordination of decision making by several people dealing with related parts of a larger problem.

3. A DSS should support decisions that are *inter*dependent as well as those that are *in*dependent. Much of the early DSS work implied that a decision maker would sit at a terminal, use a system, and develop a decision *alone*. DSS development experience has shown that DSS must accommodate decisions that are made by groups or made in parts by several people in sequence. Hackathorn and Keen [6] cite three decision types:

   - *Independent*: A decision maker has full responsibility and authority to make a complete implementable decision.
   - *Sequential interdependent*: A decision maker makes part of a decision, which is then passed on to someone else.
   - *Pooled interdependent*: The decision must result from negotiation and interaction among several decision makers.

   Different capabilities will be required to support each type of decision. These might be labeled personal support, organizational support, and group support, respectively.

4. A DSS should support all phases of the decision-making process. A popular model of decision-making is given in the work of Simon [7]. He characterized three main steps in the process:

   - *Intelligence*: Searching the environment for conditions calling for decisions. Raw data are obtained, processed, and examined for clues that may identify problems.
   - *Design*: Inventing, developing, and analyzing possible courses of action. This involves processes to understand the problem, to generate solutions, and to test solutions for feasibility.

- *Choice*: Selecting a particular course of action from those available. A choice is made and implemented.

Although the third phase includes implementation, many authors feel that it is significant enough to be shown separately. It has been added to Figure 2-1 to show the relationships between the steps. Simon's model also illustrates the contribution of MIS and MS/OR to decision making. From the definition of the three stages listed above, it is clear that EDP and MIS (in the narrow sense) have made major contributions to the intelligence phase, whereas MS/OR has been primarily useful at the choice phase. There has been no substantial support for the design phase, but this seems to be one of the primary potential contributions of DSS. There has also been very little support from traditional systems for the implementation phase, but some experience has shown that DSS can make a major contribution here also.

5. DSS should support a variety of decision-making processes but not be dependent on any one. Simon's model, although widely accepted, is only one model of how decisions are actually made. In fact, there is no universally accepted model of the decision-making process, and there is no promise of such a general theory in the foreseeable future. There are too many variables, too many different types of decisions, and too much variety in the characteristics of decision makers. Consequently, a very important characteristic of DSS is that they provide decision makers with a set of capabilities to apply in a sequence and form that fits each person's cognitive style. In short, DSS should be process independent and user driven (or controlled).

6. Finally, a DSS should be easy to use. A variety of terms have been used to describe this characteristic, including flexible, user-friendly, and nonthreatening. The importance of this characteristic is underscored by the discretionary latitude of DSS clientele. Although systems that require heavy organizational support or group support may limit the discretion somewhat, users of DSS have much more latitude to ignore or circumvent a system than do users of more traditional transaction systems or required reporting systems. Therefore, DSS must earn user allegiance by being valuable and convenient.

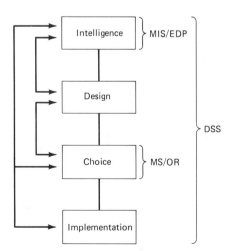

FIGURE 2-1   Phases of Decision Making

The Builder's View: Technical Capabilities

The DSS Builder has the responsibility of drawing on computer-based tools and techniques to provide the decision support required by managers. DSS Tools can be used directly, but it is generally more efficient and effective to use DSS generators for this task. A generator must have a set of capabilities that facilitates quick and easy initial creation of a Specific DSS, followed by modification in response to changes in the manager's requirements, environment, tasks, and thinking approaches. A conceptual model can be used to organize these capabilities, both for builders and for the toolsmith who will develop the technology to provide these capabilities.

The old "black box" approach is helpful here, starting with the view of the system as a black box, and successively "opening" the boxes to understand the subsystems and how they are interconnected. Although the decision support system is treated as the black box here, it is important to recall that the overall system is the decision-*making* system, consisting of a manager/user who uses a decision support system to confront a task in an organizational environment (see Figure 2-2).

Opening the large DSS box reveals a data base, a model base, and a complex software system for linking the user to each of them (see Figure 2-3). Opening each of these inner boxes reveals that the data base and model base have some interrelated components and that the software system is comprised of three sets of capabilities: data base management software (DBMS), model base management software (MBMS), and the software for managing the interface between the user and the system, which might be called the dialog generation and management software (DGMS). These three major subsystems provide a convenient scheme for identifying the technical capabilities that a decision support system must have. Let us con-

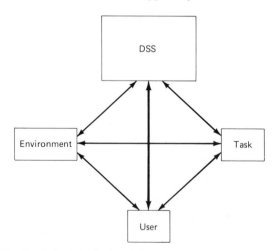

FIGURE 2-2   The Decision-Making System

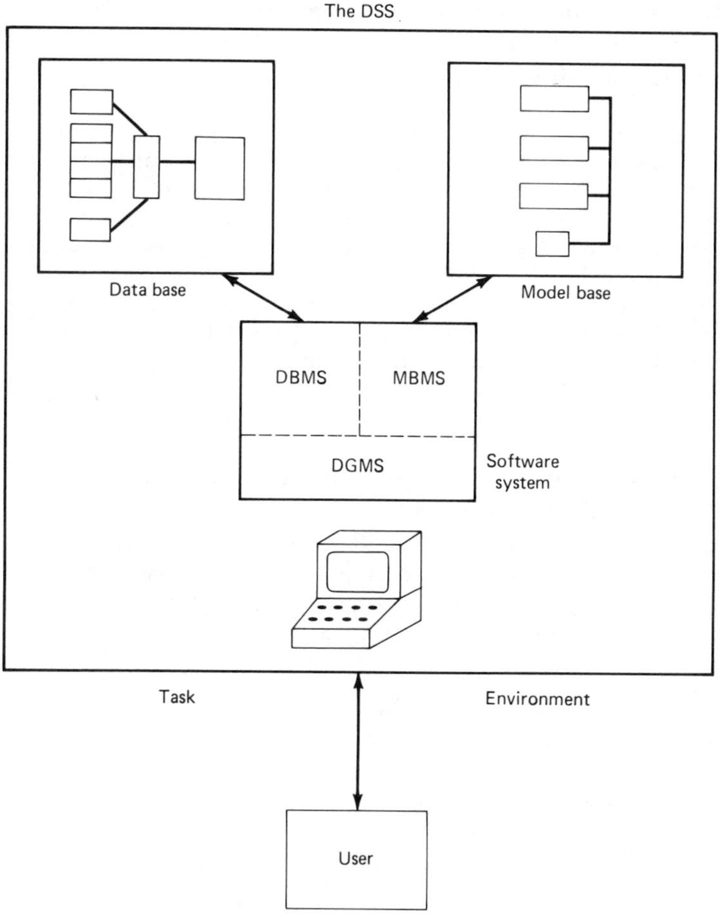

FIGURE 2-3 Components of the Decision Support System

sider the key aspects in each category that are critical from the Builder's point of view, and then list a set of capabilities that are required in each category.

The Dialog Subsystem. Much of the power, flexibility, and usability characteristics of a decision support system derive from capabilities in the interaction between the system and the user, which we call the dialog subsystem. We start here because it is clearly the most important subsystem. For years there have been systems with strong computational algorithms or excellent data access routines but whose effectiveness was limited because they were difficult to use. In fact, from the DSS users' point of view, *the Dialog is the System.* All the capabilities of the system must be articulated and implemented through the Dialog.

29

Bennett identifies the user, the terminal, and the software system as the components of the dialog subsystem [1]. He then divides the dialog experience itself into three parts (see Figure 2-4):

1. *The action language*: what the user *can do* in communicating with the system. It includes such options as the availability of a regular keyboard, function keys, touch panels, joy stick, voice command, and so on.
2. *The display or presentation language*: what the user *sees*. The display language includes options such as a character or line printer, a display screen, graphics, color, plotters, audio output, and so on.
3. *The knowledge base*: what the user *must know*. The knowledge base consists of what the user needs to bring to the session with the system in order to use it effectively. The knowledge may be in the user's head, on a reference card or instruction sheet, in a user's manual, in a series of "help" commands available upon request, and so on.

The "richness" of the interface will depend on the strength and variety of capabilities in each of these areas.

Combinations of these capabilities comprise what might be called a "dialog style." Examples include the question-and-answer approach, command languages, menus, and fill-in-the-blanks. Each style has pros and cons depending on the type of user, the task, and the decision situation.

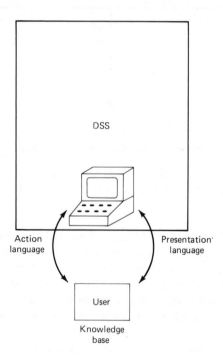

FIGURE 2-4   The Dialog Subsystem

Although we have just scratched the surface in this important area, a partial set of desirable capabilities for a DSS generator to support user/system dialog includes:

- The ability to handle a variety of dialog styles, perhaps with the ability to shift among them at the user's choice.
- The ability to accommodate user actions with a variety of input devices.
- The ability to present data with a variety of formats and output devices.
- The ability to provide flexible support for the user's knowledge base.

In Chapter 7 we present a more detailed discussion of dialog styles and the process of building the dialog capability.

The Data Subsystem.   The data subsystem is thought to be a well-understood set of capabilities because of the rapidly maturing technology related to data bases and their management. The typical advantages of the data base approach and the powerful functions of the DBMS are also important to the development and use of DSS. There are, however, some significant differences between the data base/data communication approach for traditional systems and those applicable for DSS. Opening the data base box summarizes these key characteristics, shown in Figure 2-5.

First is the importance of a much richer set of data sources than are usually found in typical non-DSS applications. Data must come from external as well as internal sources, since decision making, especially in the upper

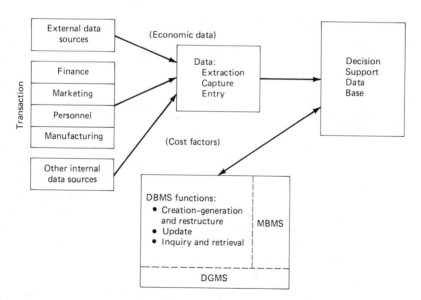

FIGURE 2-5   The Data Subsystem

management levels, is heavily dependent on external data sources such as economic data. In addition, the typical accounting-oriented transaction data must be supplemented with nontransactional, nonaccounting data, some of which have not been computerized in the past.

Another significant difference is the importance of the process of data capture and extraction from this wider set of data sources. Most successful DSS have found it necessary to create a DSS data base which is logically separate from other operational data bases. The nature of DSS requires that the extraction process and the DBMS that manages it be flexible enough to allow rapid additions and changes in response to unanticipated user requests. A partial set of capabilities required in the data base area can be summarized as follows:

- The ability to combine a variety of data sources through a data capture and extraction process.
- The ability to add and delete data sources quickly and easily.
- The ability to portray logical data structures in user terms so that the user understands what is available and can specify needed additions and deletions.
- The ability to handle personal and unofficial data so that the user can experiment with alternatives based on personal judgment.
- The ability to manage this wide variety of data with a full range of data management functions.

These abilities, and the techniques for building them, are discussed more fully in Chapter 8.

The Models Subsystem. A very promising aspect of DSS is their ability to integrate data access and decision models. They do so by embedding the decision models in an information system that uses the data base as the integration and communication mechanism between models. This characteristic unifies the strength of data retrieval and reporting from the EDP field and the significant developments in management science in a way that decision makers can use and trust.

The misuse and disuse of models have been widely discussed for many years. One major problem has been that model builders were frequently preoccupied with the structure of the model. The existence of the correct input data and the proper delivery of the output to the user was assumed. In addition to these heroic assumptions, models tended to suffer from inadequacy because of the difficulty of developing an integrated model to handle a realistic set of interrelated decisions. The solution was a collection of separate models, each dealing with a distinct part of the problem. Communication between these related models was left to the decision maker as a manual and intellectual process.

A more enlightened view of models suggests that they be embedded in an information system with the data base as the integration and communication mechanism between them. Figure 2-6 summarizes the components of the models subsystem. The model creation process must be flexible, with a strong modeling language and a set of building blocks, much like subroutines, which can be assembled to assist the modeling process. In fact, there are a set of model management functions very much analogous to data management functions. The key capabilities for DSS in the model subsystems include:

- The ability to create new models quickly and easily.
- The ability to access and integrate model "building blocks."
- The ability to catalog and maintain a wide range of models, supporting all levels of users.
- The ability to interrelate these models with appropriate linkages through the data base.
- The ability to manage the model base with management functions analogous to data base management (e.g., mechanisms for storing, cataloging, linking, and accessing models).

In Chapter 9 we present a more detailed discussion of the model base and its management.

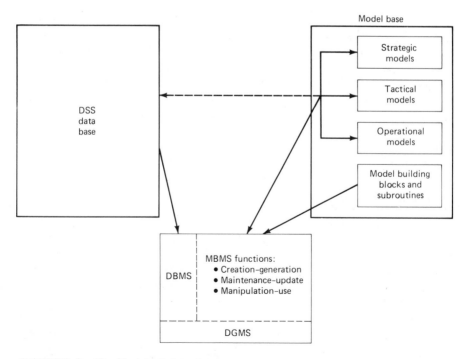

FIGURE 2-6   The Models Subsystem

The Toolsmith's View:
The Underlying Technology

The toolsmith is concerned with the science and engineering involved in creating the information technology to support DSS, and the architecture of combining the basic tools into a coherent system—the DSS Generator. We can use the same three-part model to describe the toolsmith's concerns because the tools must be designed and combined to provide the three sets of capabilities.

Each of the three areas (dialog, data handling, and model handling) has received a fair amount of attention from toolsmiths in the past. The topics of DSS and the requirements they impose have put these efforts in a new light, revealing how they can be interrelated to increase their collective effectiveness. Moreover, the DSS requirements have revealed some missing elements in existing efforts, indicating valuable potential areas for development.

It is important for builders and users, as well as toolsmiths, to understand the technology development thrusts that will be needed, and to recognize those architectural approaches that are being used in these developments. We summarize some issues briefly here, and then deal in substance with them in Part Three.

Dialog Management. There has been much empirical and some theoretical work on systems requirements for good dialog management. Many of these studies are based on watching users' behavior in using terminals, or surveying users or programmers to ascertain what they want in interactive systems. In a recent study the authors examined a series of interactive applications, several of which are DSS, to assess the *types* of software capabilities required by the applications [8]. This study led directly to some creative work on the software architecture for dialog generation and management systems (DGMS) [3]. This research uses a relation as a data structure for storing each picture or "frame" used in a dialog and a decision table for storing the control mechanism for representing users' options in branching from one frame to another.

Data Management. Most of the significant work in the data base management area during the past several years has been aimed at transaction processing against large data bases. Large DBMS generally have inquiry/retrieval and flexible report preparation capabilities, but their largest contribution has been in the reduction of program maintenance costs through the separation of application programs and data definitions. On the other hand, DBMS work has generally had a rather naive view of users and their requirements. DSS users will not be satisfied merely with the capability to issue a set of retrieval commands that select items from the data base, or even to display those selected items in a report with flexible definitions of format and headings. Users need to interact repeatedly and creatively with a relatively small set of data. They may need only 40 to 100 data variables, but the variables must be the *right ones*. Significantly, what is right may change from day to day and week to week. Required data will probably include time-series data, which are not handled comprehensively by typical DBMS. We need better ways to handle and coordinate time series data as well as mechanisms for capturing, processing, and tagging judgmental and probabilistic data. We also need better ways of extracting data from existing files and capturing data from previously noncomputerized sources. As we will see in Chapter 8, the critical area is data extraction which allows additions and deletions to a DSS data base from a large transactional data base. In short, the significant developments in data base technology need to be focused and extended in some key areas in order to serve directly the needs of DSS.

Model Management. The area of model creation and handling may have the greatest potential contribution to DSS. So far, the analytic capability provided by systems has evolved from statistical or financial analysis subroutines that can be called from a common command language. Modeling languages provide a way of formulating interrelationships between variables in a way that permits the creation of simulation or "what if" models. As we noted earlier, many of the currently viable DSS Generators have evolved from these efforts. Early forms of "modeling management" seem to be evolving from enhancements to some modeling languages which permit a model of this type to be used for sensitivity testing or goal seeking by specifying target and flexibility variables.

The model management area also has the potential for bringing some of the contributions of artificial intelligence (AI) to bear on DSS. MYCIN, a system designed to support medical diagnosis, is based on AI "production rules" which play the role of models in performing analytic and decision guidance functions [4]. A more general characterization of "knowledge management" as a way of handling models and data has also been tentatively explored [2]. More recent work proposes the use of a version of semantic networks for model representation [5]. Although the latter work is promising, usable capabilities in model management in the near future are more likely to evolve from modeling languages, expanded subroutine approaches, and in some cases, production rules.

ISSUES FOR THE FUTURE

At the end of this framework section of the book, and before discussing the process of building DSS in Part Two, it is appropriate to identify several crucial issues that will affect the success of DSS efforts. The issues given here, phrased as difficult questions, must be dealt with as we build DSS, lest the promise and potential benefits be diluted or seriously delayed.

What is a Decision Support System? Earlier we noted that some skeptics regard "DSS" as just another buzz word. We have shown that there is a significant amount of content behind the label. The danger remains, however, that the bandwagon effect will outrun our ability to define and develop potential contributions of DSS. The market imperatives of the multi-billion-dollar information systems industry tend to generate pressures to create simple labels for intuitively attractive ideas. It happened in many cases (but not all, of course) with MIS. Some companies are still trying to live down the aftereffects of the overpromise–underdelivery–disenchantment sequence from the MIS bandwagon of the late 1960's.

The implications are clear. First, by their very nature, DSS efforts should start small and grow. What is *not* needed is a major funding program, a reorganization, and a lot of ballyhoo about the DSS era. Managers, users, and decision makers are generally not interested in whether they are using the MIS, the DSS, or whatever. They are primarily interested in results. Second, a lot of systems and products that carry the DSS label will be "catching the bandwagon" with only marginal enhancement of last year's product. In subsequent chapters we identify a set of minimal capabilities or characteristics that characterize a DSS. Managers and builders should and must ask sharp, critical questions about the capabilities of any purported DSS, matching them against what is really needed.

What is Really Needed? After nearly two decades of advancements in information technology, the real nature of information system requirements is not well understood. The issue is further complicated by the realization that managers' needs and the needs of other "knowledge workers" with which they interact are heavily interdependent. The DSS philosophy and approach has already shed some light on this issue by emphasizing "capabilities"—the ability for a decision maker to *do things* with an information system—rather than just "information needs," which too often implies data items and totals on a report.

Nevertheless, it is tempting to call for a slowdown in the development of DSS until decision making and related managerial activities are fully understood. Although logically appealing, such a strategy is not practical. Neither managers, who face increasingly complex tasks, nor the information systems industry, which has increasingly strong technology to offer, will be denied. They point out that a truly comprehensive theory of decision making has been pursued for years with minimal success.

A potential resolution of this problem is to develop and use DSS in a way that reveals what decision makers can and should receive from an information system. For example, the system should be designed to capture and track the steps taken by users in the process of making key decisions. Such a strategy would serve both as an aid to the analysis of the process and as a potential education device for new users.

The counterpart of the "needs" issue is the extent to which the system meets those needs, and the value of the performance increase that results. Evaluation of DSS will be just as difficult—and important—as evaluation of MIS has been. The direct and constant involvement of users—those in the best position to evaluate the systems—provides a glimmer of hope with regard to this tough problem. Pursuit of these two tasks together may yield progess on both fronts, with the kind of synergistic effect often sought from systems efforts. The iterative design approach and the three levels of technology afford the opportunity, if such a strategy is developed from the beginning.

Who Will Do It?   A series of organizational issues will revolve around roles and organizational placement of the people who will take the principal responsibility for the development of DSS. Initiative and guidance for DSS development frequently comes from the user area, not from the EDP/MIS area. Yet current technology still requires technical support from the information system professional. The DSS builder may work for the vice-president of finance, but the technical support role is still played by someone in the MIS department. To some extent, the demand for DSS supports the more general trend to distribute system development efforts out of the MIS department into the user department. The difference is that many DSS software systems (generators) specifically attempt to reach the end user directly, without involvement of the MIS group. The enlightened MIS administrator considers this a healthy trend and willingly supplies the required technical support and coordination. Less enlightened data processing administrators often see it as a threat; the resulting political negotiation obviously limits the advancement of DSS development. Some companies have set up a group specifically charged with developing DSS-type applications. This strategy creates a team of DSS Builders who can develop the necessary skills in dealing with users, become familiar with the available technology, and define the steps in the development approach for DSS.

How Should It be Done?   One of the pillars on which the success of DSS rests is the iterative development or adaptive design approach. The traditional five- to seven-stage system development process and the system life-cycle concept have been the backbone of systems analysis for years. Most project management systems and approaches are based on it. The adaptive design approach, because it combines all the stages into one quick step that is repeated, will require a redefinition of system development milestones and a major modification of project management mechanisms. Since many traditional systems will not be susceptible to the iterative approach, we also need a way of deciding when an application should be developed in the new way instead of in the traditional way. The outline of the approach is conceptually straightforward for applications that require only personal support.

It becomes more complicated for group or organizational support when there are multiple users. In short, DSS builders will need to develop a set of milestones, checkpoints, documentation strategies, and project management procedures for DSS applications, and recognize when they should be used.

How Much Can be Done?   The final issue is a caveat dealing with the limitations of technical solutions to the complexity faced by managers and decision makers. Information systems professionals must be careful not to feel, or even allow others to feel, that they can develop or devise a technological solution to all the problems of management. Decision makers will always "deal with complexity in a state of perplexity"—it is the nature of the job. Information technology can, and is, making a major contribution to improving the effectiveness of people in this situation, but the solution will never be total. With traditional systems, we continually narrow the scope and definition of the system until we know it will do the job that it is required to do. If the specification/design/construction/implementation process is done correctly, the system is a success, measured against its original objectives. With a decision support system, the user and the system's capability are constantly pursuing the problem, with the systems analyst or builder acting as facilitator. But the underspecified nature of the problem ensures that there will never be a complete solution. Systems analysts have always had a little trouble with humility, but the DSS process requires a healthy dose of modesty with respect to the ability of technology to solve all the problems of managers in organizations.

CONCLUSION

The introduction and framework described in the first two chapters shows the dimensions and scope of DSS in a way that sets the stage for the *development* of this highly promising type of information system.

1. The relationships among EDP, MIS, and DSS show that DSS is only one of several important technology subsystems for improving organizational performance, and that DSS development efforts must carefully integrate with these other systems.
2. The three levels of technology and the interrelationships between people that use them provide a context for organizing the development effort.
3. The iterative design approach shows that the ultimate goal of the DSS development effort is the installation of an *adaptive system* consisting of all three levels of technology and the people that use them adapting to changes over time.
4. The performance objectives show the types of decision making to be served by, and the types of support that should be built into DSS as they are developed.

5. The three technical capabilities illustrate the fact that development efforts must build DSS with capabilities in dialog management, data management, and model management.

6. The issues discussed at the end of this chapter identify some potential roadblocks that must be recognized and confronted to permit continued development of DSS.

   In the remaining chapters we put "meat on the bones" of this framework, supplying guidance for the steps in development, with specifications for the capabilities that must be built and the technical strategies for building them.

QUESTIONS AND PROBLEMS

REVIEW QUESTIONS

1. What are the six performance criteria that Specific DSS as a group should satisfy? Which of the key players in DSS development is most concerned with these?

2. What are the three types of capabilities that a DSS Generator should have? Who is most concerned with these?

3. List examples in each of the three areas of capabilities.

4. Why has the use of models been troublesome in the past, and how does DSS make it less troublesome?

5. What are the potential technology improvements in each of the three capability areas?

6. Summarize the issues that are important in the future development of DSS.

DISCUSSION QUESTIONS

1. Should DSS have separate data bases or should they be part of the main data base managed by a large DBMS such as IMS, ADABAS, or SYSTEM 2000? Why?

2. We do not understand enough about how managers make decisions to try developing DSS. We first need a better understanding of what managers and users need and want to assist them in decision making. Then we can develop the necessary information technology capabilities. Do you agree or disagree? Why?

3. There really is no need for DSS builders. That job can easily be done by typical systems analysts. Do you agree or disagree? Why?

4. Should DSS development be managed by the MIS/EDP department, or does the nature of the technology and applications suggest that it should be developed entirely by user groups?

5. Is it wise to start developing DSS capability with current technology, enhanced and supplemented if necessary? Or is it better to wait until the toolsmiths have responded to some of the needs that are now apparent and a full-service DSS Generator is available in the software market?

EXERCISES

1. For the examples of Specific DSS, DSS Generators, and DSS Tools that you identified in Chapter 1, list the capabilities of each. Use the three categories presented in this chapter. (If you are using a description from a journal article, you may have to make some inferences or educated guesses.)
2. Contact someone in your business community or in your organization who has *used* a Specific DSS. Find out what they liked or did not like about the system. Could the dislikes (or shortcomings) have been eliminated with additional capabilities in one of the three areas? Did you discover any other capabilities that do not seem to fit into the three areas?

REFERENCES

1. BENNETT, J. "User-Oriented Graphics, Systems for Decision Support in Unstructured Tasks," in *User-Oriented Design of Interactive Graphics Systems*, S. Treu (ed.), Association for Computing Machinery, New York, 1977, pp. 3–11.
2. BONCZEK, H., C. W. HOLSAPPLE, and A. WHINSTON. "Evolving Roles of Models in Decision Support Systems," *Decision Sciences*, Vol. 11, No. 2, April 1980, pp. 337–56.
3. CARLSON, ERIC and WOLFGANG METZ, "A Design for Table-Driven Display Generation and Management Systems," in *Display Generation and Management Systems (DGMS) for Interactive Business Applications*, E. Carlson et. al., Fried, Vieweg and Sohn, Braunschweig/Wiesbaden, 1981, pp. 17–53.
4. DAVIS, R. "A DSS for Diagnosis and Therapy," *Data Base*, Vol. 8, No. 3, Winter 1977, pp. 58–72.
5. ELAM, J., J. HENDERSON, and L. MILLER. "Model Management Systems: An Approach to Decision Support in Complex Organizations," *Proceedings, Conference on Information Systems*, The Society for Management Information Systems, Philadelphia, December 1980.
6. HACKATHORN, RICHARD and PETER KEEN, "Organizational Strategies for Personal Computing in Decision Support Systems," *MIS Quarterly*, Vol. 5, No. 3, Sept. 1981.
7. SIMON, H. *The New Science of Management Decision*, Harper & Row, Publishers, New York, 1960.
8. SUTTON, J. A., and R. H. SPRAGUE. "A Study of Display Generation and Management in Interactive Business Applications," in *Display Generation and Management Systems (DGMS) for Interactive Business Applications*, E. Carlson et. al., Fried, Vieweg and Sohn, Braunschweig/Wiesbaden, 1981, pp. 1–16.

THE GEODATA ANALYSIS AND
DISPLAY SYSTEM (GADS)

This example describes GADS from the three points of view discussed in Chapter 2 (user, builder, toolsmith). For the users' view, we will use one application of GADS—its use for decisions relating to allocating IBM customer engineers to geographic territories, which constitutes a specific version of GADS, i.e., a Specific DSS. This example is taken from a research report by Jim Sutton.* For the builders' view, we describe GADS as a DSS Generator. It is important to note that GADS was not originally designed as a DSS Generator, and thus it does not exactly match the framework described in this chapter. Because GADS evolved into a Generator, however, it does have the three major components of Dialog, Data, and Models. It is in the Models Subsystem that GADS deviates most from the framework. The toolsmiths' view describes the hardware and software tools used to build GADS.

The User's View of GADS: A Scenario

GADS is a DSS for decisions related to geographic areas. Examples of such decisions are resource allocation, facility location, and natural resource management. From the users' point of view, GADS provides support for manipulating maps of geographic areas, and data related to those areas. An example of a map is a set of zones in a city (Figure 2-7), and an example of data related to that map is installed equipment (by zone). In the GADS application described by Sutton, the map was a set of zones covering the city of San Jose and adjacent areas, and the data consisted primarily of zone summaries of the number of IBM office products (by product group). To understand the users' view of GADS, we include Sutton's scenario of how IBM Field Managers used GADS. The particular decision involves designing a set of territories for the Customer Engineers (CEs) working for a Field Manager. A territory is a set of (usually contiguous) zones. The territory design decision involves considering factors such as:

- Adequate workload for a particular CE;
- Balancing workload among CEs with a variety of skills and training;
- Providing for backup of CEs;
- Providing the best possible service times for customers;
- Providing for individual CE job satisfaction.

*Sutton, J. A. "Evaluation of a Decision Support System: A Case Study With the Office Products Division of IBM," RJ2214 (3/30/78) IBM Research Division, San Jose, CA.

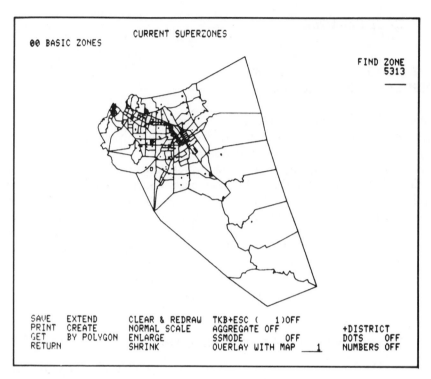

FIGURE 2-7   Zone Map of City

Each CE manager had a different set of variables and a different process for making the decision. Thus there was no single manager's view of GADS. Figures 2-7 through 2-16 give a sample usage scenario; the following three paragraphs are Sutton's description of the scenario.

Figure 2-7 shows the computer representation of the zone map with which the Field Manager dealt. The Field Manager might gather *intelligence* concerning the nature of the problem and the alternatives available to him by viewing tabular displays of one or more data items (Figure 2-8) and/or by viewing these data displayed on the relevant area of the map (Figure 2-9). Using these data and representations, the Field Manager would *design* alternative sets of CE territories. Figure 2-10 shows the use of GADS to define a subset of zones to be grouped into a trial territory. To do this grouping, the Field Manager applied data shown to him by the computer as well as data he felt was important but was not in GADS. GADS maps showed the Field Manager the new territory boundaries and the aggregate values of the data item selected (Figure 2-11). The Field Manager might choose to view the same territory in light of other data items (Figure 2-12). When the Field Manager had completed a set of territories (Figure 2-13), or at any time, a territory map could be saved for later use.

Choice among alternative maps was facilitated by viewing the same data items on alternative maps (Figure 2-14) or by overlaying maps. GADS also gave the Field Manager the ability to view data on histograms, scatterplots, and projected 3-D graphs. The data shown on such graphs could be aggregated by a given alternative map to aid in the evaluation of alternatives. Figure 2-15 illustrates the use of a scatter plot to show the loading by CE (each "*") for one product group. The horizontal displacement of each point shows the expected service load for each CE and the vertical displacement identifies the CE and associated Field Manager (each horizontal "band" represents the CEs under one Field Manager). Examples of the uses of the histograms include:

- the Field Manager would rescale it by changing the minimums or maximums on either axis
- they would change the data items displayed
- they would locate the point on the graph representing a given zone
- they would find the zones represented by any given point
- they would cause the displayed points to represent aggregations to any set of stored territories

PAGE AHEAD BACK	CANCEL CHANGES	BASELINE	1	PRINT	RETURN
SHOW DATA FROM	4000 TO 4211				
4000	0.00	4046	179.00	4110	26.00	4150	39.00
4001	48.00	4047	182.00	4111	45.00	4151	0.00
4003	246.00	4050	4.00	4112	39.00	4152	10.00
4004	20.00	4051	50.00	4113	19.00	4153	31.00
4005	7.00	4053	0.00	4114	0.00	4154	73.00
4006	51.00	4054	15.00	4115	56.00	4155	24.00
4010	12.00	4055	0.00	4116	177.00	4156	9.00
4011	1.00	4056	93.00	4117	0.00	4160	350.00
4012	36.00	4057	1.00	4120	0.00	4161	0.00
4013	0.00	4060	0.00	4121	118.00	4162	2.00
4014	0.00	4061	50.00	4122	32.00	4163	52.00
4015	72.00	4062	73.00	4123	0.00	4164	36.00
4016	0.00	4063	66.00	4124	32.00	4165	230.00
4020	0.00	4064	40.00	4125	48.00	4166	21.00
4021	0.00	4065	0.00	4126	0.00	4167	23.00
4022	22.00	4066	78.00	4127	53.00	4171	28.00
4023	17.00	4067	11.00	4130	0.00	4172	0.00
4024	0.00	4071	46.00	4131	46.00	4173	60.00
4025	93.00	4072	4.00	4132	99.00	4174	151.00
4026	60.00	4073	29.00	4133	21.00	4175	13.00
4030	22.00	4074	55.00	4135	42.00	4176	23.00
4032	626.00	4075	13.00	4136	33.00	4177	1.00
4033	0.00	4077	22.00	4137	0.00	4200	60.00
4034	0.00	4100	200.00	4140	42.00	4201	22.00
4035	50.00	4101	4.00	4141	0.00	4202	21.00
4036	23.00	4102	13.00	4142	0.00	4203	42.00
4037	4.00	4103	197.00	4143	140.00	4204	163.00
4040	9.00	4104	86.00	4144	21.00	4206	0.00
4041	0.00	4105	15.00	4145	44.00	4207	0.00
4042	420.00	4106	18.00	4146	37.00	4210	74.00
4043	0.00	4107	452.00	4147	0.00	4211	78.00

FIGURE 2-8   Tabular List of Data by Zone

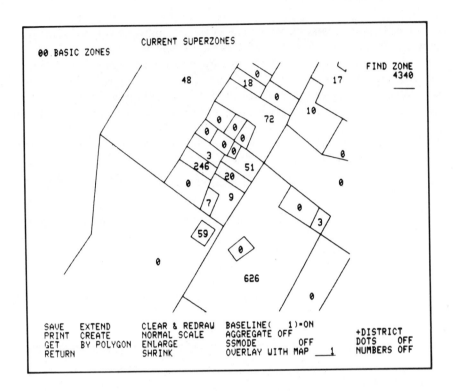

FIGURE 2-9   Zone Date Displayed on City Map (expanded scale)

- they would cause the symbols displayed at the data points to represent any third variable or combination of variables

Once an alternative had been chosen, the DSS could be used to aid in *implementation*. Figure 2-16 shows the boundaries of a new territory, and hard copies of this map were given to the appropriate CE showing his new territory boundaries and expected workload.

This scenario of the use of GADS can be used to illustrate how GADS supported the DSS capabilities described in this chapter. Note that the way GADS supported these capabilities differed in other applications of GADS.

1. The CE territory decision was semi-structured (underspecified) because the decision process differed among decision makers. GADS allowed each Field Manager to select the data in GADS which he thought was relevant; and to use that, plus other data (not in GADS) to develop and evaluate alternative solutions.

2. GADS was used by both CEs and Field Managers, although primarily by the latter. Field Managers were first or second line managers, not executives.

3. The CE territory decision was pooled interdependent, because the Field Managers had to work out a negotiated decision on one set of territories for the Branch Office.

4. As illustrated in Sutton's scenario, GADS supported intelligence, design, choice and implementation. Intelligence was supported by displaying data as maps, histograms, and tables. Design was supported by manipulating maps. Choice was supported by comparing alternatives quantitatively and visually. Implementation was supported by involving CEs in choice and by making choice data available to CEs.

5. GADS did not force the Field Managers to follow any specific decision making process, and observation of their usage patterns indicated a wide variety among Field Managers in how they used GADS.

6. Ease of use is hard to measure. Sutton reported that all the Field Managers used GADS, and that they thought of additional uses. Field Managers helped each other. They were not forced to use GADS, but none chose to make the territory decisions without it.

The Builder's View of GADS

Sutton was one of the builders of GADS and Figure 2-17 shows how he described the version of GADS used for the CE territory decision (the

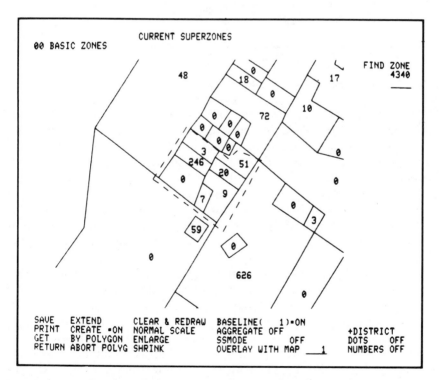

FIGURE 2-10   Defining a Trial Territory as a Set of Zones

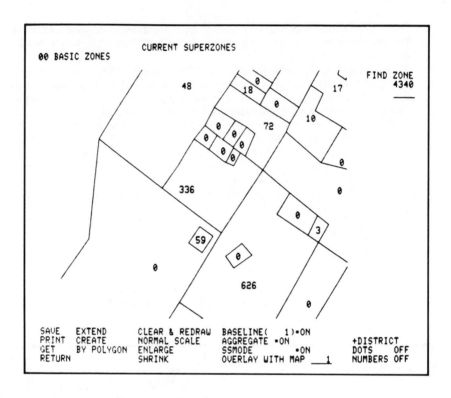

FIGURE 2-11   Zone Data Aggregated by Territory

OPD DSS). In Sutton's diagram the DSS consists of a data base and a set of operations which the Field Manager accessed via a display terminal with joystick (for manipulating a screen cursor) and hard copy unit. The operations listed by Sutton can be divided into dialog (display), model (transformation and aggregation), and data base (query). In Figure 2-18, we describe GADS in terms of dialog, models, and data. The dialog component is used to create a variety of output representations (e.g., Figures 2-7 through 2-16) and to support user input by pointing (via the joystick-controlled cursor) or typing. The modeling component consists of a simple arithmetic and logical transformation system that can be used to compute new data or create symbols on a map. In addition, data can be aggregated (summed) for arbitrary combinations of data and zones. The data base stores the zone maps, the data associated with the maps, any aggregate maps (e.g., territory maps), parameters for the dialog component (e.g., the scale at which to display a map), and any models created by the user (e.g., arithmetic and logical statements in the modeling language). Figure 2-17 indicates that the data for the Specific DSS used by the Field Managers came from two main sources (current CE territories and Installed Machine Inventory).

The Toolsmith's View of GADS

The builders put together GADS (as shown in Figures 2-17 and 2-18) from a variety of tools. The primary tools were:

1. a display management subroutine package which isolated the rest of the GADS software from changes in the display output and input hardware
2. the FORTRAN programming language which was used to write the dialog, modeling, and most of the data base functions
3. the PL/1 programming language which was used to write the programs for extracting data from source files to form a GADS data base
4. a laboratory-enhanced, raster-scan color graphics display device with full keyboard, function keys, and a light pen.

Figure 2-19 shows the dialog, modeling, and data base components of GADS from the toolsmith's view. For each major GADS function (user's view), one or more modules (toolsmith's view) is used to implement the appropriate dialog, modeling, and data base components (builder's view).

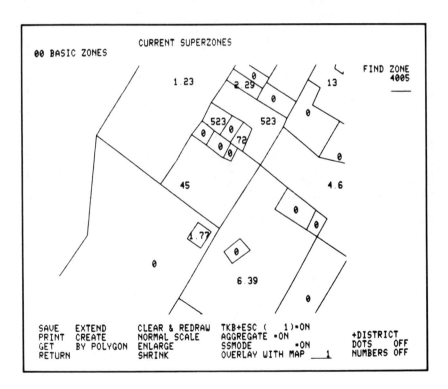

FIGURE 2-12   Another Data Item Aggregated by Territory

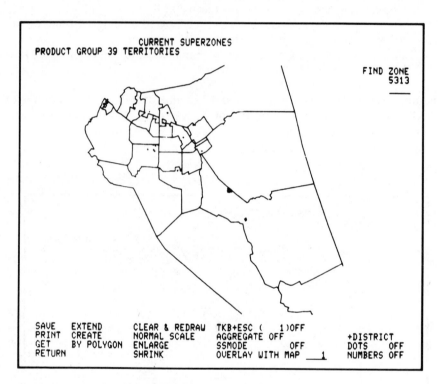

FIGURE 2-13   A Complete Set of Territories

48

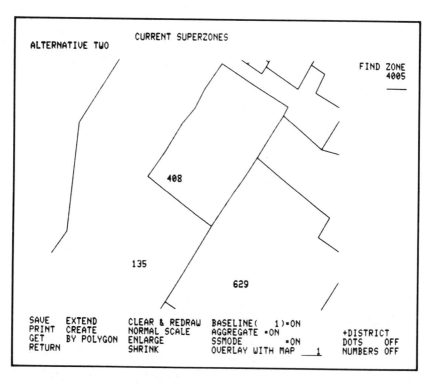

FIGURE 2-14   Aggregated Zone Data for an Alternative Territory (for specific part of city)

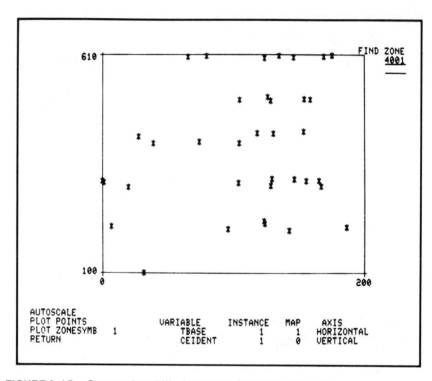

FIGURE 2-15   Scatterplot of Workload per Customer Engineer

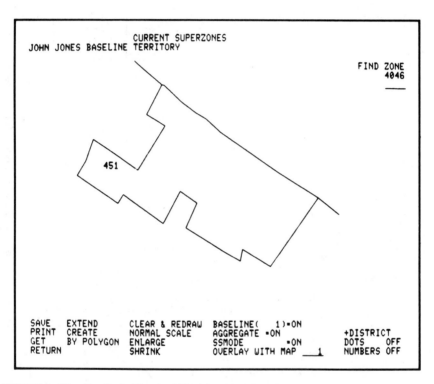

FIGURE 2-16   Territory Map and Workload for One Customer Engineer

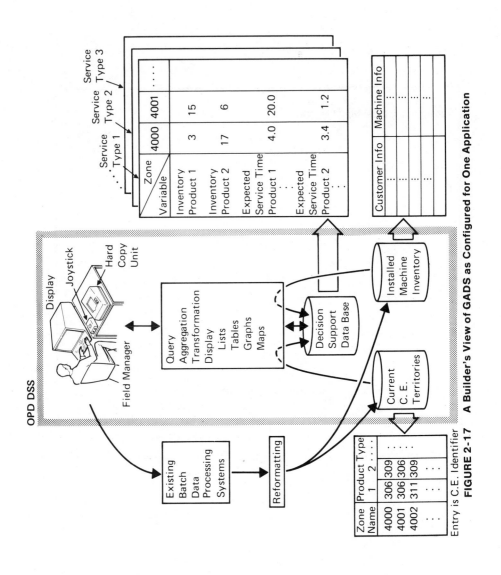

FIGURE 2-17 A Builder's View of GADS as Configured for One Application

52

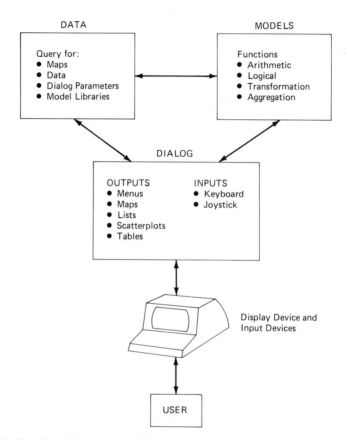

FIGURE 2-18   Builder's View of GADS

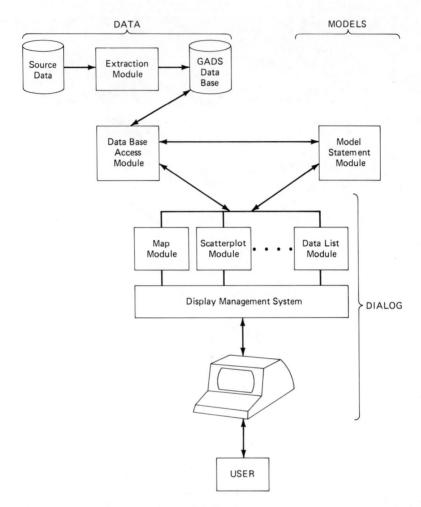

FIGURE 2-19   Toolsmith's View of GADS

PART TWO
THE PROCESS OF BUILDING DSS

Part Two of the book deals with the *process* of building DSS. With the structure of the framework from Part One in mind, we can begin to explore the processes and steps which will lead to the development of DSS.

Chapter 3 is a discussion of getting organized for DSS development. Included are:

- how to ascertain if a DSS is for you,
- how to get organized, with a list of alternative approaches and the pros and cons of each alternative,
- how to develop a plan of action

Chapter 4 suggests an approach for the process of *systems analysis* or the requirements definition for DSS. It is a user-oriented and procedure-independent model for defining what the DSS should do for a user and how.

Chapter 5 deals with the *systems design* phases of developing DSS. It emphasizes the process of iterative design which allows systems development to fit the ill-defined needs of users facing complex decision making and problem solving tasks, and to track changes in those needs over time.

Chapter 6 deals with the *implementation* process of building DSS. When DSS are to be used by a number of people, and when they affect institutional practices and procedures, they must be integrated into the organization. Two critical aspects of this integration process are emphasized in Chapter 6: user education and evaluation.

Because of its emphasis on the process of building DSS, Part Two should be read by all those in the organization that will play one of the roles in DSS development. However, DSS builders and their managers will be most directly in charge of managing and monitoring these processes, so Part Two is of most direct importance to them.

CHAPTER THREE

PLANNING AND ORGANIZING FOR DECISION SUPPORT SYSTEMS

OUTLINE

INTRODUCTION

The sophistication and complexity of decision-making and problem-solving tasks in organizations have been increasing for several years. To some observers, the MIS effort was always a few steps behind real managerial needs for information system support. This has led to the feeling that DSS is attempting to do what MIS failed to do. Similarly, the technology for supporting these needs has been increasing rapidly. Application of this technology on an ad hoc basis has lead to the comment that "DSS is what we have been trying to do all along but didn't have a name for." As these two evolutionary trends converge, we need to develop better ways to organize and manage their interaction.

Observers continue to debate which trend is the driving one. Is DSS development characterized by "demand pull" or "technology push"? To some extent this is a chicken-and-egg argument, and the pragmatist might feel the question is more philosophical than useful. There is a good reason for raising the issue, however, especially as we begin the chapter on organizing the DSS development effort. The market imperatives of the information technology industry, coupled with the technical background of most systems development people, create strong pressures to use all the fancy technology that is becoming available. In addition, many organizations are large enough to have developed a fair amount of bureaucratic inertia. Getting a new effort started may require an overstatement of the problem and an overselling of the solution. This is the bandwagon effect discussed in Chapter 2. A bandwagon approach to DSS development may generate short-run visibility, but it will lead to a seriously shortened life expectancy.

It is critical, in organizing for the development of DSS, to avoid the bandwagon tendency and maintain a user-needs focus, responding to those needs as they develop, change, and mature over time. Fortunately, the very nature of DSS supports a development approach that tracks user needs closely. It is characterized by a small initial system which evolves and grows over time. The organizational questions this approach raises are:

- How can current needs susceptible to DSS be recognized?
- How can the likely extent of their growth be assessed?
- What type of DSS are required to support the needs, now and in the future?
- What are the minimum startup capabilities required, both organizational and technical?
- What kind of plan can be developed to establish the long-term direction, yet respond to unanticipated developments in managerial needs and technical capabilities?

This chapter addresses these questions and provides guidance for assessing the advantages and disadvantages of several alternative answers.

GETTING STARTED

Needs and Tools

Since tough problems and decisions (which are susceptible to DSS) have been evolving for some time, there are examples in most firms of attempts to provide answers and support. They have taken the following forms:

- Requested revisions to EDP or MIS systems (additional reports, new features, etc.). In many cases, system upgrades of this type are used as part of a more complex process of decision-making or problem-solving support. The request may reflect a need for DSS-type support, but in the absence of a DSS capability in the organization, it takes the form of an incremental improvement to an existing system. Of course, to the extent that the requested change is merely a change in the processing of transactions or a needed revision in the routine reporting process, it is merely an EDP or MIS function, not a DSS application in disguise. These requests are usually made to the EDP group, perhaps through a functional information specialist or liaison person.

- Requests from managers for special studies or reports. An especially good clue is an increasing number of studies and reports that are special or one-time, but similar in nature or structure. These requests may be directed to an external consulting group (if they are large, special purpose, and technical), to a management science or operations research group (if they require quantitative analysis), to a financial analysis group (if they require traditional financial analysis), or to a departmental staff analyst.

- Requests for external data. Managers are increasingly seeking external data such as competitors' performance, industry financial or marketing data, regional or local economic and financial data, and so on. A request of this type might go to the computer people if the data are in machine readable form, to consultants if they require a special data gathering effort, or to a staff group.

As part of the evolving technology to support these types of requests, many companies have developed technology-based tools or mechanisms to make some contributions. For instance:

- A time-sharing contract to provide access to external data bases and to libraries of analysis programs.

- A financial planning language to support analysis based on spread sheets and financial reports.

- An interactive facility on the in-house EDP system so that staff analysts can have direct access to internal computer data.

- A query language and/or a report generator on the in-house computer system to allow the preparation of special-purpose inquiries and reports from internal computerized data. These capabilities may be part of a data base management system.

- Turnkey applications, based on a mini- or microcomputer, that support a designated small set of problems on a regular basis.

- A personal computer to support an individual manager's need for fast response analysis (e.g., an APPLE or TRS-80 microcomputer with VISICALC).

Any one of these tools can be an instance of a Specific DSS if it adequately supports a decision maker or group of them facing a set of related tasks. However, no one of them can constitute general DSS capability for the organization over a wide variety of decision-making and problem-solving situations. Such a set of tools, if properly managed and integrated, could constitute general DSS capability. Usually, however, because they have evolved in response to different needs at different times, they will not be well integrated. Eventually, the continued accumulation of decisions/problems and tools to meet them raises a crucial question. Is it better to continue developing tools and capabilities in response to needs as they are expressed, or to get organized, integrating the tools and promoting their use to develop a general DSS capability for the organization?

Ad Hoc or Integrated Approach

The decision can be made, of course, by default. If no one in the organization notices the trend and takes the responsibility for raising the question, ad hoc development will continue as a matter of course. Managers in well-run organizations, however, are likely to recognize the trends and identify the opportunity to do a more effective and efficient job of meeting their increasingly complex needs with the increasingly powerful technology.

There are, in fact, a variety of tactical options for developing DSS in an organization, including the following three.

1. The quick-hit. If it is not clear that a general DSS capability is needed, but there is a recognized high-payoff area for decision support, develop a Specific DSS directly using the most appropriate tools, capture the benefits, then consider what to do next.
2. The staged development approach. Build one Specific DSS, but with some advanced planning, so that part of the effort in developing the first system can be reused in developing the second. With appropriate planning, a DSS Generator evolves from the development of several successive Specific DSS.
3. The complete DSS. Before building any Specific DSS, develop a full-service DSS Generator, and the organizational structure for managing it.

Each of the three tactics has advantages and disadvantages. To a large extent the best tactic will depend on a combination of four factors.

1. The organization. The extent to which the organization is in a stable or volatile industry, whether it is willing to use technology that is not yet fully established, whether it has a history of using computer-based technology and quantitative analysis approaches, and so on.
2. The tasks. The extent to which DSS-susceptible problem-solving and decision-making tasks are presently recognized and expected to prevail in the future.

3. The users. The extent to which managers and users are willing to *participate* in the development of DSS, beyond mere support, ratification, or approval of the general effort.
4. The builders. The extent to which there is a group of people willing and able to become promoters and champions of this special way to use information technology to support decision making.

Considering the three development tactics in the light of these four factors gives some obvious guidance. For example, the quick-hit approach is clearly preferred if there is an immediate problem area but no evidence of long term need. Also, any approach is likely to be difficult or impossible without users' willingness to participate in the development, or without a group of DSS builders.

The Quick-Hit. Even if the basic conditions make a development tactic feasible, however, there are some more subtle advantages and disadvantages, as summarized in Figure 3-1. The quick-hit approach clearly has the lowest risk and highest potential payoff in the short run. The required tools and techniques can be developed in-house or purchased in the hardware/software market and applied directly to the problem. Since there is no carryover from the first Specific DSS, the second DSS can be developed using the latest technology at that time. The lack of carryover also counts as a disadvantage, however. The development experience will be useful but there is no assurance that any of the tools used in one Specific DSS will be directly helpful in the next. Moreover, the Specific DSS created directly with basic tools is likely to be less flexible and require more maintenance effort over time than if it had been developed with an integrated set of tools or a DSS Generator.

The Staged Development Approach. The principal advantage of the staged development approach is that it leads to the accumulation of a general DSS capability while minimizing the risks and giving a somewhat early payoff through the completion of one Specific DSS. In addition, it allows the overlapping development of successive Specific DSS with an integration between them whenever appropriate. Because it is an iterative approach with frequent opportunities to change direction, it allows some assimilation of new technology as it becomes available. The disadvantages include the need for some up-front development costs and some delay in the completion of the first Specific DSS.

The Complete DSS. The development of a complete DSS Generator as a major project is likely to result in the most efficient generator with the best integration of basic tools and the best architecture. It is also most likely to reach "full strength" before either of the other two approaches. Counterbalancing these advantages are the long development time before any bene-

QUICK-HIT

ADVANTAGES	DISADVANTAGES
• Fast payoff	• One shot—no likely carryover to next SDSS
• Low risk	
• Easier to apply technology and development procedures	• Specific DSS may require more effort to change and modify
• Latest technology always available	

STAGED DEVELOPMENT

ADVANTAGES	DISADVANTAGES
• Leads to development of DSS Generator	• Requires some additional cost up front
• Gives early success and visibility	• Delays initial success somewhat
• Allows overlapping of SDSS and integration between them	
• Ability to assimilate evolving technology	

COMPLETE DSS

ADVANTAGES	DISADVANTAGES
• Likely to be best integrated and have best architecture	• Long development time before first benefits are realized
• Will reach "full strength" soonest	• High risk of technological obsolescense
	• High risk of unknown pitfalls

FIGURE 3-1   Development Tactics: Advantages and Disadvantages

fits are attained. Current software systems that approach the concept of a DSS Generator have taken 6 to 10 years to develop. Although a direct development project begun at the present time could be completed more quickly, it is certainly a multi-year effort. It is also the most risky option, susceptible to technological obsolescence and to unknown development pitfalls. For example, a system using color graphics terminals just a few years ago incurred high hardware costs and software complexity compared to the units available in the market today.

Any of the three approaches may be best in a given organization. Most of the early DSS described in the literature illustrate the first approach—they were the direct development of a Specific DSS using available tools. Pacific Diversified Industries, a case illustration in this book, used the staged development approach, illustrated in more detail at the end of this chapter. The development of the GADS system, the other case example in this book, was similar to the third option—development of a large DSS Generator as a vehicle for researching the characteristics and nature of DSS. We recommend the staged development approach because we feel it is more balanced than the other two approaches. However, the ideas, procedures, and techniques in this book are equally applicable to all three tactics.

Make or Buy

The word "development," used repeatedly in the preceding section, should not be construed to exclude the purchase of software products and services in the marketplace. In fact, flexible DSS software is proving to be quite expensive to develop from scratch. At the same time, however, there are extensive efforts in the software and time-sharing industries to provide these products and services. Together, these trends make the development of DSS capability through purchase in the software marketplace a very viable option.

Because the products produced by the marketplace are evolving from pre-DSS software, however, there are currently no packages of well-integrated tools or DSS Generators as we describe them in this book. Therefore, in most organizations, the process of "developing" or building general DSS capabilities will be a combination of software purchase and internal development to integrate and fill in the gaps. A plan for this process is illustrated in the PDI case at the end of this chapter.

GETTING ORGANIZED

In this section we discuss the organizational steps and procedures for managing the DSS development effort. These procedures are relevant for all three of the development options outlined above, but most directly fit the staged development approach. For simplicity, we assume that the organization has decided to create a general DSS capability using the staged approach. Early organizational effort will be needed to create three things:

1. A DSS group
2. A plan of action
3. A minimal set of startup tools and data sources

We will not need a major reorganization of the systems group, a lot of new hardware and software, or a major campaign to usher in the "DSS era."

The DSS Group

A conscious, purposeful DSS development effort will require a group of people to take the responsibility for managing it. The number of people in the group will depend on the size of the effort and the tactical development option they will use. Some companies have initiated a DSS effort with as few as two or three people; others have used as many as 12 to 15 people. Notice that even the upper limit of this range is quite small compared with typical applications systems development departments. Fewer people will be required because of the different roles they will play, the nature of the technology, and the size of the systems. DSS development depends on heavy user participation and is usually based on technology that is "end-user" oriented. Typically, these tools enable rapid creation of a system that is usually much smaller than a transactions processing system.

In general, the responsibilities of the DSS group will include the following:

1. To develop a good understanding of the DSS philosophy and formulate a group mission based on that philosophy.
2. To become familiar with the procedures for implementing DSS.
3. To manage the DSS Generator or integrated collection of tools in order to provide DSS services to users.
4. To play the role of facilitator to help the user bring the technology to bear on his or her problems.

The builder role is the center of the spectrum of five roles discussed in Chapter 1. It bridges the gap between the technology and the user. This is the role applications-oriented systems analysts have played in building traditional systems. In this central role, there are some aspects of both the liaison roles (technical support and intermediary) embedded in the builder's role. Sometimes the builder must act as the intermediary and counsel with the user. Sometimes the builder must play the technical support role in dealing with the toolsmith.

In some companies, the builders' role is beginning to develop a double focus, one which is technology oriented to develop and manage the DSS Generator, and the other, which is sales oriented, to promote the use of DSS, working directly with the users or intermediaries in developing them. This tendency should not be surprising; it also happened with systems analysts for traditional systems as the applications became more complex and the users' needs became more sophisticated. In the DSS group, however, both functions are more user oriented and require special procedures and tactics.

The DSS group can be formed by redefining and extending the charter of an existing group, or it can be newly initiated. In either case, the group or individuals can come from several sources.

1. A special purpose team of applications systems analysts
   - In a manufacturing firm, one of the application development teams in the MIS department was given the responsibility for all DSS type applications that were requested by users. Instead of passively waiting for requests, they soon became active in advertising the availability of their skills and expertise.
2. A reoriented tools group
   - A small group of programmers in a bank developed an interactive reporting system using APL. After several iterations, the system had several characteristics of a DSS Generator, so the group began to promote its use for other similar applications.
   - A food-processing firm noticed that the use of its time-sharing service had grown substantially, and that many of the applications were DSS-like. The coordinator of time-sharing services was designated the head of a new DSS group. In effect, he was asked to focus on the DSS needs of users, drawing on a broader set of technology than he had previously managed.
3. A management science or operations research group
   - A management science group at a diversified conglomerate was expanded and redirected to become a DSS group.
   - The financial analysis section of the management science department in an oil company developed a set of integrated financial analysis tools and began functioning as a DSS group.
4. The planning department
   - The strategic planning department of a major airline developed a data analysis and forecasting system which became the DSS Generator for a DSS group that was spun out of the planning department.
   - The chief planning officer at a medium-size bank became a one-man DSS department for executive officers through his use of an external planning/analysis system from a consulting firm.
5. A staff analysis group from one of the functional areas such as a market research group, or a budget analysis group from accounting/finance

Organizational Location

The organizational placement of the DSS group will depend greatly on its origin, the people in the group and their philosophical heritage, and the overall organizational structure. In fact, most DSS groups will begin working on DSS without a major change in organizational location. The nature of their activities merely evolves as indicated in several of the examples listed above.

In spite of the fact that "it all depends on the situation," a few general comments on the location of the DSS group are appropriate. Perhaps the theoretically best location is within the information services division (ISD) because of the advantage of coordinating the availability of data and evolving technology. This assumes that the ISD actually takes the broad view inferred by its name and is concerned with managing the information resources for the entire organization. Such a broad-based department would have jurisdiction over word processing and office automation efforts, permanent records management, and perhaps even copiers and printing facilities. If the department is a narrow-minded MIS department, or basically a relabeled EDP department, it is less likely that its managers will understand or appreciate the special nature of DSS activities, needs, and technical requirements.

Another likely organizational location is a highly placed executive staff group. This is a relevant alternative because many DSS groups and people have evolved from such a position. In this location, users are more likely to view the group as a source of problem solving assistance, and less likely to view them as just computer types in the EDP sense. A third location is within the finance area. In the early days of EDP, computer departments were often formed within the accounting and finance areas because most of the work was there. Similarly, early DSS applications and technology have found most frequent use in the finance area. Although there are good reasons to put the DSS group where most of the users are in the short run, it will probably be relocated eventually for the same reasons that MIS departments are now seldom within the finance area.

Regardless of the organizational location, the DSS group will have to deal with the issue of centralization versus decentralization. As usual, the primary determinant is the structure of the organization itself and to what extent it has a declared policy on centralization or decentralization. In a centralized organization, the DSS group is more likely to have the full responsibility for developing and maintaining the DSS Generator or Tools and for dealing with all users. In a decentralized organization the group may provide the technical expertise to manage the Generator and Tools while supporting some groups that deal directly with users in each division or geographic region. In the latter case, the Generator or Tools may be centralized and available through data communications or they may be distributed. In a fully decentralized firm, the DSS effort may be carried out by totally separate smaller groups in each division. These, of course, can be considered central DSS groups for each division.

THE ACTION PLAN

The DSS group may be formed as the first step in a DSS effort based on upper management's conviction that such an effort is needed. More often the decision to form a group will be a step in a broader plan to evaluate potential benefits and the feasibility of a DSS effort. Because the cardinal rule in DSS is to be driven by user needs, a DSS effort should not be undertaken unless the need is apparent. Assessing the extent of need, however, requires some understanding and commitment to DSS in advance (another chicken-and-egg issue). The plan outlined below suggests forming the DSS group as part of Phase II in an overall plan. In our experience, Phase I often is done by one of the origin groups mentioned earlier, or it evolves from a set of events which together constitute Phase I. The PDI case at the end of this chapter illustrates a combination of these origins. The choice of development tactic (quick-hit, staged development, complete DSS) is likely to be determined by the DSS group after it is formed, but we have shown the plan that would be most appropriate to the staged development tactic. Neither of these simultaneities is serious because the structure of the plan follows another of the key principles of the DSS philosophy. It is iterative, with frequent checkpoints for midcourse corrections and redirection.

Let us outline the general phases of the plan at this time, illustrating one example of a detailed plan in the PDI case at the end of the chapter.

Phase I: Preliminary Study and Feasibility Assessment

1. Survey the "user base" to determine the extent of DSS-type applications and assess the likelihood that these needs will continue or increase in the future. This step is usually based on an inventory of requests, projects, and studies as mentioned earlier in the chapter, perhaps supplemented by interviews with key managers and users.

2. Conduct a few pilot projects (or analyze some of the existing projects) to ascertain their general characteristics and the implications to DSS needs. This step is important in determining the starting point for the first Specific DSS. It is also a good opportunity to explain the nature and purpose of DSS and to test the receptivity of potential users to the DSS effort.

3. Assess the results of Phase I and prepare a detailed plan for Phase II.

Phase II: Developing the DSS Environment

1. Assuming that the DSS effort is warranted, form the DSS group, articulate its mission, and define the relationships between it and other organizational units.
2. Establish a minimal set of tools and data and operationalize them. The make-or-buy decision discussed earlier is particularly important at this stage. It is also a tricky step because of the tendency to overprepare. There is a temptation for builders to implement in advance all the capabilities and data that users might want so as not to be caught unprepared. However, there is no way to identify users' desires until they begin to use the system, requesting additions, deletions, and modifications in response to that use under real conditions. At the same time, it is not feasible to start discussions with users about support from a DSS with no available tools or data; the inevitable delay before real work can begin would result in a loss of credibility. Builders must find a middle ground, bringing up a "minimal set" of tools and data that users of the first Specific DSS are *highly likely* to want and use.
3. Prepare a tentative plan for the evolution of the tools toward a DSS Generator. The plan is tentative because it will respond to the users' needs as they become apparent, and to evolving technology as it becomes available. It will be somewhat specific in defining the minimal starting point and the initial enhancements, but the specifications for 6-, 12-, and 18-month checkpoints will be successively more general. See the PDI case illustration for an example of an evolutionary plan.
4. Assess the results of Phase II and prepare a detailed plan for Phase III.

Phase III: Developing the Initial Specific DSS

1. Based on the activities in Phase I, decide where to start. The identification of the initial Specific DSS is important. It should address a recognized need, with a high probability of early observable benefits. The managers or users should be motivated and willing to participate directly, and the builders should know something about the functional application.
2. Begin working with the users on the system analysis and design for the first Specific DSS.
3. Upgrade the tools and the data in response to needs that evolve from dealing with the users.
4. Assess the results of Phase III and prepare detailed plans for Phase IV.

Phase IV: Developing Subsequent Specific DSS

The choice of the second SDSS is nearly as important as the first. In addition to criteria used in choosing the first, the second might need to "fit into" the first system in some way. For instance, a Specific DSS for a higher or lower organizational level in the same area as the first would help define the data flows and interrelationships between them. On the other hand, replicating the same system in another division with a different group of users would probably be easier and yield a quicker payoff.

It may not be necessary to wait until the first Specific DSS is completed before beginning the second. PDI found it appropriate and beneficial to initiate three separate Specific DSS at three different levels of the organization with staggered starting times (see the case example).

CRITERIA FOR A DSS GENERATOR

The staged development approach leads to the development of a DSS Generator which evolves from the process of building several Specific DSS. To do this requires a target. What does an ideal DSS Generator look like, and what should it do? Identifying the necessary and desirable characteristics of a DSS Generator is a crucial step in Phase II of the plan (development of the DSS environment). A typical but *inappropriate* approach to this task would be to list all possible features a DSS Generator should have, then prepare a checklist to see which existing software system has the most features. Such an approach is inappropriate for two reasons. First, there is no rationale for choosing items on the initial list, and no way to assess the importance of their presence or absence in a given DSS Generator. Second, we feel that there is no "full-service" Generator, currently available, either in the software market or in a user organization, so there is no way to identify serious shortcomings by merely examining existing systems. Thus we need a way to identify capabilities of a Generator so that some can be fulfilled from the marketplace and others can be developed in-house. In short, guidelines for building a DSS Generator should evolve from this criteria identification scheme.

A Four-Step Process

The approach we suggest is a form of "top-down" analysis at four levels.

1. Identify the *overall objectives* for a DSS Generator. Identify what it should accomplish and why. In this step we focus on a large set of *decision-making systems*, each consisting of a user, facing a task, in an organization setting, using a Specific DSS.
2. Infer from number 1 the *general capabilities* that a DSS Generator must have to respond to the objectives. In this step and the following steps, we focus on the DSS Generator from which the Specific DSS are built.
3. Infer from number 2 a set of *specific capabilities* that are required to accomplish the general capabilities.
4. Infer from numbers 2 and 3 specific devices, strategies, and hardware/ software *features* that can be used to implement the specific capabilities.

Each of the inference steps is subject to discussion and judgment, but the process leads to a set of *defendable* characteristics or criteria against which to judge the existing hardware and software, and guidelines for filling the gaps. Figure 3-2 is a schematic representation of the process.

We begin this process by discussing the upper two levels—overall objectives and general capabilities—in this chapter. Two overall objectives lead to three general capabilities which correspond to the Dialog–Data–Model paradigm developed in Chapter 2. The specific capabilities required in each of these areas are discussed more fully in Chapters 7, 8, and 9, respectively.

In Figure 3-2, the features of the ultimate DSS Generator are combined in one list and are no longer aligned with the Dialog–Data–Model paradigm. Individual features may contribute to more than one of the three capabilities depending on the architecture of the Generator.

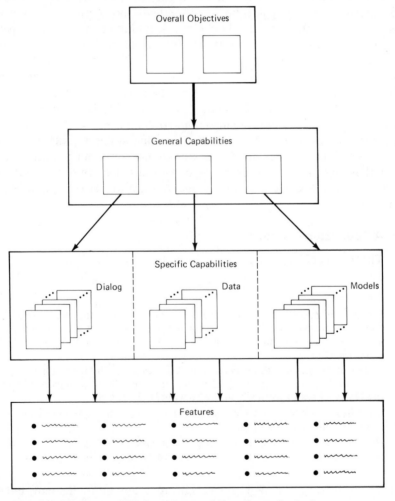

FIGURE 3-2   Criteria for DSS Generators: A Top-Down Analysis

Overall Objectives

There are two basic objectives of the DSS Generator:

1. To permit quick and easy development of a wide variety of Specific DSS. As we have mentioned earlier, there is no way to generalize or define a "typical" Specific DSS. Each specific DSS must serve a decision maker, with a decision-making approach or style, facing a set of tasks or problems, in an organizational environment. *As a group*, however, the Specific DSS built with a Generator must satisfy the six performance criteria discussed in Chapter 2. Therefore, the Generator must permit construction of Specific DSS that meet those criteria.
2. The Generator must be flexible and adaptive enough to facilitate the iterative design process by which Specific DSS can respond quickly to changes—in the organizational or physical environment, in the style of the user, or the nature of the task. The Generator must also facilitate the communication and interaction between the user and the builder. The iterative design process requires this communication to allow the Specific DSS to evolve and grow over time. Specifically, the Generator should:
   a. Facilitate creation of an initial version of a Specific DSS to support decision making or problem solving for a critical subproblem.
   b. Facilitate the users' evaluation of the performance of the system and specifications for needed changes, modifications, and enhancements.
   c. Facilitate the implementation of these changes by the user or builder.

General Capabilities

In order to satisfy the overall objectives given above, the DSS Generator must have three general capabilities:

1. It should be easy to use. Specifically,
   a. The Generator should create Specific DSS which are easy and convenient for nontechnical people to use in an active and controlling way.
   b. The Generator should be easy and convenient for a builder to use for building and modifying Specific DSS.
2. A DSS Generator should provide access to a wide variety of data sources, internal and external, transactional and nontransactional. These data should be available in a way that supports problem-solving and decision-making activities for a variety of users, problems, and contexts.
3. A DSS Generator should provide access to analysis capabilities to the extent that some "suggestion" is available to the user if requested. The analysis capability should support problem-solving and decision-making activities for a variety of users, problems, and contexts.

Notes on General Capabilities. Some additional comments are appropriate for the general capabilities. The underlying model is the three-part framework that focuses on dialog, data, and analysis capabilities developed in Chapter 2. Strength in only one or two of the areas, however, is not sufficient. A DSS Generator needs to have minimal capability in all three of the areas; it needs to be "balanced." There are many examples of systems with strength in one or two areas but with a debilitating weakness in another. Second, the three general capability areas must be integrated and available through the same mechanism, implying an underlying communication facility among all parts of the system.

The Dialog–Data–Model paradigm is a useful and relevant way to organize capabilities in the short run, because it aligns well with state-of-the-art theory and technology. "Intelligence" capability is likely to increase in all three areas, perhaps coalescing into a separate function. In the short run, however, the primary guidance and control function will remain with the user. The user must still decide what decision style is preferred, and draw (perhaps with the help of the builder) on a variety of mechanisms (dialog styles) to support it. Some "intelligence" is available currently in the analysis area because of the relatively advanced stages of statistical and management science modeling.

Capabilities and Features.   The overall objectives and general capabilities for an "ideal" DSS Generator define the general nature of the long-range target. Discussion of the specific capabilities in dialog, data management, and model management, and how they can be implemented with hardware/software features is the subject of Part 3.

SUMMARY

Interest in DSS results from intersection of the increasing complexity of decision-making and problem-solving tasks in the organization, and the increasing power of information systems technology which can support those tasks. Perceptive managers are recognizing that planning and organizing to develop a DSS capability will be more effective than treating each project on an ad hoc basis.

This chapter outlines a plan of action that includes phases to assess the potential value of such a DSS effort, create an environment to support DSS development, and build the initial Specific DSS to support problem solving and decision making. We presented several development and organizational tactics along together with the advantages and disadvantages of each.

Finally, we discussed a top-down approach for identifying the general nature of the ideal DSS Generator, which may be the target for development of general DSS capabilities in the long run.

QUESTIONS AND PROBLEMS

REVIEW QUESTIONS

1. What is some evidence that a general DSS effort might be needed?
2. What kinds of information systems tools and technologies have been applied to DSS-type problems in the past?
3. What is the difference between the ad hoc approach and the integrated approach to the development of DSS?
4. Who makes the decision of which approach to use, and on what basis is it usually made?
5. Identify three tactics for the development of DSS. What are the advantages and disadvantages of each?
6. What are the responsibilities of the DSS group? What kinds of expertise will be required of the people in the group?
7. Outline the action plan for the development of a general DSS capability using the staged development approach.
8. Summarize the two overall objectives and the three general capabilities required for an "ideal" DSS Generator.

DISCUSSION QUESTIONS

1. Since the DSS group usually evolves from a previously existing group, why should we bother to form a new group? Is it not better to just let the existing groups build DSS? Discuss the advantages and disadvantages of formally organizing a DSS group.
2. If a DSS group is organized, where is the best place for it to reside in the organization? Why?
3. Since the development of DSS Tools and Generators is very expensive, it makes no sense to develop them internally. An organization should always wait until the right tools are available in the marketplace. Discuss.

EXERCISE

1. Read the PDI case example at the end of this chapter. Develop a Gantt chart or a PERT network for PDI's action plan. Be sure to show where the steps and phases overlap and how the adaptive nature of the checkpoints at the end of each phase are accomplished.

CASE EXAMPLE

PDI, INC.

In the annual meeting with the staff of the Information Services Division, Mr. Victor outlined his thinking about DSS. Specifically, he:

- Summarized the one-half day seminar on DSS which he had attended, particularly emphasizing the types of problems and users they were designed to support, and the three levels of technology that can be used to support them.
- Identified the series of recent projects that seem to have some DSS characteristics. (See Chapter 1.)

After some discussion and questions, they decided to form a small task force to consider building a generalized DSS capability. The group consisted of the ISD manager, the manager of systems analysis, two major potential DSS users (the director of the planning and analysis group from HQ staff and a manager from the construction division), plus the manager of the management science department.

Although Mr. Victor could easily justify the project and fund it from his existing budget, he decided to solicit reactions from his boss, the executive vice-president, Mr. Campbell. He found that several recent developments among top management were also suggesting the need for DSS.

- At its yearly strategic planning meeting at a mountain retreat, the executive management committee had spent one day discussing information technology and assessing its potential value and impact on the organization.
- As a result of that meeting, the CEO had formed an ad hoc committee to explore better ways to use information systems and analysis capability for himself and his office.
- Mr. Campbell himself had taken on the job of developing a more flexible system for analyzing and evaluating the performance of operating divisions, in cooperation with each group vice-president. From what he had heard about DSS, he thought it would directly support that effort.
- Several of the financial executives at headquarters had indicated an interest in better access to current data on economic and financial conditions, and a better way to analyze those data for planning purposes.

At the end of the discussion Mr. Victor and Mr. Campbell observed that each of these needs could be met with a separate systems development project or special study in the usual way, but that such a fragmented approach in this case would be partially redundant and inefficient. They decided that it would be more sensible to explore the feasibility of developing a flexible "delivery system" to provide the information and analysis capabilities executives need to manage the critical aspects of their responsibilities. The DSS approach Mr. Victor had described seemed like the right way to address this general task.

At the first meeting of the DSS task force a few days later, Mr. Victor shared Mr. Campbell's comments and reactions with the rest of the group. Encouraged by top management's support of the effort, they began to identify a tentative plan of action. After several meetings they developed the following general plan.

PHASE I: Preliminary Study

1. Do a preliminary study to find out how much need for DSS there might be.
2. Conduct a few pilot studies, probably chosen from the needs identified in Step 1, to "test the water" and explore some of the key aspects of DSS.
3. Assess the results of Phase I, prepare a detailed plan for Phase II, and reassess the plans for Phases III–V.

PHASE II: Develop the DSS Environment

1. Organize a DSS group.
   a. Define organizational roles and interrelationships within ISD.
   b. Define interrelationships between ISD and other departments.
2. Identify a minimum set of startup tools and data, and get them up and running.
3. Develop a tentative plan for evolving the Generator as SDSS are developed.
4. Assess the results of Phase II, prepare a detailed plan for Phase III, and reassess the general plan for Phases IV and V.

PHASE III: Develop a System for a Group
Vice-President (GVP)

1. Select the GVP.
2. Develop a personal Specific DSS for the GVP using the iterative design approach.
3. Assess the results of Phase III and prepare a detailed plan for Phase IV. Specifically:
   a. Reassess the Generator and data sources.
   b. Reassess the relationships between DSS and other ISD thrusts.
   c. Decide on the focus of the next phase, particularly whether to expand horizontally or vertically.

PHASE IV: Develop Operating Division
System (most likely option)

1. Extend the system downward to one division president.
2. Evaluate Phase IV and select the focus of Phase V.

PHASE V: Extension and Replication

Although the plan was quite general, the group felt that it gave overall direction which could be refined or changed as it progressed. They felt that the short preliminary study as Step 1 of Phase I would allow assessment of directional strategies without consuming a large amount of time and resources. To implement that objective, they allowed one person in the group a whole month to prepare the report for Step 1.

The Preliminary Study

The report from the preliminary study was based on interviews with all the group vice-presidents, the executive vice-president, the CEO, and several members of the corporate staff groups. An excerpt from the report follows.

The interviews with executives revealed a desire for better information system support, including flexible data access and analysis, both for tracking current operations and analyzing problems and opportunities. At the present time, only a few of these needs are perceived as urgent. These urgent needs are partially met by manual methods or by parts of the pilot projects described later. However, all the executives felt that significant improvements are possible and that the need for additional information systems capability will become increasingly important in the future. The absence of current urgency coupled with the perceived future importance of these needs permits careful, planned development of a flexible set of systems capabilities for meeting them. A partial list of the needs cited in the interviews includes the following:

1. Increasing need to track and analyze the performance of competitors as a guide to planning and decision making.
2. Quick and flexible access to key economic and financial data with analysis capability.
3. Ability to assess the impact of economic conditions of related businesses: for example, the impact of a recession on the pulp and paper industry which affects tug and barge business.
4. Need for detailed data and a powerful set of analytic capabilities to support the planning decisions and capital appropriation requests at the division levels throughout the company. Many of these now require special studies.
5. Better support for merger and acquisition analysis, which includes assessment of long range impact on the entire company.
6. Better ways to handle and analyze some of the complex reports currently produced for planning and control: for instance, the construction progress report.
7. The capture and analysis of historical data to guide in the competitive bidding process.
8. A generally increasing need for information systems that focus on decision making rather than just reporting and summarizing activities and transactions.

Some of these needs are partially met by a manual or computer-based technique. They are, however, separate or nonintegrated and each is partially deficient.

In summary, the interviews reveal that there is currently a need for flexible information support for analysis and decision making, and that the need will be increasing rapidly in the future. The development of a DSS capability will permit PDI to meet these needs effectively and efficiently now and as they evolve in the future.

Pilot Studies

Based on the report from the preliminary study, Mr. Victor and the task force decided to proceed with Step 2, the pilot studies. One of them was already in process, and the other two were to be done in a month or two to provide quick feedback for guiding the project. The three pilot studies were:

1. Develop and refine the interactive reporting system that had been developed for the CEO under the guidance of his information systems committee. By this time the CEO had identified a set of internal and external data that he would like to look at and analyze. In the course of one month, a member of the management science department had entered a subset of these data onto the Executive Information Services (EIS) system available on a time-sharing basis from Boeing Computer Services in Seattle. The system allowed a wide variety of analysis, report formatting, graphing, plotting, and modeling capabilities on these data. The CEO was impressed with an initial interactive demo in which he asked for computations, analysis, and displays of the limited but real and up-to-date data. This project would increase the amount of internal data and add some external data before the next monthly demonstration for the CEO.

2. Provide a system for the presentation and analysis of key economic and financial data for all executives at headquarters. This group included the CEO, the executive vice-president, all the group vice-presidents, and the vice-president of finance, Mr. Randall. The interviews indicated that this capability was a high-priority item for Mr. Randall, so it should be implemented quickly to capitalize on his interest. The focus of this project will be to investigate and install, on a test basis, a computer-based wire service and stock quotation system. It was expected to yield some valuable experience with executives' use of such a system.

3. Add some competitive data and some of the new financial performance measures to the EIS system so that Mr. Campbell and Mr. Randall could use it. It should be easy to extend the system in this way and it would give both executives a flexible tool for examining the effectiveness of the new performance evaluation approach. It should also give the DSS team some experience in using different versions of the same system (EIS) for several executives at the same time.

Two months later, as the pilot projects were under way, the group met to assess the results of Phase I and reconsider the rest of the plan. After some discussion, they concluded that:

- The CEO would probably continue to use some type of DSS capability, but probably not on a daily or weekly basis and probably not without an intermediary.
- The people in the management science department were very positive toward DSS and its potential, especially the analyst who had worked with the CEO as his intermediary.
- The outside time-sharing service was very powerful and flexible, but they expected Mr. Campbell to urge that the capability be provided on their in-house computer system.

- The use of the system by the executives in projects 2 and 3 was quite encouraging. In fact, as a result of the discussions in the executive suite, another group vice-president had shown considerable interest in participating in some way.

At the end of the meeting, it was clear that the DSS effort should continue. Before tackling the detailed plan for the development of the DSS environment (Phase II), Mr. Victor wanted to complete the reassessment of the entire plan by giving some more thought to the development of the Specific DSS in Phases III and IV. At the close of the meeting he asked one of the group members to prepare a detailed plan for Phase II, and another to articulate Phases III and IV more fully. An excerpt from the latter report follows.

Phase III: The Group VP System

The experience with DSS development during the pilot test will lead into the development of a system for one of the group vice-presidents (GVP) (perhaps the one who has indicated an interest). It should start as a personal system for the GVP and begin with the concept of a *delivery system* for critical success factors (CSF), as explained by Jack Rockart at MIT. The CSF concept is fairly easy to describe and has some history at PDI because of the seminars on the subject held last year. It must be made clear, however, that CSF is not just a reporting system. In fact, there are three important parts of the CSF approach:

1. Identification of the factors that are critical.
2. Identification of the appropriate unit of measure for each factor and designation of the level that constitutes success or nonsuccess.
3. Identification of the data that must be gathered and processed to track progress in meeting the CSF.

Even more important, it must be made clear that a Specific DSS can and should be more than just a delivery system for CSFs. It must also serve a problem- or opportunity-finding function, and the decision-making or problem-solving functions necessary to pursue success over time. In short, the DSS effort can begin with the CSF delivery concept but should not become limited to merely a personal reporting system. The design of the procedure for interviewing the executive and developing a mature understanding of DSS is an important part of this phase.

The selection of the GVP to participate in this initial system development will be important. Some of the selection criteria should include:

- The potential value of improved decision making and problem solving in the group.
- The attitude, capability, imagination, and creativity of the individual executive.
- The commonality of the divisions in the group.

- The working relationship between the GVP and the division presidents.
- The quality of the computer-based information systems in the divisions of that group.

Phase IV: The Division Level System

It is likely that the development of the Specific DSS for the GVP will require data transfers from the division. It would thus be easy to extend the group-level system downward into the division level. Again the initial focus of the effort will be the development of a personal system for the division president using criteria similar to those above. At this time the problems of data transfer, ownership of data, and confidence in the system will become an important part of the design process. At the conclusion of this phase, all of the key processes and issues will have been encountered. The result will be a personal system for the GVP, another for one of his division presidents, plus the linkages between them.

Phase V: Extension and Replication

Based on the experience from the foregoing steps, the DSS effort can be extended or replicated in several ways.

1. Add more division presidents in the same group to build a full group system.
2. Replicate the GVP system for all other groups.
3. Extend upward to the CEO (may not be too useful until all GVPs have been done).
4. Replicate from the bottom up by developing the individual divisions and then the GVP for all other groups.

The specific growth option will be chosen based on experience and a set of criteria that evolve in the process of doing one vertically integrated set of personal systems.

The system can also be extended along a different dimension. Thus far, each Specific DSS has been characterized as a "personal" DSS for the individual executive with linkages and data transfers when appropriate or when required as a result of negotiations between that person and his superior. Their usage will be for CSF tracking and measurement, opportunity finding, and problem solving, as outlined earlier. It is also possible to "institutionalize" the DSS by using it to:

1. Become a flexible alternative output system for the financial reporting system (FRS). Although the DSS will never completely replace the FRS, it may displace some of the reporting and output.
2. Extend the system to become a support facility for the "plan-making process" each year: that is, the five-year plan.

It is important to recognize that these are specific options for extending the use of the DSS. It is likely that some people intuitively feel that the entire DSS effort is no more than number 1 or 2 above, so the development effort must specifically decide whether to support these activities. This decision should, of course, respond to the needs of users as the system evolves.

Cautions and Constraints

The DSS must be developed to support the corporate policy and management style of decentralization. It must give no evidence or appearance that upper management (primarily corporate) is undercutting the role of the group vice-president. It must not permit staff units to access too much data from a lower level in the groups or divisions.

In addition, the system must carefully control the structure and release of information between organizational levels. There must be mechanisms to control the upward flow of data with respect to detail, timing, need to know, privacy, and so on. The mechanisms can be implemented by negotiations that provide variability and flexibility in what is reported and when.

The confidence problem is a big one here. Executives at each level must be confident that unauthorized data transfers or access *cannot* be made. These considerations could impact on the selection of hardware and software for DSS. For example, the distributed concept might help if a division or group is given absolute control over a distributed data base. A central system in company headquarters, on the other hand, might be inherently suspect.

It will also be important to anticipate the tendency to view the DSS effort in a limited way. Based on the nature of their direct contact and experience with the system, DSS will be viewed by some people as:

- An information retrieval system
- A convenient way to do interactive modeling
- An automated spread sheet
- Interactive reporting of financial data
- Graphs and plots instead of tables and reports

A DSS is all the above and more. It will be important during the development of DSS to neutralize any attempts to limit DSS to merely one of them.

The tendency for managers to have a limited view of DSS has two important advantages, however. First, the more limited uses may provide a starting point that generates early practical results leading to more comprehensive use later. Second, if a particular executive is unwilling or unable to utilize the DSS as a flexible set of tools to assist in CSF tracking, opportunity finding, and problem solving, one of the limited uses is legitimate and valuable. This characteristic becomes a built-in hedge, reducing the risk of failure in the overall DSS development effort.

Creating the DSS Environment

Over the course of the next few months, Mr. Victor concentrated on Phase II, creating the DSS environment. The general plan called for formation of the DSS group, establishment of a minimal set of startup tools and capabilities, and construction of a technical plan for evolving the startup tools into a DSS Generator as the first few Specific DSS were built.

The DSS Group. There were two groups at headquarters that had people with expertise and experience in decision-making and problem-solving assistance. One was the management science (MS) group within ISD, and the other was planning and analysis services (PAS) attached to the controller's office. The MS group had always handled a full range of MS and operations research (OR)-type problems, and used the computer regularly. For instance, recent projects included an oil tank car simulation model for an energy division, and a linear programming-based barge scheduling model for a maritime division. They had also developed a financial risk analysis system using Monte Carlo methods that had been used directly by decision makers in the construction and property divisions.

The PAS group dealt primarily with financial analysis. Their services were heavily used by the divisions because they were also responsible for advising the executive committee on capital requests. The divisions apparently felt that it would be helpful to get analysis assistance from PAS in the preparation of these requests. PAS also managed the budgeting and planning process, which included a five-year plan with detail in the first year, which then became the budget. It seemed likely that the early Specific DSS would heavily involve financial data and financial analysis, so this experience and contact with the users would be valuable.

After discussing the decision with the manager of PAS, Mr. Victor decided to assign the DSS responsibility to the existing MS group. The predominant reasons were:

- They had shown an interest in the early DSS work and were excited about its possibilities.
- They were within ISD, thus easing the coordination and communication in obtaining internal computer data and technical assistance from the systems group.
- They had technical experience and computer programming ability to enhance and integrate the DSS Tools.
- Mr. Victor believed that the DSS approach and the DSS Generator eventually could be used to do most of the traditional MS/OR consulting, and that the group should evolve in that direction.

It was clear that the DSS group would play several roles as the effort began. The intermediary role might be required in some cases as it was with the CEO. The builder and technical support role would obviously fall to them as the early Specific DSS evolved. In the long run, the builder role might be partly assumed by the PAS group, especially if the SDSS was used heavily to support the planning process, or by some members of the controller's office if the SDSS partially replaced the financial reporting system. It was likely that the DSS group would always manage the Generator and play the technical support role, even if some of the intermediary and builder roles became distributed into other staff groups or into the user areas.

Startup Tools and Technology.   The required technology to get the DSS effort under way would include some hardware, some software, and some data. The pilot studies had used a commercial time-sharing service, so no hardware or special software had been required. Data were entered manually as needed. Although this process could continue with higher volumes of data transferred directly over telecommunication lines when necessary, Mr. Victor decided to again merge the DSS effort with an existing system. He had recently requested funds to purchase a Hewlett-Packard 3000 to run the three analysis systems built by the MS group. They were currently implemented on a commercial time-sharing service, but the use was heavy enough to justify bringing them in-house. The HP3000 was to be run by the computing center operators but primarily used by members of the MS group. By adding some primary memory, disk drives, and ports, the system could handle the expected DSS load also. The data transfer links between the large machine and the minicomputer would also be easier.

The software to start the DSS effort was more troublesome. Mr. Taylor, the manager of the newly named DSS group, suggested expanding and enhancing the user-oriented risk analysis system to serve as a starting point. After some discussions, they decided that it would require too much programming time from the DSS group. They then considered adapting the financial planning system (IFPS) that the PAS group had recently purchased. The manager of PAS had recently made IFPS available to all divisions on a time-sharing system as a way of standardizing the format and analysis approaches used by the divisions in submitting their capital requests. He was now about to base the procedure manual for submitting capital requests on IFPS, and so had authorized its purchase for in-house use. Although Victor knew that IFPS was not a DSS Generator in the "ideal" sense, it was further along than many other systems and it had several advantages.

- If the DSS group and the PAS group both used the same system, it would promote communication and coordination between them.
- IFPS already had gotten good reviews from many of the users in the divisions because of its easy-to-use language.
- The vendor had offered to supply PDI with source code on the system and provide them with early copies of all new enhancements.
- It seemed to be fairly strong in modeling and dialog, but relatively weak in data. Considering the skills of the people in the DSS group, he felt they could develop a plan to enhance the data area in the short run, and strengthen the other areas later.

After discussing the prospects with PAS and the DSS group, they decided to install IFPS on the HP3000 and make it available to all division users through telecommunication lines. Through a multi-installation agreement with the vendor, a large division could install the system on their local computer in the future at a preferred price.

That left the data sources. The identification of specific data sources had to be postponed, because it would depend on the nature of the SDSS and its users' needs. A general approach was determined, however, consisting of data availability at three levels.

1. A relatively small set of data available immediately because it would be loaded into the data base maintained by the DSS Generator. The initial set of data would be chosen because of the high likelihood that it would be useful to the user of the Specific DSS.
2. A larger set of data available on a 24-hour basis because it could be loaded to the DSS data base over night (e.g., after an extraction run against a major transaction input file or master file).
3. A catalog or inventory of data sources that could be loaded on a few days' notice.

The latter category would be important because much of the benefit of DSS is likely to derive from data that has not been computerized. Some of it would need to be accumulated over time and managed by someone familiar with a large variety of noncomputer data sources. For these reasons, Mr. Victor planned to make the corporate library an important part of the DSS environment as it matured.

With this general plan for data extraction and availability in mind, the DSS group decided that the most likely type of data to be used in the early stages of the SDSS would be the financial reporting data. They therefore made plans to develop a limited extraction program against the financial reporting system master files.

DSS Generator Development Plans. With plans for the starting hardware, software, and data under way, the only element of the DSS environment remaining was a general plan for evolving the startup tools into a DSS Generator over time. The Generator development plan is given as an appendix to this case example.

Selecting the Specific DSS

As the DSS environment began to fall in place, Mr. Victor and the DSS group began to look ahead to the implementation of first Specific DSS. The group vice-president who had become interested during pilot test was still interested, but he had admitted his needs were not pressing. Meanwhile, Mr. Victor had begun to get strong interests from one of the divisions in the energy group. Deregulation of oil and natural gas had thrown many typically routine management tasks into a constant state of change. The president needed access to financial and operating performance data, with quick and flexible analysis by geographic distribution, organizational unit, and product line. When he heard about the DSS project, he invited Mr. Victor and two members of the DSS group to make a presentation about the project and what it promised to do. By the end of the meeting he was "selling" his needs as an interesting and important test bed for the project, and offering to participate in the development of the first Specific DSS. Mr. Victor realized that the division president probably would be a better starting point than the group vice-president because of the frequency and nature of the problem solving and decision making the job required. The GVP responsibilities were mostly coordination and communication among division presidents in each group, and between the CEO and the division presidents.

Meanwhile, one of the members of the DSS group, while on a routine MS task, saw an opportunity to help the marketing manager in the same division with an immediate problem. With the prices for oil and natural gas changing several times a day, they needed a better way to quote prices to their customers as orders were received. Pricing was based on a weighted average of supply costs which had to be recalculated every time suppliers announced a price change. In less than a week, the DSS builder implemented a system with an APPLE II and VISI-CALC that gave the marketing manager exactly what he wanted. Always a skeptic about computers in the past, the marketing manager became an overnight zealot, pressing the DSS group for two other related applications that he thought could be done on the APPLE.

Pleased by the response of the two managers at the energy division, Mr. Victor returned to his office to find a message from Mr. Campbell. He too was pleased by his experiences in the pilot project and wondered when the full development of his system would begin. Mr. Victor called a meeting with the DSS group to discuss how to handle this excess of success. After much deliberation, they decided that none of the requests could be postponed for very long. Moreover, there were strong advantages to tackling SDSS at several levels of the organization. They decided, therefore, to pursue all three SDSS with staggered starting times. The APPLE system could be expanded first because it was self-contained and needed no external data and only simple programming. The next expansion to the APPLE system would require some data transfer to/from the division president. By that time the data extraction programs and IFPS would be implemented, allowing the start of the SDSS for the division president. Soon thereafter, with the same software but different data, they could begin the SDSS for the executive vice-president.

As he pondered the major differences between this plan for Phases III–V compared with the way it looked just three months ago at the end of Phase I, he was glad he had not gotten locked in too early.

STAGED DEVELOPMENT OF THE
DSS GENERATOR FOR PDI

Introduction

In keeping with the philosophy of the iterative design approach that characterizes DSS efforts, the DSS Generator (DSSG) will start small and evolve over time. The initial stage will be relatively simple, basic, and available soon to build the first Specific DSS (SDSS). As the needs of the users evolve, the strength of the SDSS and the capabilities of the DSSG will evolve together.

Decision and Constraints

Previous decisions by ISD and PAS have created several constraints and boundaries for the planned evolution of the DSS Generator. They include:

- The purchase of the HP3000 and its designation as the in-house time-sharing computer. The Generator will therefore be resident on the HP3000.
- The formation of the DSS group within ISD and its responsibility to manage the Generator on the HP3000.
- The purchase of IFPS by PAS and its use to support planning activities throughout the company.
- The subsequent purchase of the multi-installation license for IFPS.
- The agreement of Execucom to provide the use of advanced copies of all new product releases.

As a result of these decisions and developments, we have decided to use IFPS as the starting point for the DSS Generator.

Level 1

Level 1 of the DSS Generator is the minimal technology required to begin building a Specific DSS. It should be operable by late summer or early fall. The basic characteristics are (see Figure 3-3):

- IFPS as the heart of the system. It is to be used at first with little or no internal modification.
- Foreign file interface (FFI) as the data extraction program to tap computer-based files. The initial version will not use any files that cannot be processed with FFI.
- A mechanism for transferring the data from the IBM 4331 to HP3000 (before or after the extraction run).

85

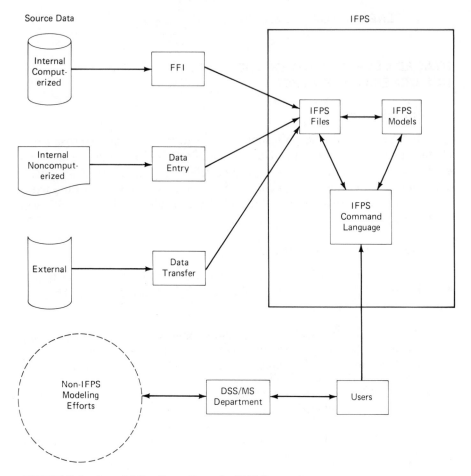

FIGURE 3-3   Level 1 Configuration of a DSS Generator

- A flexible data entry system (perhaps form-based) for capturing noncomputer data. Output from this program is also an IFPS data file. This program can probably be purchased in the market, perhaps from Hewlett-Packard.
- External data sources *as needed* by the initial users.

Data sources of all three kinds (internal computerized, internal non-computerized, and external) can be identified only after initial discussions with the user(s) of the first Specific DSS. However, it is highly likely that they will need some data from the financial reporting system (FRS). Consequently, we should identify a common set of financial data from FRS and build the extraction/transfer routines necessary, probably FFI, to create IFPS files on the HP3000. As the SDSS is developed, FFI is applied originally by the DSS builder to tap a data file and create appropriate IFPS files.

Once "installed," the extraction routines run regularly on an update schedule defined as part of this original setup. Additional extractions are defined *as needed* by users.

Level 1 Enhancements

As the Level 1 Generator capabilities are used to build the SDSS, shortcomings in dialog, data, or modeling will begin to appear. Incremental enhancements to Level 1 will constitute movement toward Level 2. Although these depend on what is needed and required by users, likely enhancements are as follows:

- Level 1.1 (see Figure 3-4)
    - Add an extraction routine to build a KSAM (or other) file from the source file. This is a "workspace" file which acts as an early version of the DSS data base.
    - Build a FORTRAN utility to create IFPS files from that workspace file. The utility can be built as an EXECUTE function in the IFPS command language. Thus it can be utilized by some sophisticated users during an IFPS session or set up in advance by the builders in response to a user's request.
- Level 1.2
    - Add a data model (probably a multidimensional cube) with some built-in consolidation operations and other user-efficient data operations.
- Level 1.3
    - Add data dictionary capability.
- Level 1.4
    - Add a simple query facility.

The improvements described above deal primarily with data handling because IFPS is weakest in that area. Each of these improvements should be kept as simple as possible, responding directly to user's needs. It is possible that they will be replaced by the addition of a full-service DBMS in establishing Level 2.

It may also be necessary to add a few enhancements in Dialog and Modeling to respond to user's needs. For example:

- The ability to handle a variety of stored models (model base), or the ability to string IFPS models together with something like common statements and a procedure (command string).
- The ability to graph model output in several formats.

Level 2

The DSS Generator will have evolved to a Level 2 set of capabilities when the enhancements constitute a full set of DBMS functions or a DBMS

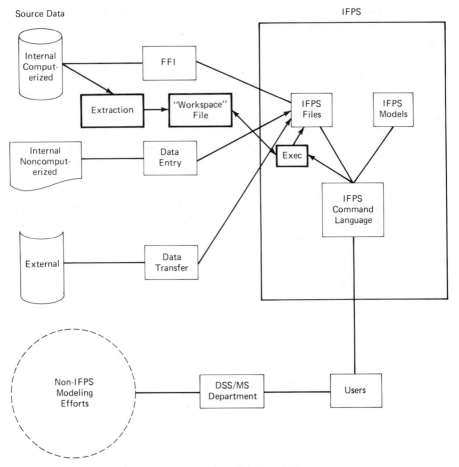

FIGURE 3-4   Initial Enhancements to Level 1 Capability

can be purchased and installed on the HP3000. The characteristics of the Level 2 Generator will include (see Figure 3-5):

- A full DBMS for the HP3000. The choice will result from a make-or-buy decision which balances the efficiency of the evolved enhancements against the function and cost of a purchased system. Special attention should be given to the possibility of a system that uses a relational data model.
- A full set of data query and display capabilities. We may shift some data query and display functions from IFPS to the DBMS depending on the capabilities that come with the DBMS.
- A transitional implementation which is transparent to existing IFPS users, to be accomplished by:
    a. Attaching the DBMS to the existing system so that copies of the existing data files are managed both by IFPS and by the DBMS.

  b. Converting the extraction programs one at a time to produce data files directly for the DBMS.

- A data dictionary for the three levels of data availability: immediate, 24-hour, and one-week. Characteristics include:

  a. A three-level catalog.

  b. The data model (hierarchic, network, relational) that best fits the user's needs.

  c. A data dictionary directly accessible by the user without IFPS.

  d. Automatic update whenever the source data or extraction process changes.

  e. Overlapping data bases in agreement with an authorization/privacy scheme.

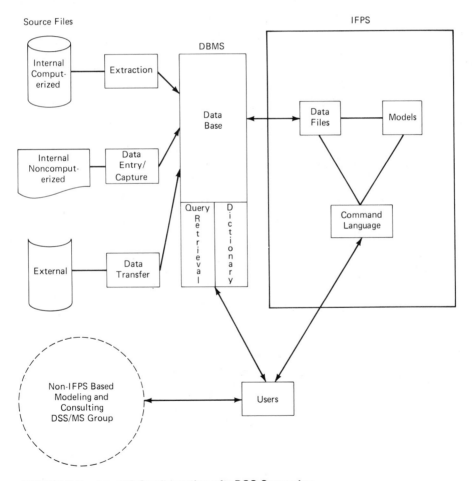

FIGURE 3-5   Level 2 Configuration of a DSS Generator

Level 3

Level 3 capability results from adding a full-service dialog generation and management system (DGMS) to the system of Level 2 (see Figure 3-6).

- The DGMS should have all the capabilities that we outlined at the specific capability level of our design document.
- The DGMS might use the ROMC approach, especially if the DBMS is relational, because it could handle representations and control structures as relations.
- The DGMS implies some strong hardware capability in the terminals, which should be available economically by that time.
- The system will still have linkage into IFPS and DBMS, but the DGMS will absorb all dialog functions, duplicating some functions of IFPS if necessary to

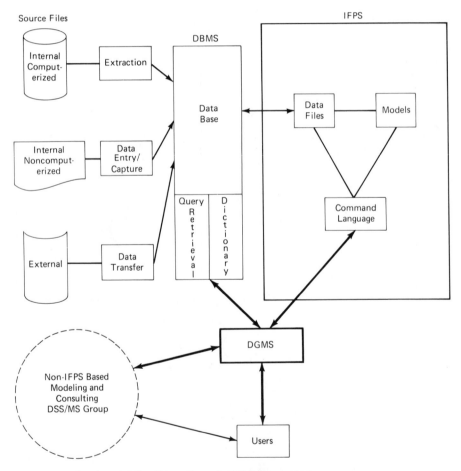

FIGURE 3-6   Level 3 Configuration of a DSS Generator

maintain transparency for what should be a strong body of IFPS users by this time.
- By this time analysis and modeling functions that are not IFPS compatible will be performed separately and linked through the DGMS.

Conclusions

Levels 3 and 4, which might add a full-service model base management system (MBMS), are distant enough to be highly speculative. There will undoubtedly be much activity in the development of DSS Generators by vendors in the software industry over the next few years. We should follow these developments closely and revise this plan every few months if necessary.

CHAPTER FOUR

SYSTEMS ANALYSIS FOR DECISION SUPPORT SYSTEMS

OUTLINE

INTRODUCTION

Chapter 3 dealt with planning and organizing for DSS. We next address the process of systems analysis for DSS using any of the specific action plans identified in Chapter 3.

The process of developing a computer-based system starts with systems analysis and design. Systems analysis refers to the initial steps, which include 1) analyzing the existing activities or problem area, and 2) defining the performance requirements of the system that will be applied to those activities. The tools used for systems analysis also define the structure within which the system will be designed. Design refers to the process of identifying the parts of the system and how they will work together.

We have said that decision makers and decision-making processes have characteristics that make unusual demands on DSS. In fact, because computer-based DSS are so much different from traditional computer-based systems (EDP or MIS), the systems analysis and design process must be substantially different. This chapter deals with an approach to system analysis that recognizes the special nature of the users and tasks that DSS will support. The approach presents a set of attributes that help define the requirements and identify specific capabilities which DSS can provide to support these users and tasks.

DSS OBJECTIVES REVISITED

The special characteristics of DSS that have an impact on the analysis and design approach begin with the overall objectives that they must satisfy. In Chapter 2 we discussed a set of performance objectives for Specific DSS (as a group). To review the six objectives:

1. To support hard, underspecified or unstructured decisions as well as structured decisions. We used Simon's definition of "unstructured" as a decision-making process that cannot be described in detail before making the decision [19]. A decision may be unstructured because of novelty, time constraints, lack of knowledge, large search space, need for nonquantifiable data, or other reasons.
2. To support decision making at all levels of the organization and to integrate between levels when appropriate. A well-known classification scheme for decision levels and tasks comes from Anthony [2]. Based on Anthony's paradigm, we classify decisions as:
    - *Strategic Planning*: decisions related to setting policies, choosing objectives, and selecting resources.
    - *Management Control*: decisions related to assuring effectiveness in acquistion and use of resources.
    - *Operational Control*: decisions related to assuring effectiveness in performing operations.

- *Operational Performance*: decisions that are made in performing the operations.
3. To support the communication between decision makers so as to support interdependent decision making. We used Thompson's classification scheme as interpreted by Hackathorn and Keen [11].
    - *Independent.* A decision maker has full responsibility and authority to make a complete implementable decision.
    - *Sequential Interdependent.* A decision maker makes part of a decision which is passed on to someone else.
    - *Pooled Interdependent.* The decision must result from negotiation and interaction among decision makers. Different capabilities will be required to support each type of decision—personal support, organizational support, and group support, respectively.
4. To support all phases of the decision-making process and facilitate interaction between the phases. Here we use Simon's stages of decision making [19]:
    - *Intelligence.* Searching the environment for conditions calling for decisions. Raw data are obtained, processed, and examined for clues that may identify problems.
    - *Design.* Inventing, developing, and analyzing possible courses of action. This involves processes to understand the problem, generate solutions, and test solutions for feasibility.
    - *Choice.* Selecting a particular course of action from those available. A choice is made and implemented.
5. To support a variety of decision-making processes but not be dependent on any one. In other words, to provide support that is process independent and under full control of the user.
6. To be easy to use and modify in response to changes in the user, the task, or the environment.

In the early 1970s, G. A. Gorry and M. S. Scott Morton [8] combined Anthony's levels of management and Simon's types of decision. The combination can be extended as shown in Figure 4-1. Gorry and Scott Morton claimed that most existing computer support for decision making was for structured decisions, that some progress was under way for supporting semistructured decisions, but that almost no computer support was used for unstructured decisions. They argued that it is the semistructured and unstructured decisions (especially management control and strategic planning) that are of the greatest concern to decision makers. Yet these are the most difficult to support with a computer system, because they tend to be based on ill-defined processes, whereas computer programs are based on strictly defined processes and sequences of instructions.

More recently, Alter surveyed 56 systems with DSS characteristics and divided them into two general categories: data-oriented and model-oriented [1]. Data-oriented DSS provide functions for data retrieval, analysis, and presentation. Systems in this category are usually developed by persons with data processing or computer science backgrounds. The model-oriented DSS provide accounting, simulation, or optimization models to help make decisions. These systems usually are developed by persons with management science or accounting backgrounds.

In general, neither data-oriented nor model-oriented DSS have had complete success in supporting decision making. The main problem seems to be a mismatch between the capabilities of the DSS and the requirements of decision makers or decision making. The causes of the mismatch may be technical (e.g., poor response times) or nontechnical (e.g., different personal preferences). Because of the mismatch, many systems which are developed ceased to be used or are used for routine report generation rather than for direct support of decision makers. In terms of our three capability areas from Chapter 3, they do not have *balanced* strength in dialog, data, and modeling capabilities. In addition, the standard approaches to the identification of system requirements are deficient because users cannot specifically define the decision support requirements in advance.

To design a DSS in this environment of poorly specified requirements, we advocate an approach to systems analysis which is intended to identify requirements in each of the three major capability areas of DSS. The approach is based on a set of four user-oriented entities: Representations, Operations, Memory Aids, and Control Mechanisms. The capabilities of the DSS from the user's point of view derive from its ability to provide *representations* to help conceptualize and communicate the problem or decision situation, *operations* to analyze and manipulate those representations, *memory aids* to assist the user in linking the representations and operations, and *control mechanisms* to handle and use the entire system. For obvious reasons, we call it the ROMC approach. Before discussing the approach in more detail, let us consider the nature of the gap between decision support requirements and DSS capabilities which the ROMC approach will help reduce.

	OPERATIONAL PERFORMANCE	OPERATIONAL CONTROL	MANAGEMENT CONTROL	STRATEGIC PLANNING
STRUCTURED	Payroll Production	Accounts Receivable	Budget Analysis	Tanker Fleet Mix
	Airline Reservations	Inventory Control	Short-Term Forecasts	Site Location
	Dispatching	Production Scheduling	Long-Term Forecasts	Mergers
UNSTRUCTURED	Solving Crime	Cash Management	Budget Preparation	Product Planning

FIGURE 4-1   Different Types of Decisions and Degree of Decision Structure [8]

DECISION SUPPORT
REQUIREMENTS

In developing the ROMC approach, we analyzed a variety of studies of decision-making processes and of decision makers.

Decision Processes

Three paradigms of decision making illustrate the wide variety of decision-making processes. The first is the rational (economic) paradigm, which postulates that decision processes attempt to maximize the expected value of a decision by determining payoffs, costs, and risks for alternatives [4]. A second paradigm asserts that the decision-making process is one of finding the first cost-effective alternative by using simple heuristics rather than optimal search techniques [5]. A third paradigm describes decision making as a process of successive limited comparisons to reach a consensus on one alternative [12].

Additional evidence of the variety of decision-making processes can be found in published studies of decision making. L. A. Gordon and his associates [7] identified 40 processes in looking at nine types of decisions. H. Mintzberg and associates [16] analyzed 25 decisions and identified seven basic processes with many variations. Carlson and Sutton [3] observed different processes among individuals working on the same decision.

Different levels and types of decisions have different information processing requirements. That is, a structured operational control decision would have different requirements than a semistructured one. Strategic planning decisions tend to require more varied, more aggregate, and more qualitative data than management control decisions. Structured decisions tend to utilize more calculations or algorithms than do unstructured decisions. Finally, a given decision may be of a different type in different organizations, at different times, or for different decision makers.

The conclusion that there is a wide variety of decision-making processes is not surprising; the evidence merely supports our earlier assertions and fits common experience and conventional wisdom. Because of the variety of decision-making processes, a DSS is more likely to be useful and cost effective if it supports multiple processes. If a Specific DSS is designed for only one type of decision, any change in the decision requires a change in the DSS to accommodate changes in information processing requirements. Therefore, designing a DSS for a specific decision reduces the number of decisions it can support. At the very least, it leads to increased cost if there is a change in the type of decision that it is intended to support.

Decision Makers

Decision processes are dependent on variations in decision makers as well as types of problems or tasks. Five observations from our analysis of decision makers were important in developing the ROMC approach. First, decision makers have trouble describing a decision-making process, but they do seem to rely on conceptualizations, such as pictures or charts, when making or explaining a decision [3]. In some cases the conceptualizations are not physically represented, but we can infer their existence from verbal communication (e.g., "bottom line," "payoff curve," "quick ratio"). Thus a DSS should not require that a decision maker be able to describe the decision-making process before the DSS is built, but DSS should help a decision maker conceptualize a problem.

Second, Simon's intelligence–design–choice scheme can be useful in categorizing decision makers' activities, even though the decision-making process may be difficult to explain. Studies of decision making that use this paradigm indicate that intelligence, design, and choice activities are interleaved and interrelated, but that these activities can be identified [18]. Identifying intelligence, design, and choice activities is a useful method for selecting operations to be provided in a DSS. We must not assume, however, that these activities, and therefore the operations, will always be carried out in the same sequence.

A third observation is that decision makers need memory aids [17]. These memory aids may be physical, such as scratch paper, memos, or reports. They may be mental rules that a decision maker applies, or they may be reminders from a decision maker's staff. By observing the memory aids used by decision makers, we can identify memory aids that DSS should provide to be compatible with the needs of decision makers. A DSS may provide memory aids which are "richer," or faster, or easier to use.

The fourth observation about decision makers is that there are differences in their styles, skills, and knowledge [14]. These differences are a likely explanation for the wide variety of decision-making processes mentioned earlier. Therefore, if a DSS is designed to support a specific process, it would probably support a specific set of styles, skills, and knowledge rather than supporting the variety observed to exist. Decision makers would have to conform to the style, skills, and knowledge assumed by the DSS.

An alternative approach would be to design the DSS to match a specific decision maker's style, skill, and knowledge. Because of the variety among decision makers, this approach is likely to require that the DSS be redesigned (or retailored) for each decision maker, and that there be techniques for characterizing a decision makers' style, skills, and knowledge. Such techniques are still not reliable or well known [20].

Thus we conclude that if a DSS is to support varying styles, skills, and knowledge, it should not attempt to enforce or to capture a particular pattern. Rather, the DSS should help decision makers use and develop their own styles, skills, and knowledge. If this requirement can be met, the cost effectiveness of DSS should improve because several decision makers could make effective use of the same DSS.

Finally, a fifth observation is that decision makers expect to exercise direct, personal control over their support [6,15]. This observation suggests that the decision maker should be able to personally control what the DSS does. Direct user control of a DSS allows the DSS to accommodate the different styles mentioned above, and it allows the user to accommodate changes in behavior over time due to the learning curve. This requirement does not necessarily imply that the decision maker needs to operate the DSS personally [9]. It implies that the decision maker must understand what the DSS can do and be able to interpret its outputs. With such an understanding, the decision maker can direct and evaluate the operation of a DSS and can integrate the information provided by the DSS with other information sources.

Requirements versus Capabilities

There are important parallels between the observed requirements of decisions and decision makers (left column of Figure 4-2) and the ROMC components (right column). The requirements indicate characteristics of decision makers and decision making which can be observed (and recorded) in a systems analysis process preceding the design of a DSS. The ROMC components identify the computer support that can be provided for each of these characteristics.

Notice there are still some differences between the requirements and the components, as illustrated by the examples under each of the four parallel headings (e.g., a map outline contains less information than does a city map). There are two reasons for these differences. First, a DSS will be only one of many alternatives for providing support for decision makers. Second, technology and costs limit the support that a DSS can provide. For these two reasons the DSS will probably never be "complete": (1) representations will not be as detailed as the decision makers' conceptualizations, (2) the DSS operations will support only some of the decision-making activities, (3) the DSS memory aids will be activated differently from those to which the decision maker is accustomed, and (4) using the DSS control aids will require learning new skills, making some changes in styles, and adding to the decision maker's knowledge base.

We postulated earlier that the many deficiencies of DSS were caused by a mismatch between the requirements of decision makers and decision making and the support provided by DSS. The mismatch can be analyzed and illustrated using the parallels shown in Figure 4-2. For example, in our analysis of early DSS efforts, such as the 56 described by Alter, we identified the following problems:

DECISION MAKERS' USE	DSS PROVIDES

1. Conceptualizations
  • A city map
  • Relationship between assets and liabilities
	1. Representations
	  • A map outline
	  • A scatterplot of assets vs. liabilities
	  • A graph of monthly asset/ liability ratios

2. Different Decision-Making Processes and Decision Types, All Involving Activities for Intelligence, Design, and Choice
  • Gather data on customers
  • Create alternative customer assignments for sales personnel
  • Compare alternatives
	2. Operations for Intelligence, Design, and Choice
	
	  • Query the data base
	  • Update list to show assignments
	
	  • Print summary statistics on each alternative

3. A Variety of Memory Aids
  • List of customers
  • Summary sheets on customers
  • Table showing sales personnel and their customer assignments
  • File drawer with old tables
  • Scratch paper
  • Staff reminders
	3. Automated Memory Aids
	  • Extracted data on customers
	  • Views of customer data
	  • Workspace for developing assignment tables
	  • Library for saving tables
	  • Temporary storage
	  • DSS messages

4. A Variety of Styles, Skills, and Knowledge Applied Via Direct, Personal Control
  • Accepted conventions for interpersonal communication
  • Orders to staff
 	
  • Standard operating procedures
 	
  • Revise orders or procedures
	4. Aids to Direct, Personal Control
	
	  • Conventions for user–computer communication
	  • Training and explanation in how to give orders to the DSS
	  • Procedures formed from DSS operations
	  • Override DSS defaults or procedures

FIGURE 4-2   Decision Makers' Requirements and ROMC Components

1. Representations
    Early DSS do not provide decision makers with familiar representations which support conceptualization. In addition, the decision maker often is forced to deal with concepts (e.g., flowcharts) and representations (e.g., printouts) which are unfamiliar and have little to do with the way the decision maker usually conceptualizes the decision.

2. Operations
    a. Early DSS tend to segment intelligence, design, and choice activities,

whereas decision makers tend to integrate them. For example, Alter's data-oriented DSS primarily support intelligence activities, but not design or choice, and the model-oriented DSS primarily support design or choice assuming that intelligence has been completed.

    b.   Early DSS tend to support a single decision-making process.

3. Memory Aids

    a.   Early DSS provide long-term memory aids (e.g., data base) but do not provide short-term memory aids. For example, the scratch paper and staff reminders to which a decision maker is accustomed usually are not available in most DSS.

    b.   Early DSS impose *additional* memory requirements, such as learning the names of the data in the DSS or learning a new command language, and often the DSS does not provide memory aids to support these requirements.

4. Control Mechanisms

    a.   Early DSS do not provide enough control aids to help the decision maker learn the new skills (e.g., signing onto a computer terminal), new styles (e.g., automated support rather than manual), and increased knowledge base (e.g., learning what the operations do) which a DSS introduces.

    b.   Early DSS replace direct control with indirect control where one or more intermediaries interpret the DSS capabilities and outputs for the decision maker. This type of control introduces well-known communication problems [6, 13].

The ROMC approach is intended to help overcome these problems. The parallels in Figure 4-2 indicate where support is needed and highlight the design challenges in providing support which reduces the differences between the requirements of decision makers and the capabilities of the DSS. The ROMC approach may not overcome all the differences or totally replace manual support with automated support. We do expect it to reduce the differences to an acceptable level and to provide support that results in displaced cost or added value.

THE ROMC APPROACH

The most important characteristic of the ROMC approach is that it is a *process-independent* approach for identifying the necessary capabilities of a Specific DSS. The typical sequence-of-steps model, usually represented by a flowchart, is an excellent systems analysis tool for transaction processing systems. It is a process model for a process-based system. Flowcharts can be used at several levels of detail to support top-down analysis—system flowcharts, program flowcharts, and detailed coding flowcharts, for example. In fact, the combination of flowcharts and the hierarchial input–process–output model form the basis for the traditional system development life-cycle approach which has become an industry standard (with many variations, of course). For all the reasons we have just explored, however, no process model can serve as a paradigm for systems analysis and design of DSS because DSS must be process independent. The ROMC approach provides a process-independent model for organizing and conducting systems analysis in DSS. Let us look more closely at each of the four components and then consider some examples of its usage.

The Components

Representations.   Any activity in a decision-making process takes place in the context of some conceptualization of the information used in the activity. The conceptualization may be a chart, a picture, a few numbers, an equation, and so on. The conceptualization may be mental, but in many cases it is physically represented on scratch paper, blackboards, graph paper, foils, and so on. A physical representation is particularly important when the decision maker wants to communicate some aspect of the decision to another person. Figure 4-3a gives examples of representations associated with some intelligence, design, and choice operations used in analyzing bad debts. Figure 4-3b gives examples of intelligence, design, and choice operations associated with a graph representation. Figure 4-3c lists instances of representations.

Representations provide a context in which users can interpret outputs and invoke the operations. Representations can also be used to supply parameters for the operations. For example, a point selected on a graph or

---

INTELLIGENCE

- A *list* of customers with bad debts
- A *graph* of bad debts over time
- *Cross-tabulation* statistics on attributes of customers

DESIGN

- A *scatterplot* of customers by two attributes associated with bad debts used to partition customers into risk groups

CHOICE

- A *pie chart* of percentage of loans by customer risk groups used to evaluate the partition
- A *report* on simulated bad-debt losses for each alternative risk group partition

---

FIGURE 4-3a   Representations for Analyzing Bad Debts

INTELLIGENCE

- *Identify* data to be graphed
- *Scale* the graph
- *Plot* data on graph

DESIGN

- *Draw* polygons to partition the lines on the graph
- *Forecast* future data based on each partition

CHOICE

- *Print* summary statistics for each partition
- *Display* each partition on the graph

FIGURE 4-3b   Operations Associated with a Graph Representation

Histograms	Balance sheets
Scatterplots	Spread sheets
Line graphs	Schedule boards
Maps	Engineering drawings
Surfaces	Architectural drawings
PERT charts	Aerial photographs
Organization charts	Seismic plots
Data entry forms	Scratch paper
Tabular reports	Memos

FIGURE 4-3c   Instances of Representations

locations on a map can identify a key value that will be used to retrieve detailed information. Subdividing a list of employees or reconnecting groups on an organization chart can serve as an input mechanism for a personnel scheduling algorithm.

Operations. As described previously, intelligence, design, and choice is a well-known paradigm which can help classify the operations used in decision making. The categories are "complete" in that all decision-making operations can be classified into one or more of the three categories. Figure 4-4a lists some general decision making operations usually associated with intelligence, design, and choice. Figure 4-4b illustrates the use of the categories to describe the operations used in a specific decision-making process for allocating police officers to areas of a city. Note that an operation may be used in more than one activity and that there is no prespecified ordering

```
┌─────────────────────────────────────────────────────────┐
│                                                         │
│    INTELLIGENCE                                         │
│                                                         │
│     • Gather data                                       │
│     • Identify objectives                               │
│     • Diagnose problem                                  │
│     • Validate data                                     │
│     • Structure problem                                 │
│                                                         │
│    DESIGN                                               │
│                                                         │
│     • Gather data                                       │
│     • Manipulate data                                   │
│     • Quantify objectives                               │
│     • Generate reports                                  │
│     • Generate alternatives                             │
│     • Assign risks or values to alternatives            │
│                                                         │
│    CHOICE                                               │
│                                                         │
│     • Generate statistics on alternatives               │
│     • Simulate results of alternatives                  │
│     • Explain alternatives                              │
│     • Choose among alternatives                         │
│     • Explain choice                                    │
│                                                         │
└─────────────────────────────────────────────────────────┘
```

FIGURE 4-4a   General Decision-Making Operations for Intelligence, Design, and Choice

of the operations. The operations may involve complicated decision aids, such as simulation models or forecasting algorithms.

Memory Aids. Several types of memory aids can be provided in a DSS to support the use of representations and operations. The following are examples:

- *A data base* from sources internal and external to the organization
- *Views* (aggregations and subsets) of the data base
- *Workspaces* for displaying the representations and for preserving intermediate results as they are produced by the operations
- *Libraries* for saving workspace contents for later use
- *Links* for remembering data from one workspace or library that is needed as a reference when operating on the contents of another workspace
- *Triggers* to remind a decision maker that certain operations may need to be performed
- *Profiles* to store default and status data

INTELLIGENCE

- Gather data on calls for police service
- Divide city into small geographic zones
- Select subset of data
- Aggregate subset by zones
- Validate data by checking familiar zones
- Plot data values on map of zones

DESIGN

- Set objectives for combining zones into police beats
- Develop quantitative measures for some of the objectives
- Plot data values on map of zones
- Combine zones into police beats based on objectives

CHOICE

- Print summary statistics on each police beat alternative
- Plot aggregate data on maps of police beat alternatives
- Modify alternatives
- Select an alternative
- Plot data on map for chosen alternative to explain choice to others

FIGURE 4-4b Intelligence, Design, and Choice Operations in a Police Personnel Allocation Decision

A data base is a memory for data compiled from sources which the decision maker thinks may be relevant to the decision. Views are memory aids containing specifications for partitions (groupings), subsets, or aggregations of data in the extracted data base which may be relevant to the decision alternatives. A decision can often be represented as a view. For example, a personnel allocation decision can be represented as a partition of a personnel data base where each group in the partition is allocated to a particular task. A hiring decision can be represented as a subset of an applicant data base where the subset is the list of those applicants to be hired.

Workspaces act as transient memory aids which provide a vehicle for accumulating results of the operations on the representations. For example, a "spread sheet" workspace could be used to develop product plans. A library associated with each workspace provides long-term memory for useful intermediate or final results created in the workspace.

Often, information from one workspace or library may be needed in another workspace or library. For example, a customer list may be used to identify a customer for whom the decision maker wants a graph of assets over time. Or a starting point on a map may be needed as an input to an algorithm that performs a districting operation on the map. Links are memory aids for information needed to make such associations. When a user identifies a customer's record in a list, or a point on a map, the link memory preserves the relevant data (e.g., customer identification number, or the x, y coordinates of the point) for later use.

Triggers are memory aids used to invoke operations automatically or to remind the user to invoke operations. A trigger may be a message telling the user that before a profit forecasting operator can be invoked, rates of return must be assigned to various projects. Or a trigger may be a message that is displayed quarterly, reminding the user to invoke the profit forecasting operation.

The profile memory aids store initial defaults for using the DSS, such as the axes labeling for a graph or the number of columns in a report. These defaults may be user-specific to help personalize use of the DSS for a decision maker. A "log file" used to record a user's actions for backup or "replay" can be considered as a profile memory.

Control Mechanisms. The representations, operations, and memories of a DSS are intended to support a variety of decision-making processes and a variety of types of decisions. The DSS control aids are intended to help decision makers use representations, operations, and memories to synthesize a decision-making process based on their individual styles, skills, and knowledge. The control aids may be crucial to the success of the DSS because they help the decision maker direct the use of the DSS and because they must help the decision maker acquire the new styles, skill, and knowledge needed to make effective use of the DSS.

There are a variety of control aids that can be helpful. One type is comprised of aids that facilitate the mechanics of using the DSS. Examples are menus or function keys for operation selections, standard conventions for user–system interactions (such as editing or accessing libraries) which are enforced across representations and operations, and use of the representations as the context for operation selection.

A second type includes aids to support training and explanation for using the DSS. These aids help the decision maker learn how to control the DSS. Natural language error messages, "help" commands, and a training method that permits the decision maker to "learn by doing" are examples of this type of control aid [10].

Decision-maker control of the DSS can also be supported with aids that permit combining operations associated with one or more representations into procedures. A "procedure construction language" for combining the DSS operations using standard programming language control techniques, such as iteration and case statements, is one example of this type of control aid. Procedure construction also is a mechanism for adding new operations.

Another type of control aid is comprised of operations that help the decision maker change the results of other operations, such as the ability to edit results of a forecasting model. Finally, control aids can include operations for changing any DSS default values. For example, if a DSS provides operations to automatically draw a graph with a default scale and axes labeling conventions, it should provide operations to change these defaults.

Using the ROMC Approach

The ROMC approach is a tool for focusing the systems analysis (of the decision-making system) preceding the design of the DSS and for structuring the actual DSS design. We will assume an interactive, graphics environment for DSS in describing the use of the ROMC approach. Although such an environment is not required, both interactive systems and computer graphics expand the options available to the DSS designer. Interactive graphics helps provide control aids because user–system communication options are enhanced. Interactive graphics also enables a wide range of representations to be used in the DSS.

Scatterplot Example. As a simple example of the use of the ROMC approach, consider the dialog required in an interactive DSS to define and draw scatterplots. Figure 4-5 gives an example of a process-oriented dialog (a "20 questions" approach) for creating a scatterplot. The dialog leads the user through all the operations possible for this representation. Each time a scatterplot is drawn, the same process must be followed.

The interaction requires that the decision maker have a mental picture of what is going to appear. (For example, what is the *x*-axis; do the data need to be scaled?) Once the scatterplot is drawn, any changes require that the dialog sequence be repeated. Figure 4-6 gives an example of the same set of operations, presented in the context of the scatterplot representation and supported by a set of memory and control aids. The advantages of the approach illustrated here include:

1. The representation makes it convenient for the user to respond only to those of the "20 questions" which are relevant.
2. It does not require that changes to answers be made in a particular order.
3. It does not require that all questions be answered each time the scatterplot is drawn.
4. It presents the parameters (the questions) together with the scatterplot (the results of the answers to the questions).

Exactly the same capabilities (inputs, operations, and outputs) are provided in each dialog approach. The process-oriented dialog is based on the assumption that leading the user through a *process* makes the capabilities easier to use. The representation-oriented dialog is based on the assumption that *context* makes the capabilities easier to use.

System:	*Choose function*	*1 = Table, 2 = Graphs, 3 = Plots*
User:	3	

System:	*Do you want a tutorial?* *(Y or N)*
User:	N

System:	*Enter data name for X axis*
User:	$ LIABILITIES

System:	*Enter data name for Y axis*
User:	$ ASSETS

System:	*Do you want default scaling?* *(Y or N)*
User	Y

System:	*Do you want default labels?* *(Y or N)*
User:	Y

System:	*Do you want descriptive statistics?* *(Y or N)*
User:	Y

System:	*Select stats* *1 = Mean, 2 = Median, 3 = Range,* *4 = Standard Deviation, 5 = Variance*
User:	1 3 4

System:	*Do you want to execute a procedure?* *(Y or N)*
User:	N

System:	*Do you want to save results?* *(Y or N)*
User:	N

System then erases display screen and draws scatterplot

FIGURE 4-5   **Process-Oriented Dialog for Creating a Scatterplot**

Investment Decision Example. To use a more substantive example, Figure 4-7 illustrates the results of a hypothetical analysis for investment decision making in which a flowchart of the existing or desired decision process is used as a tool for analysis. The focus is on the decision-

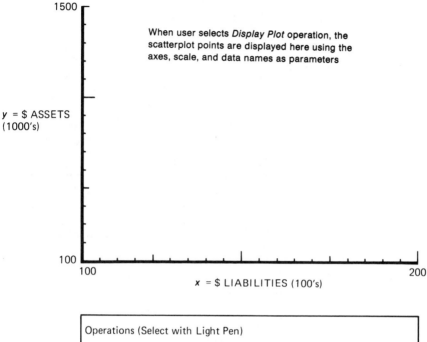

FIGURE 4-6   ROMC Dialog for Creating a Scatterplot

making process, particularly the inputs, operations, and outputs of each task. For different decision-making processes, the flowchart would be different. The same set of inputs, operations, and outputs might appear, but their relationships and sequencing would be different.

If the flowchart, or any other tool that focuses on the process, is used as a systems analysis tool, the resulting DSS is likely to mimic the process captured in the flowchart. That is, the DSS is likely to impose a sequencing of tasks. If the decision-making process changes, the DSS has to be changed. If different decision makers who have different processes want to use the DSS, they will have to conform.

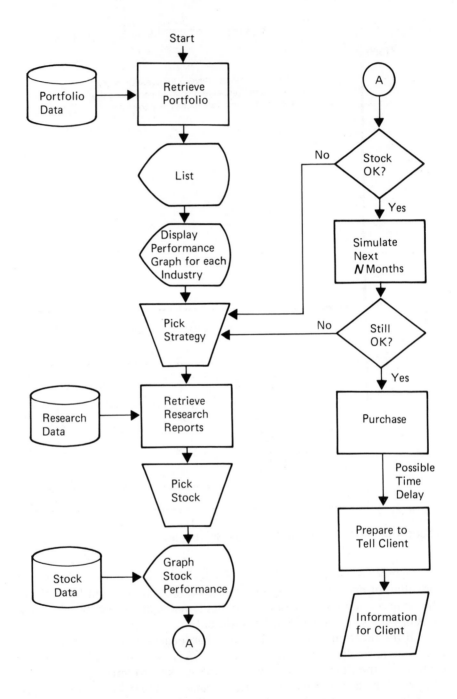

FIGURE 4-7 Analysis of an Investment Decision Using a Flowchart

Figure 4-8 illustrates a schematic resulting from using the ROMC approach to analyze the same decision. The representations and operations are chosen as in the process-oriented analysis, but they become the basis for the DSS structure. The ROMC approach attempts to make the DSS into a decision-making scratch pad that decision makers can use for a variety of decision-making processes.

Note that in Figure 4-8 there is a representation for a procedure construction language. A procedure construction language allows the DSS to create procedures which are sets of operations. An example would be a procedure to compute the average price of three related stocks for the past 12 months and plot the average and the individual stock prices. The representation for the procedure construction language might be a "blank pad" where the user could type in procedures using a syntax such as

AVG = (STOCK A + STOCK B + STOCK C)/3
PLOT: AVG, STOCK A, STOCK B, STOCK C

Representations

Portfolio Lists	Graphs	Research Reports	Simulation Outputs	Procedure Construction Language Syntax

Operations

Set of Operations on Portfolio Lists	Set of Operations on Graphs	Set of Operations on Research Reports	Set of Simulation Operations	Set of Procedure Construction Operations

Memory Aids

- Workspace for each representation
- Library for each representation
- Data bases: portfolio data
              research data
              stock data

Control Aids

- Use menus to display operations
- Provide a training manual giving examples of how to use the system to make a decision

FIGURE 4-8   DSS Schematic Resulting from Using the ROMC Approach to Analyze an Investment Decision

Or the representation might be a fill-in menu, such as:

STEP 1 Operation: AVG Operands: STOCK A, STOCK B, STOCK C
STEP 2 Operation: PLOT Operands: AVG, STOCK A, STOCK B,
STOCK C

Thus, like other representations, the representation for the procedure language is a context in which procedure operations are specified and invoked.

In the ROMC approach, the memory and control aids help the user develop the decision-making process. If the decision maker wants to follow a specific process, such as the one flowcharted in Figure 4-7, this process can be "programmed" in the procedure construction language and executed under the decision maker's control.

Thus a DSS based on Figure 4-8 is more general than the one based on Figure 4-7 because it can support a variety of decision-making processes. The DSS based on Figure 4-8 might also be useful for other decisions, such as mergers and acquistions, where the same representations and operations are used but the processes differ. The cost of the generality is that it may be more difficult to use than the DSS based on a flowchart because the user must learn to develop a process with the DSS. The memory and control aids are intended to help reduce this difficulty.

A Single Representation Example. An expanded version of the scatterplot example shows how the ROMC components fit together (see Figure 4-9). Assume that the scatterplot is the only representation required. Results of operations on the scatterplot are displayed in the workspace. These results may be a scatterplot of data, a scatterplot of data filtered through a view, or transformations of a scatterplot (e.g., scaling). The scatterplot can be displayed and modified in the workspace by using the operations.

The operations are commands that the user selects, such as draw plot, label axes, scale, print summary statistics, and so on. Intelligence, design, and choice activities identified in the system analysis for this DSS could serve as a guide in selecting the operations to be provided.

Intelligence operations might include displaying data using a scatterplot and identifying the "keys" and numeric values of points on it. Design operations might include creating groups of points on the scatterplot and making temporary ("what if") changes in values of points on the scatterplot. Choice operations might include fitting a regression curve to the scatterplot and computing ratios based on values of points selected from the scatterplot.

Another method of identifying operations is to list possible transformations of the scatterplot representation: for example, plot points, label axes,

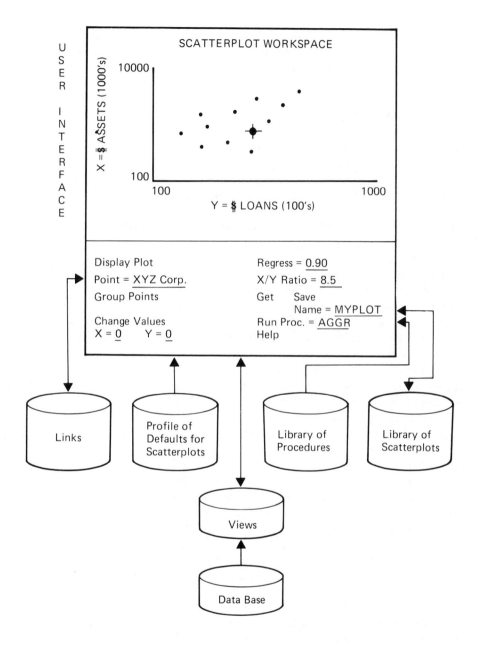

FIGURE 4-9   Relationships Among ROMC Components for a Single Representation

scales axes, plot regression line, identify points on plot, compute ratios for a point on the plot, save plot, and so on.

A library allows the user to name, save, and retrieve the contents of a workspace. Thus an interesting scatterplot can be named, saved, and retrieved using the library facilities. A procedure library, which is associated with a representation (e.g., an alphanumeric syntax used to construct procedures) can be accessed to execute "macro" operations which may or may not be associated with the scatterplot. For example, a sequence of labeling, scaling, and drawing operations that produce a scatterplot may become a procedure. Or there may be a procedure that aggregates data for use in displaying a scatterplot.

The extracted data base contains the data that can be accessed for a scatterplot, and the view memory stores specifications for subsets (e.g., customers with more than $100,000 in loans) and aggregations (e.g., combine domestic and foreign customers). The link memory is used to store data that might be useful with another representation.

For example, the customer identification number associated with a point on the scatterplot could be stored in the link memory for use in retrieving a summary report about that customer. The profile memory would contain initial defaults for the scatterplot workspace, such as axes labeling and scaling, scatterplot colors, or symbols used in the scatterplot. Defaults are required when the user wants a new scatterplot but forgets to specify some parameters.

Specific control aids include the menus that present the set of operations available to a user and a "help" operation for learning how to use other operations. Note that the memory aids often serve as control aids. For example, the procedure library can serve as a control aid for invoking a sequence of operations to create a scatterplot. The memory containing defaults can help reduce the time and effort needed to display a scatterplot (such as providing axes scaling and labeling for draw scatterplot). The workspace and library memories make it easier to recreate a scatterplot.

The representation (as displayed in the workspace) is the context in which operations are used, and the memory and control aids help the decision maker invoke the operations and use the results of the operations. If the parallels shown in Figure 4-2 are valid, it is the combination of the four components that will help the decision maker make effective use of the DSS. That is, for any one of the four components to help improve decision making, the other three components seem necessary.

Multiple Representations. It seems likely that every DSS will require more than one representation. Figure 4-10 shows a DSS design consisting of four types of representations: tables, graphs, maps, and a procedure construction language. Each representation has operations for intelligence, design, and choice and an associated workspace for presenting the results of applying the operations to the representations. For each representation there are workspace, library, and profile memory aids.

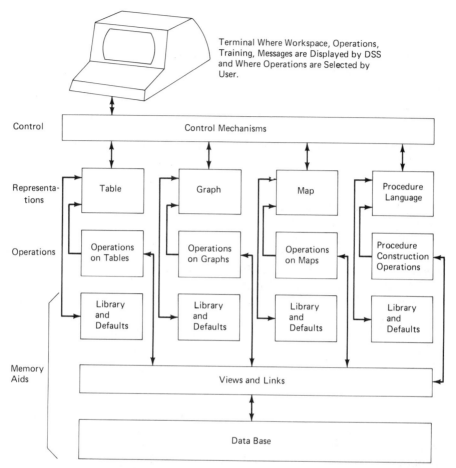

Terminal Where Workspace, Operations, Training, Messages are Displayed by DSS and Where Operations are Selected by User.

FIGURE 4-10 **Relationships Among DSS Design Components for Multiple Representations**

The operations in each representation can access a data base, possibly through a view. Views can be constructed using a representation (e.g., select points on a graph to specify subsetting) or via the procedure language.

With multiple representations, link memory is very important. Information presented on a graph may lead to questions best answered using a map (e.g., "Where is that high crime area?"), or using a table (e.g., "Give me a list of total crimes for each zone"). Links can help the user transfer data among representations. Control aids are provided by modules that give error messages and provide training sequences and by user–system communication (dialog) conventions. Note that the control aids cover all representations, operations, and memory aids.

ROMC and the DSS Framework

We have outlined the ROMC approach, described each of the four components in some detail, and illustrated their use with examples. Let us now review how the ROMC concept fits into the overall framework for building DSS developed in Chapters 1 and 2. ROMC directly affects the three key concepts in the framework.

1. The three levels of technology—Specific DSS, DSS Generators, and DSS Tools.
2. The three types of technology capabilities required from the Generator or Tools—dialog, data, and models.
3. The iterative design approach.

(1) The ROMC approach is a user-oriented and process-independent way to *define* the components of a Specific DSS. Stated another way, a specific set of Rs, Os, Ms, and Cs constitute a Specific DSS. The process of designing a Specific DSS is the process of identifying the set of ROMC required by the user to face the decision-making and problem-solving tasks.

(2) Although the ROMC approach is a good model for organizing the capabilities of the Specific DSS from the user's view, it does not specify how Rs, Os, Ms, and Cs will be built. The Dialog–Data–Model paradigm (DDM) is a framework for organizing the technologies and techniques that the builders/toolsmiths provide via DSS Generators and/or Tools to build the desired set of ROMCs. In general, the dialog component is used to build R and C capabilities, the modeling component is used to build the O capabilities, and the data base component is used to build the M capabilities.

(3) Iterative design of a Specific DSS consists of the iterative addition and deletion of specific instances of Rs, Os, Ms, and Cs from the Specific DSS. The users request these additions and deletions, which are implemented by the builder using the DDM capabilities in the Generator or from the Tools.

Figure 4-11, an expanded version of a diagram from Chapter 1, illustrates these conceptual relationships. It is possible that DSS Generators will eventually become a "superset" of ROMCs from which builders (or users) can select to build a Specific DSS. In the near future, however, it is clear that Generators will continue to be a synthesis of Tools to provide capabilities that fit the DDM paradigm.

SUMMARY

In summary, the ROMC approach is a framework for identifying the required characteristics and capabilities of a Specific DSS. It is a process-independent approach which does not require the users to be able to describe how they make decisions. Use of the ROMC approach seems to help avoid four major deficiencies of early DSS efforts.

- Early DSS did not provide the representations that decision makers need for semistructured and unstructured decisions.

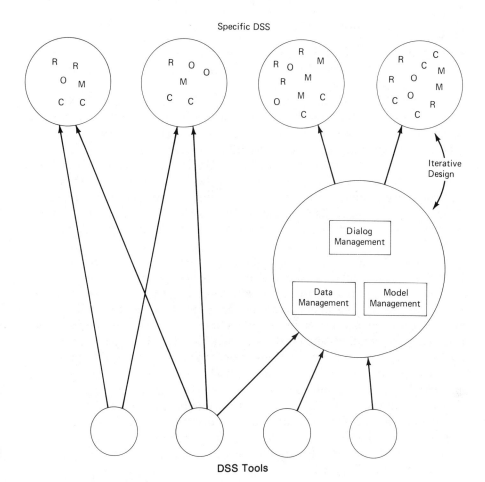

FIGURE 4-11   ROMC and the DSS Framework

- Early DSS usually supported only one or two of the three basic activities (intelligence, design, and choice) of decision making.
- Early DSS did not provide enough support (and actually introduced additional requirements) for conceptualization and memory, two areas where decision makers are observed to need help.
- Early DSS required specification of the decision-making process in advance and did not support a variety of styles, skills, and knowledge; thus they did not help decision makers exercise the personal control to which they are accustomed when making semistructured or unstructured decisions.

The ROMC approach overcomes these problems by providing representations as the context for DSS use; operations on the representations to support intelligence, design, and choice activities; a variety of memory aids to support use of the representations and operations; and aids for controlling the representations, operations, and memories.

The ROMC approach for specifying the required capabilities of Specific DSS has several advantages over other approaches. It is easier for a DSS builder to identify representations and the associated operations which are used in decision making than to identify completely all possible decision-making processes. Instead of designing a DSS as a set of operations that result in representations, the DSS is designed as a set of representations with associated operations. The process-based approach is more likely to impose a sequencing of the operations on the decision maker—yet we see that to support a variety of processes, a large number of possible sequencings must be available.

The ROMC approach is more likely to let the decision maker select the sequencing of the operations, and a new sequencing (i.e., a new process) is less likely to require programming modifications to the DSS. Moreover, one set of representations and operations can support a variety of decision-making processes because the differences among processes are more in the sequencing of operations and the decision makers' interpretation of representations than in the set of representations or operations to be used in the process.

The ROMC approach also may help DSS builders and users segment the decision problem and identify the relevant intelligence, design, and choice operations. Providing operations for intelligence, design, and choice activities helps the DSS support the entire decision-making process and makes it easier for the decision maker to integrate these activities.

The different types of memory aids act as note pads or file drawers for decision makers. They make it possible to retrieve useful results without having to repeat the operations that produced the results. They reduce the memory load on the decision maker, reduce the complexity of using representations and operations so that the decision maker can concentrate on interpretation, help personalize use of the DSS, and help the DSS support a variety of decision-making processes. Providing control aids helps the decision makers direct the use of the representations, operations, and memory aids according to their own styles, skills, and knowledge.

Finally, user involvement is often cited as an objective for successful DSS design and use. All four components of the proposed approach for DSS design are intended to encourage user involvement. The representations provide a familiar frame of reference for designing and using the DSS. Operations for intelligence, design, and choice provide support for common decision-making activities. Memory aids help develop and store useful results. Control aids help the decision maker personally direct the use of the DSS.

The ROMC approach for designing Specific DSS is directly linked with the Dialog–Data–Model paradigm for DSS Generator and Tools. DDM defines techniques and technologies which are used to provide ROMC capabilities. Thus the ROMC approach is not only the analysis framework for Specific DSS, but the specification of the capabilities that DSS Generators and Tools must provide for building effective DSS.

QUESTIONS AND PROBLEMS

REVIEW QUESTIONS

1. What are the characteristics of decision making and decision makers that make it difficult to design a DSS?
2. What is the ROMC approach?
3. How does the ROMC approach match known characteristics of decision makers and decision making?
4. How does the ROMC approach solve the DSS design problems you listed in Question 1?
5. What is the link between the ROMC approach for designing Specific DSS and the Dialog–Data–Model paradigm for DSS Generators and Tools?
6. Why would you expect a DSS designed using the ROMC approach to be more effective than one designed using a process-oriented approach?
7. Why would you expect a DSS designed using the ROMC approach to be less expensive to build than one designed using a process-oriented approach?

DISCUSSION QUESTIONS

1. A Specific DSS *should* be data oriented or model oriented because the problem or decision it is designed to support requires more strength in one area or the other. Do you agree or disagree?
2. The process-based approach is actually easier for a new or nontechnical user of a DSS because it requires only response to questions instead of initiative on the part of the user. Therefore, the ROMC approach is a step away from the easy-to-use criterion of DSS. Agree or disagree?

EXERCISES

1. Review the usage scenario of GADS at the end of Chapter 2. Identify the Rs, Os, Ms, and Cs in that scenario.
2. Choose a problem or decision with which you are familiar. List a set of representations, operations, memory aids, and control mechanisms used in making that specific decision.

REFERENCES

1. ALTER, S. "A Taxonomy of Decision Support Systems," *Sloan Management Review*, Vol. 19, No. 1, Fall 1977, pp. 39–56.
2. ANTHONY, R. N. *Planning and Control Systems: A Framework for Analysis*, Harvard University Graduate School of Business Administration, Studies in Management Control, Cambridge, Mass., 1965.
3. CARLSON, E. D., and J. A. SUTTON. "A Case Study of Nonprogrammer Interactive Problem Solving," *IBM Research Report RJ1382*, IBM Research Division, San Jose, Calif., April 1974.
4. CYERT, R. M., and J. G. MARCH. *A Behaviorial Theory of the Firm*, Prentice-Hall, Inc., Englewood Cliffs, N.J., 1963.
5. CYERT, R. M., et al. "Observation of a Business Decision," *Journal of Business*, Vol. 29, 1956, pp. 237–248.
6. EASON, K. D. "Understanding the Naive Computer User," *The Computer Journal*, Vol. 19, No. 1, February 1976, pp. 3–7.
7. GORDON, L. A., D. MILLER, and H. MINTZBERG. *Normative Models in Managerial Decision Making*, National Association of Accountants, New York, 1975.
8. GORRY, G. A., and M. S. SCOTT MORTON. "A Framework for Management Information Systems," *Sloan Management Review*, Vol. 13, Fall 1971, pp. 55–70.
9. GRACE, B. F. "A Case Study of Man/Computer Problem-Solving: Observations on Interactive Formulation of School Attendance Boundaries," *IBM Research Report RJ1483*, IBM Research Division, San Jose, Calif., February 1975.
10. GRACE, B. F. "Training Users of a Decision Support System," *IBM Research Report RJ1790*, IBM Research Division, San Jose, Calif., May 1976.
11. HACKATHORN, R., and P. G. W. KEEN. "Organizational Strategies for Personal Computing in Decision Support Systems," *Management Information Systems Quarterly*, Vol. 5, No. 3, September 1981.
12. LINDBLOM, C. E. "The Science of Muddling Through," *Public Administration Review*, Vol. 19, 1959, pp. 79–88.
13. LUCAS, H. C. *Why Information Systems Fail*, Columbia University Press, New York, 1975.
14. MCKENNEY, J. L., and P. G. W. KEEN. "How Managers' Minds Work," *Harvard Business Review*, May–June 1974, pp. 79–90.
15. MINTZBERG, H. *The Nature of Managerial Work*, Harper & Row, New York, 1973.
16. MINTZBERG, H., D. RAISINGHANI, and A. THEORET. "The Structure of 'Unstructured' Decision Processes," *Administrative Science Quarterly*, Vol. 21, June 1976, pp. 246–275.
17. NEWELL, A., and H. A. SIMON. *Human Problem Solving*, Prentice-Hall, Inc., Englewood Cliffs, N.J., 1972.
18. NICKERSON, R. S., and C. E. FEEHRER. "Decision Making and Training," *BBN Report No. 2982*, Bolt Beranek and Newman, Inc., Cambridge, Mass., July 1975.
19. SIMON, H. A. *The New Science of Management Decisions*, Harper & Row, Publishers, New York, 1960.
20. STABELL, C. B. "Individual Differences in Managerial Decision Making Processes," Unpublished Ph.D. dissertation, MIT Sloan School of Management, September 1974.

THE ROMC STRUCTURE OF GADS

Although GADS was not originally built using the ROMC approach, it can be described using this framework. GADS was originally designed for use by urban planners and administrators in making decisions, primarily related to land use. As GADS evolved it became evident that the representations, operations, memory aids, and control mechanisms in GADS were useful for a variety of decisions and by a variety of decision makers. To simplify the tailoring of GADS for new decisions and decision makers, the structure evolved into that of a DSS Generator supporting a set of representations, operations, memory aids, and control mechanism.

GADS supports four *representations*: maps, tables, scatterplots, and lists. An example of each is given in Figures 4-12a–d, respectively. The map representation supports display of data as symbols (alphanumerics, colors, stick symbols) on a map. The tabular representation permits single or multi-

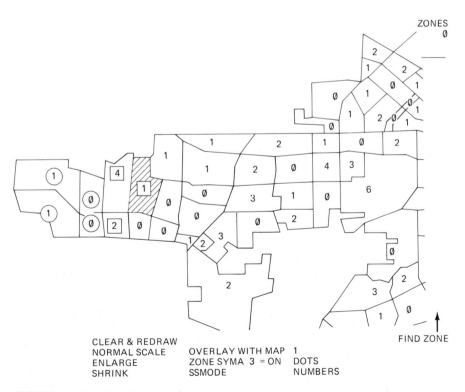

```
CLEAR & REDRAW                              FIND ZONE
NORMAL SCALE      OVERLAY WITH MAP  1
ENLARGE           ZONE SYMA  3  = ON   DOTS
SHRINK            SSMODE                NUMBERS
```

FIGURE 4-12a   Map Representation

	PAGE 1		
LABEL	UNIT -1	UNIT -2	DIFFERENCE
TOTROU	1.	1.	0.
TOT1	0.	0.	0.
TOT2	0.	0.	0.
TOT3	1.	0.	−1.
TOT4	1.	0.	−1.
TOT5	0.	1.	1.
TOTAL	2.	1.	−1.
INP1	0.	0.	0.
INP2	0.	0.	0.
INP3	0.	0.	0.
INP4	1.	0.	−1.
INP5	0.	0.	0.
TOTINP	1.	0.	−1.
CTIME1	0.	0.	0.
CTIME2	0.	0.	0.
CTIME3	57.	0.	−57.
CTIME4	28.	0.	−28.
CTIME5	0.	107.	107.
TOTCTIME	85.	107.	22.
MULTI1	0.	0.	0.
MULTI2	0.	0.	0.
MULTI3	0.	0.	0.
MULTI4	0.	0.	0.
MULTI5	0.	0.	0.
TOTMULTI	0.	0.	0.
WORKA	1.	0.	−1.
WORKB	1.	0.	−1.
WORKC	0.	0.	0.

FIGURE 4-12b   Table Representation

ple variables to be displayed as tables. Tables may be organized as either data (columns) by geographic zone (rows) or data (columns) by data (rows). Scatterplots may involve one, two, or three variables, with each point in the scatterplot representing a value for one geographic zone. List representations allow the user to list data names, map names, procedure names, and data base names.

The *operations* include a set of operations for each representation, plus a "statement language" for combining operations into procedures, and an "extraction language" for creating procedures that extract data from source files into the GADS data base. Figure 4-13 summarizes the main operations available in GADS.

The GADS *memory aids* can be divided into four categories:

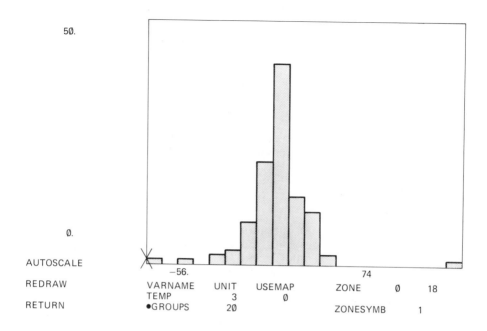

FIGURE 4-12c   Scatterplot Representation

1. Workspaces: used to store temporary results, such as overlay maps, sets of statements, and scatterplots.
2. Libraries: any workspace may be stored in a library.
3. Extracted data base: a set of data tables storing data for a set of geographic zones, plus a data dictionary and a map of basic zones from which all other maps (overlays) are formed.
4. Links: data such as symbols, zone numbers, map numbers, and parameters of representations (e.g., map scale: what data are currently in a scatterplot?) which are saved so that a user can move among representations and have the system data from one workspace that might be used in another workspace.

All the GADS memories are physically stored in the same data base, but different data structures are used.

The GADS *control mechanisms* are primarily a set of "menus" which allow the user to select operations and to enter parameters for those operations.

Figure 4-14 shows an ROMC description of GADS. This is a user's view of the structure of GADS, not a builder's view. Thus it is a view of GADS as a Specific DSS, one that provides a specific set of representations, operations, memories, and control aids that can be used to help in a set of decisions.

```
┌─────────────────────────────────────────────────────────────────┐
                                        ┌───────┐
    PAGE  │BACK│   │AHEAD│   DICTIONARY  │ PRINT │   VECTOR      ⌈1⌉
                                PAGE   1 │RETURN │   UNIT        ⌊−1⌋
                                        └───────┘

        ┌──────────┐
        │ LABEL    │      TITLE OF THE UNIT (DATA FOR A DAY)
        ├──────────┤
        │ TOTROU   │      TOTAL ROUTINE CFS       ALL DAY
        └──────────┘

        ┌──────────┐
        │ TOT1     │      TOTAL CFS 0000 TO 0300 & 2201 TO 2460
        ├──────────┤
        │ TOT2     │      TOTAL CFS 0301 TO 0000
        ├──────────┤
        │ TOT3     │      TOTAL CFS 0001 TO 1309
        ├──────────┤
        │ TOT4     │      TOTAL CFS 1301 TO 1000
        ├──────────┤
        │ TOT5     │      TOTAL CFS 1001 TO 2200
        ├──────────┤
        │ TOTAL    │      TOTAL CFS    ALL DAY
        └──────────┘

        ┌──────────┐
        │ INP1     │      IN-PROGRESS CFS 0000 TO 0300 & 2201 TO 2400
        ├──────────┤
        │ INP2     │      IN-PROGRESS CFS 0001 TO 0000
        ├──────────┤
        │ INP3     │      IN-PROGRESS CFS 0001 TO 1300
        ├──────────┤
        │ INP4     │      IN-PROGRESS CFS 1001 TO 1000
        ├──────────┤
        │ INP5     │      IN-PROGRESS CFS 1001 TO 2200
        ├──────────┤
        │ TOTINP   │      IN-PROGRESS CFS    ALL DAY
        └──────────┘

        ┌──────────┐
        │ CTIME1   │      CONSUMED TIME(MIN) 0000 TO 0300 & 2201 TO 2400
        ├──────────┤
        │ CTIME2   │      CONSUMED TIME(MIN) 0301 TO 0000
        ├──────────┤
        │ CTIME3   │      CONSUMED TIME(MIN) 0001 TO 1300
        ├──────────┤
        │ CTIME4   │      CONSUMED TIME(MIN) 1001 TO 1000
        ├──────────┤
        │ CTIME5   │      CONSUMED TIME(MIN) 1001 TO 2200
        ├──────────┤
        │ TOTCTIME │      CONSUMED TIME(MIN)    ALL DAY
        └──────────┘

        ┌──────────┐
        │ MULTI1   │      MULTIPLE-UNIT CFS 0000 TO 0300 & 2201 TO 2400
        ├──────────┤
        │ MULTI2   │      MULTIPLE-UNIT CFS 0301 TO 0000
        ├──────────┤
        │ MULTI3   │      MULTIPLE-UNIT CFS 0001 TO 1300
        ├──────────┤
        │ MULTI4   │      MULTIPLE-UNIT CFS 1301 TO 1000
        ├──────────┤
        │ MULTI5   │      MULTIPLE-UNIT CFS 1801 TO 2200
        └──────────┘
└─────────────────────────────────────────────────────────────────┘
```

FIGURE 4-12d   List Representation

Examples of ROMC Use

The value of the ROMC design as implemented (ex post facto) in GADS can be illustrated by two examples. An indication of how well the ROMC approach worked for one user group is given by a comparison of GADS with data-oriented and model-oriented DSS which preceded its use in supporting a police personnel allocation decision. The problem was to decide on a scheme for allocation of police officers to areas (beats) of a city.

The decision was first attempted using a data-oriented DSS. Reports were generated on calls for service, workload, response times, and so on. The relevant data were plotted manually on maps, and police management used the maps to develop and evaluate alternative decisions. The result was an allocation plan which was more expensive and further from the *quantitative* objectives (e.g., a balanced work load) than the existing plan.

Next, a consultant was asked to help make the decision using a model-oriented DSS to determine an "optimal" plan. The consultant interviewed decision makers, developed objective functions, collected the "relevant" data, developed an allocation model, and ran the model to make the decision. The resulting plan was rejected by police management because it violated several *qualitative* objectives which could not be incorporated into the model.

Because of dissatisfaction within the police department with the decisions made using either of these two approaches, they agreed to try GADS. GADS was used by police officers to develop a personnel allocation plan, a variation of which is still in use. This plan required fewer police officers and was closer to the objectives (quantitative and qualitative) than the plans produced with the data-oriented and model-oriented DSS.

Obviously, we cannot prove that the ROMC approach caused GADS to be more successful than the other two DSS. In follow-up interviews with the police officers who used the DSS, however, each of the four components (ROMC) was referred to in some way by each officer as being a reason why GADS was useful and valuable [3].

A second illustration of the value of the ROMC design for GADS was that it was used for 16 different applications (i.e., different users, different decisions, different data) without any changes to the basic set of representations, operations, memories, and control aids. Each application involved different decision-making processes, yet the same set of ROMCs were used.

This second illustration indicates how GADS serves as a DSS Generator, with each version as a Specific DSS. To create each Specific DSS from the GADS Generator, the builder defined and installed:

1. Specific maps (data for the map representation)

2. Starting statements, extraction specifications, and any other operations (e.g., models)

3. An extracted data base and any initial libraries that might be of value to the intended users

4. Any changes to menus to tailor/simplify control

1. Statement language

   In addition to arithmetic and logical operations, the statement language provides operations to permit the user to:

   a. Invoke dynamic aggregation using an overlay map (see 3).
   b. Save sets of display symbols.
   c. Use built-in functions (e.g., sum).
   d. Generate reports (print statement).
   e. Provide comments.
   f. Save pages of statements in a statement library.
   g. Edit statements (e.g., copy, delete).

2. Map Operations

   a. Display one or more maps and one or more sets of display symbols simultaneously or consecutively.
   b. Expand maps around any symbol.
   c. Eliminate lines between zones containing the same symbol.
   d. Display the zone number and data values for any symbol.
   e. Scale maps by positioning reference points.
   f. Create overlay maps which are combinations of the basic zones of the special-purpose map.
   g. Save overlay maps in a map library.
   h. Create polygons for use in constructing overlays or for aggregating data.
   i. Aggregate data by polygon or by overlay.

3. Graph Operations

   a. Create one-, two-, or three-dimensional graphs having one point (or line in three dimensions) for each zone.
   b. Identify points by zone number.
   c. Automatically or manually scale axes.
   d. Cumulatively sum the y-axis variable.

4. Table Operations

   a. View an index to tables and a dictionary of variable names.
   b. Display any table.
   c. Alter values in a table and log the changes.
   d. Print hard copies of tables.

5. List Operations (for all lists)

   a. Select a list for display.
   b. Update the name of an item in a list.
   c. Select an item in a list for display.
   d. Name an item and add it to the list.

6. Extraction Language

   a. Define records in a source file (fields, data type, length, position).
   b. Define a selection criterion for selecting records from a file.
   c. Define an aggregation specification for aggregating data values by geographic zone.

FIGURE 4-13   Main GADS Operations

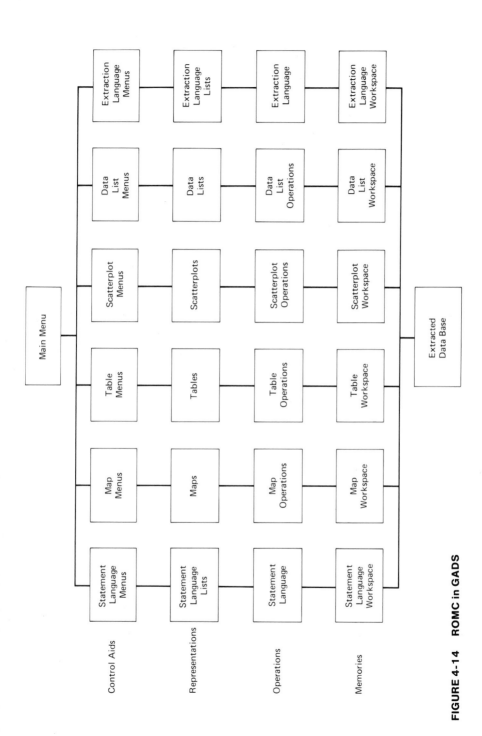

FIGURE 4-14 ROMC in GADS

CHAPTER FIVE

ITERATIVE DESIGN FOR DSS

OUTLINE

INTRODUCTION

This chapter deals with *flexibility* in DSS. It is widely recognized that DSS must be flexible because the environment, the tasks, and users of DSS are subject to frequent change. Unfortunately, beyond the obvious intuitive appeal of this assertion, there is a dearth of understanding, knowledge, and experience on the subject of flexibility. For example:

- What does flexibility really mean?
- How much flexibility is good? Is it possible to have too much?
- Are there any prescribed ways to accomplish flexibility?
- What technological capabilities are required?

This chapter provides guidance for answering questions such as these.

Flexibility affects all stages of the building and using of DSS, but it is implemented through the process of design. The ROMC approach described in Chapter 4 creates the structure within which design takes place, but the process of design results in the particular configuration of elements that become a Specific DSS. It is the configuration that must be flexible and easily changed to serve the decision-making needs of users over time. In fact, as we discussed in Chapter 1, building DSS can be viewed as the installation of an adaptive design process with several levels of technology. Thus the process of design is the mechanism for operationalizing flexibility in DSS.

THE CASE FOR FLEXIBILITY

It could be argued that flexibility and adaptability are desirable for all computer-based information systems. The maintenance costs during the life cycle of a major application system are frequently more than the original cost of its development. Many large EDP/MIS departments report that software maintenance costs are fully 50 to 75% of their *total* budget. High maintenance costs and long development schedules have led to increased interest in alternative development approaches and increased flexibility for all computer-based systems, not just DSS. Again, however, the special characteristics of DSS result in some significant differences in the need for, and the nature of, their flexibility and adaptability.

Transaction and Reporting Systems

There are several constraints that limit the desirable amount of flexibility for transaction processing systems. These constraints are related to the volumes of inputs and outputs, file sizes, activity levels, number of people that must interact with the system, and the structured or predefined nature of the tasks. For example:

- Legal, accounting, and organizational procedures determine the processes and algorithms for handling transactions. Many of these procedures are developed as a result of extensive negotiation and discussion among managers and other people inside and outside the company.
- A large number of clerical people must deal and interact with the system in data entry, auditing, control, or reporting modes. Frequent changes are likely to be more disruptive than helpful for these people.
- Contact with people outside the organization, such as customers, suppliers, and stockholders, is a primary function of transaction processing systems. Again, frequent change is disruptive.
- The high volume of transaction data increases the seriousness of all of the foregoing considerations if changes are introduced frequently.

There are also some limits to the desirability of change in traditional reporting systems, although they are not as strict as for transaction systems. There are usually a large number of managers who receive and respond to the same report, frequently using it as a context for their communication. Many traditional reporting systems produce the reports that are used to measure the performance of organizational units. It is important for these reports to permit comparisons over time with compatible definitions and formats. Therefore, frequent change in both transaction and reporting systems are troublesome.

Flexibility in DSS

In contrast to transaction systems or traditional reporting systems, DSS have characteristics that place a much higher premium on flexibility. Keen examined about 30 case studies of DSS and their usage over the past several years. In general, these case studies show that key factors explaining successful development are a flexible design and architecture that permit fast modification and a phased approach to implementation which allows users a smooth, trauma-free transition into the new system. Some observations on the characteristics of DSS users, tasks, and environment which illustrate the need for flexibility include (adapted from Keen [5]):

- Neither the user nor the builder can specify functional requirements in advance. For instance, in unstructured or underspecified tasks, either there is a lack of knowledge to define the procedures and requirements, or a lack of procedures is intrinsic to the task.
- Users do not know, or cannot articulate, what they want and need. They need an initial system to react to and improve upon.
- The users' concept of the task, and perception of the nature of the problem, changes as the system is used. The system stimulates new learning and new insights, which in turn stimulate new uses and the need for new functions.
- Actual uses of DSS are almost always different from the originally intended ones. In fact, case studies show that many of the most valued and innovative uses could not have been predicted when the system was originally designed.

- Users must believe in the solution and be able to communicate it to others. In many cases, the process of using a system to explore the problem in personalized ways is more valuable than the actual answer or solution. In fact, for unstructured tasks, there is often no absolutely right answer; the best alternative is the one with which the user/decision maker is most comfortable and willing to promote in dealing with others.
- Intended users of the system have sufficient autonomy to handle the task in a variety of ways, or to differ in the way they think to a degree that prevents standardization of process. In fact, case studies show that whether a system is recently operational or in place for some time, there are wide variations among individuals in how they use its functions.

In summary, there are two basic reasons for the importance of flexibility in DSS.

1. DSS must evolve or grow to reach a "final" design because no one can predict or anticipate in advance what is required.
2. The system can never be final; it must change frequently to track changes in the problem, user, and environment because these factors are inherently volatile.

Both of these general characteristics require flexibility and both can be accomplished with the iterative design process. In the short run, the iterative design process results in an initial usable system which is developed through active participation and communication between the builder and the user during the operation/evaluation of the system. In the long run, the iterative design process allows the system to change regularly to track changes in its users, tasks, and environment.

Let us now consider the nature of this flexibility, how it is accomplished with the iterative design process, and how it satisfies the two necessary objectives given above.

A TAXONOMY OF FLEXIBILITY

It should be clear from the preceding section that there are several varieties of flexibility. We have used the words "changeable," "adaptable," "modifiable," and "evolutionary," in addition to "flexible." We need a variety of words because there are a variety of concepts related to flexibility of DSS in supporting decision making and problem solving. Thus we need a taxonomy to organize the words and meanings behind them. Let us use the word "flexibility" as a generic word with notation to indicate different forms of flexibility. In Chapter 1 we described a full DSS as an adaptive system that changed over time. We now present a more precise definition of DSS as adaptive systems based on four types of flexibility.

Four Levels of Flexibility

The first level of flexibility, F1, gives the user the ability to confront a problem in a flexible, personal way. It is the flexibility to perform intelligence, design, and choice activities and to explore alternative ways of viewing or solving a problem. Let us use the word *solve* to describe this process. To help visualize this activity, imagine a "problem space" in which each point is a particular problem or subproblem, faced by a user, in an organizational context, using a DSS for support. A set of problems that can be handled by a Specific DSS is the "problem domain" for that system. This is a cluster of similar problems that is within the scope of a Specific DSS. The ability of a user to *search* or *browse* among the points in the problem domain in order to *solve* the problem is represented by F1. Stated another way, F1 represents the ability of a Specific DSS to handle a group of related or similar problems in the problem domain under direct control of the user. These relationships can be represented by Figure 5-1.

The second level of flexibility, F2, is the ability to *modify* the configuration of a Specific DSS so that it can handle a different or expanded set of problems (points in the problem space). This flexibility is implemented by addition and deletion of representations, operations, memory aids, and control mechanisms. Examples of F2 flexibility are the ability to add/delete a graph or a map, an operation on a graph, a scratch pad workspace, or choices on a menu. Since we have defined a Specific DSS as a unique set of ROMC, F2 flexibility permits definition of a different Specific DSS (SDSS). Figure 5-2 shows the new SDSS and its problem domain with dashed lines.

The third level of flexibility, F3, is the ability to *adapt* to changes that are extensive enough to require a completely different SDSS. In fact, F3 flexibility is implemented through changes to the DSS Generator so that it can be used to build SDSS which were not possible before. These changes

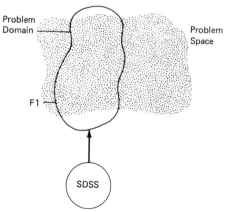

FIGURE 5-1   F1: Flexibility to Solve

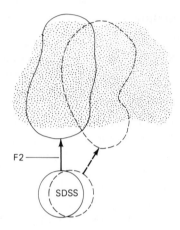

FIGURE 5-2   F2: Flexibility to Modify

take the form of new capabilities in dialog, data management, and modeling (DDM) which are increments to the Generator's repertoire of DDM facilities.

There are actually two kinds of addition/deletion of DDM components. First is the addition/deletion of an *instance* of a capability that the Generator already has. Examples include addition/deletion of a menu, addition/deletion of a data source, or addition/deletion of a modeling analysis option (a Box–Jenkins model for forecasting, for instance). The second kind of change is the addition/deletion of a *type* of capability to or from the Generator. Examples are the ability to add/delete a dialog style (such as menus) or a dialog support device (a touch panel), the ability to add/delete a logical data structure (hierarchical or network), or the ability to add/delete a modeling/analysis approach (Monte Carlo simulation). The result is a major expansion in the problem domain susceptible to DSS support. Figure 5-3 shows the expanded Generator and a new SDSS with a dashed line.

The fourth level of flexibility, F4, is the ability of the system to *evolve* in response to changes in the basic nature of the technology on which DSS are based. It is implemented with changes to the tools and technical capabilities, which can increase the power of the Generator to adapt. Here too the change may be an advancement in the speed and efficiency of an existing technological capability, or it may be a new technology completely. F4 provides the ability for the DSS Generator to absorb and assimilate technology to improve its ability to adapt. It may be a development in hardware technology (such as bubble memories or raster-scan color graphics) or software (such as a relational data base system or an improved conversational operating system). The new tools and technology are shown with dashed lines in Figure 5-4.

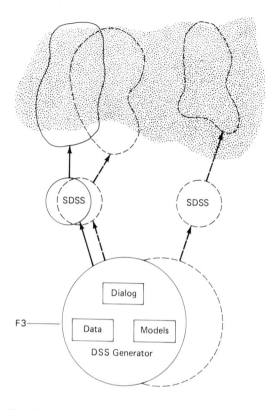

FIGURE 5-3   F3: Flexibility to Adapt

Roles in Flexibility

Obviously, these levels of flexibility are heavily dependent on the people who participate in them and implement them. Recalling our spectrum of participants in the DSS process, it is the user who utilizes the flexibility to search or browse to *solve* different variations of similar problems. An intermediary may participate in a clerical or staff assistance role, but it is the user who takes the responsibility for utilizing the F1 type of flexibility. The ability to *modify* the SDSS is a joint effort between the user (or intermediary) and the builder as they add or delete ROMCs to/from the SDSS. The builder is primarily responsible for changes to the Generator that enable it to *adapt.* In this case the changes take the form of additions and deletions of capabilities in dialog, data, and modeling. Some of these changes may require assistance from the technical support role; others may be a joint effort between the builder and the toolsmith. Finally, the toolsmith has the primary responsibility for the development of the new tools which will enable the entire DSS to *evolve.*

Figure 5-4, with the roles depicted along the right side, is an attempt to portray the dynamics of the adaptive system discussed in Chapter 1. The flexibility levels have a time horizon that increases from F1 to F4. On a daily, weekly, or monthly basis, users interact with a SDSS to assist in decision making and problem solving. During a year they work with the in-

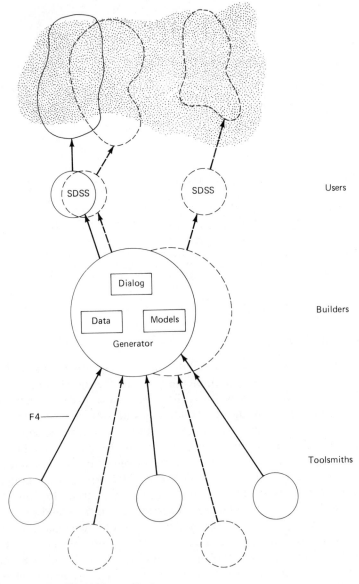

FIGURE 5-4   F4: Flexibility to Evolve

termediary or builder to modify the SDSS in response to the changes in the conditions they face or in their approach to problem solving. Builders adapt the capabilities of the Generator to create SDSS, and every few years the system evolves as a new technology is developed and absorbed. The levels are also generally hierarchical. Changes at the lower levels permit (but do not ensure) changes at the upper levels. With this conceptual view of the adaptive DSS, let us consider the process of "putting it in place."

TRADITIONAL SYSTEMS DEVELOPMENT

As a backdrop for the discussion of the iterative design process, let us briefly consider the traditional process for developing computer-based information systems. The system development life cycle (SDLC) can be called traditional in the sense that it has evolved over the past 10 to 15 years and is relatively standard. There are many versions in many textbooks and procedure manuals, but the basic sequence of events is remarkably similar among them. A good example is the version from Couger and McFadden [1]. The stages are:

1. Documentation and analysis of the existing system
2. Logical system design
3. Physical system design
4. Programming and testing the new system
5. Implementing the new system

The stages, their sequence, and the relative levels of effort over time are illustrated in Figure 5-5.

Problems

The traditional SDLC has always been a troublesome, complex, costly, and time-consuming process. The volume and complexity of applications increase together with the power and complexity of technology, so that there is a continual backlog of system development projects. Hardware and software tools in the form of "improved programming technologies" have been developed to increase programmer productivity in an attempt to solve the "software crises." Structured analysis and design and structured programming are attempts to impose enough discipline on the software development process to convert it from an art to a craft, again in the interest of improved productivity and reduced software maintenance costs.

Complex project management processes, several of them computer assisted, have been developed and widely sold as proprietary products. Their

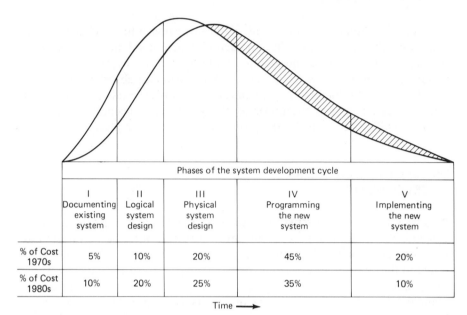

Phases of the system development cycle				
I Documenting existing system	II Logical system design	III Physical system design	IV Programming the new system	V Implementing the new system

	I Documenting existing system	II Logical system design	III Physical system design	IV Programming the new system	V Implementing the new system
% of Cost 1970s	5%	10%	20%	45%	20%
% of Cost 1980s	10%	20%	25%	35%	10%

Time ⟶

FIGURE 5-5   The System Development Life Cycle (from Couger and McFadden [1])

dual focus is to provide support for the planning and control functions in project management, and to structure the vital communications between the large number of people who must work on a project. Communication between the users of the system and the systems analysts has been a particularly difficult problem, especially in the crucial stages of identifying system performance requirements. Recently, there has been increased interest in prototyping as a more efficient way of defining the system requirements and enhancing these communication links.

In spite of these notable and effective efforts, the complete replacement of the traditional systems development approach is not likely in the near future. The traditional SDLC is costly and time consuming primarily because of the nature of the traditional systems that must be built with it. The volume of data, large files, high activity levels, many users, and predefined nature of tasks make some variation of the SDLC a necessary and appropriate approach for transaction processing and traditional reporting systems. The multiple levels of flexibility required for DSS, as outlined earlier, make the traditional SDLC inappropriate and difficult. DSS require the articulation of a new design/development approach which supports the flexibility they must have. In fact, in a popular book on data processing project management, Gildersleeve [3] points out that "projects are also to be distinguished from research efforts . . . They differ in that a project goal is predefined, whereas a research goal is necessarily vague." The development of DSS, in Gildersleeve's terms, are research efforts, not DP projects, and therefore not well suited for traditional project management procedures.

The Function of Design

The version of the SDLC depicted in Figure 5-5 divides the design steps into two phases: logical design and physical design. Logical design is the process of identifying what the system should do—the system performance requirements. Physical design is the process of specifying which pieces of technology can be used and how they can be connected to accomplish those requirements. In many ways, design is the most important step of the entire process. The most efficient programming, testing, and implementation are for naught if the performance requirements specifications are wrong.

There is usually a very distinct separation between the design steps and the steps that implement the design. The most popular project management approaches formalize the stages to the extent that there are mandatory meetings and sign-offs required to move from one stage to another. It is common at the end of the design phase for the design specifications to be "frozen" for the duration of the programming/testing/implementation phases. In this way many system performance requirements start out right and end up wrong.

Design is one of those words that can be used as a verb (the process of designing the system) or as a noun (the structure or design of the system). The word can be used in both ways for DSS as for other types of systems. For DSS, however, the process of design literally refers to all of the system development steps because the requirements (logical design) and the interrelationships between the pieces of technology (physical design) are constantly being defined by use and evaluation. It is for this reason that we focus so much attention on the process of design in DSS. At the same time, the structure of the DSS must support and facilitate this constant process of change. It is for this reason that we focus so much attention on the flexibility of the DSS architecture.

ITERATIVE DESIGN

In Chapter 1 we characterized the iterative design approach as a short development cycle, repeated many times. The process has several definable steps, but they are different from the traditional system development steps.

Steps in Iterative Design

Early research and experimentation in the iterative design process was done in France at the University of Grenoble. Courbon and associates [2] define the evolutive approach as a "methodology based on the progressive design of a DSS, going through multiple as-short-as-possible cycles, in which successive versions of the system under construction are utilized by the end-user." The steps in the process, adapted from Courbon et al., include:

1. Identify an important subproblem.
    The decision maker or user and the builder jointly identify the subproblem. This early joint effort sets up initial working relationships between them and opens the communication lines. The subproblem should be small enough that the nature of the problem, the need for some computer-based support, and the nature of that support are clear. It should have high interest value to the decision maker even if that interest may be short lived. Indeed, short-lived projects or problems are particularly susceptible to the DSS approach using iterative design.

2. Develop a small but usable system to assist the decision maker.
    Notice that no major systems analysis or feasibility analysis is involved. In fact, the builder and the user go through all the steps of the system development process quickly and on a small scale. The system will probably (of necessity) be simple. In his case study analysis, Keen found that "the functions DSS provide are generally not elaborate; complex systems evolve from simple components" [5].

3. Refine, expand, and modify the system in cycles.
    Each cycle passes through all the analysis–design–implementation–utilization–evaluation steps. The user is probably not aware of these stages because they emanate easily from usage. In terms of the ROMC approach, these modifications can be implemented by adding/deleting instances of ROMCs. Notice the balanced and cooperative effort of the user and the builder. The user takes the lead in the utilization and evaluation activities, while the builder is stronger in the design and implementation phases. The user plays a joint and active role. In conventional systems development, the user frequently operates in a reactive or passive role.

4. Evaluate the system constantly.
    At the end of each cycle, the system is evaluated by the user. Evaluation is built into the process, and it is the control mechanism for the entire iterative design procedure. It is the evaluation mechanism that keeps the cost and effort of developing a DSS in line with its value. It encourages the development of short-lived systems, for ad hoc or special studies for which computer systems were not feasible in the past. With constant evaluation, the system can die when the need for it is over or it proves not to be valuable.

Iterative Design and the Adaptive System

The iterative design process is described above in terms of a Specific DSS. The problem solver or decision maker needs flexibility F1 to *solve* each problem. The user and builder need flexibility F2 to *modify* the SDSS at the end of each iterative cycle. The same process can be applied, with a longer time horizon and longer cycles, at the Generator and Tools levels using flexibilities F3 and F4. The builder and toolsmith need flexibility F3 to *adapt* the Generator, by adding/deleting capabilities in dialog, data management, and modeling. The builder and toolsmith need flexibility F4 to integrate new tools and technologies to allow the entire system to *evolve*. The result of applying the iterative design process at all levels is an adaptive DSS capability.

Note that using the iterative design approach at the first level does not ensure that flexibility at lower levels will automatically follow. It is possible to apply a static set of tools with the iterative design approach to create and modify a Specific DSS. Over time, however, the usefulness of the tools and the SDSS are likely to decline. Experience has shown that if a tool is useful, there will be a tendency for it to be enhanced and adapted to expand its capabilities. APL, for instance, has been regularly enhanced with data base and file capability, report formatting capability, and graphical output as it became a popular DSS Tool.

Development Path of a Specific DSS

The use of the iterative design approach produces a Specific DSS which drifts or changes over time. The process is described in terms of cycles for clarity, but if the cycles are frequent, short, and continuous, they may actually blend into an ongoing process with no distinct checkpoints over time. Conversely, if the cycles are longer and less frequent, they may be distinct enough to constitute *versions* of the SDSS. Whether the change is continuous or in discrete steps will depend on the nature of the task, the frequency of data update, and the number of people involved as users. For convenience in discussing the development path, let us assume that versions are discernible.

The initial workable, usable system might be called version 0. It is a starting system to support a small problem or a small part of a bigger problem. The system is then modified through successive cycles and versions, say 1 through S. Version S is a relatively satisfactory version which then becomes somewhat stable. The frequency of modification cycles and the incremental change with each cycle will decrease (but not stop). At this point, the iterative design approach has satisfied the first of its general requirements—to create a usable system when the system performance requirements could not be defined in advance. Note that version S can be attained with only flexibilities F1 and F2.

Versions S + 1 and beyond result from modifications of the system in response to changes in the user, the task, or the environment. These versions satisfy the second general requirement of iterative design—to track changes in the key factors in the decision-making system. Some versions beyond S will be available with only F2 flexibility but, eventually, continual change will require adaptation of the Generator through F3, and evolution of the entire system through F4.

Interdependent Tasks

The iterative design approach is fairly straightforward for those SDSS requiring only personal support. The process is complicated somewhat, but not invalidated, for SDSS that need to provide group support or organizational support. Specifically, there is a stronger need for mechanisms to support communication among users and builders. There is also a need for mechanisms to accommodate personal variations of a system while maintaining a common core system which is standard for all users. Mechanisms that provide personal, group, and public data files have been a standard part of time-sharing systems for years. In a similar way, SDSS for group or organizational support need to provide personal as well as group instances of ROMCs. The former are defined by and for individuals, while the latter are standard for all individuals in the group, created by the builder with consensus by the group. This concept can be illustrated by Figure 5-6.

As the number of users for a given system gets large, the communication links required to operate the iterative design process must become more formal and more structured. It may be necessary to establish checkpoints to define the beginning of each usage-evaluation cycle. Changes may need to be accumulated and implemented in batches, thereby clearly defining distinct versions. For DSS with many users, iterative design may take on some of the characteristics of prototyping, which is gaining popularity as an approach for defining and refining the performance requirements for traditional systems. In fact, when a DSS has many users and is designed for organizational support, it must be *integrated* into the organization by formalizing some of the stages in the systems development process. Chapter 6 deals with three of these integration processes: installation, user education, and evaluation methods.

Mechanisms to Support Iterative Design

It is apparent that the iterative design approach requires a variety of support mechanisms, both technical and organizational. Most of them are part of the necessary capabilities for decision support, but enumerating them in the context of iterative design reveals some additional dimensions.

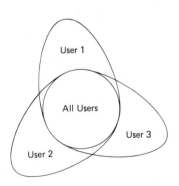

FIGURE 5-6   SDSS Boundaries for Personal and Group Support

Definition of Roles. The interpersonal relationships are crucial in iterative design. There must be a clear definition of the users, the intermediaries (if any), the builders, and the technical support people. Each person should know who the others are, and understand his or her role and responsibilities with respect to the others. The proper alignment of organizational units and reporting responsibility is also important in some cases. The interaction will be frequent and intense enough to make personality styles a dominant consideration.

The Technology. The need to build a small usable system and change it constantly makes heavy demands on the technology. It is, in fact, advances in technology that have made the iterative design approach and DSS feasible in the past few years. DSS Tools and/or a DSS Generator with DDM and ROMC capabilities will be required for this task.

Communication Mechanisms. Because of the compressed sequence of steps and rapid cycling of the iterative design approach, communication among users and builders is particularly important. There are a variety of mechanisms to support these communications, including the proximate location of builders' and users' offices, frequent informal meetings, bulletin boards, and electronic message systems (EMS). The latter are particularly promising, especially if they are built into the DSS and utilize the capability of a strong dialog component in the Generator. A general EMS capability can also be used to support documentation, user education, and evaluation if they are an integral part of the system.

Documentation Capability. The iterative design approach requires a dynamic documentation capability so that users and builders can always access a description of the current configuration of the system. For the SDSS, the documentation system should permit the user to call for an enumeration of all the ROMC elements that are currently part of the system, as well as the description of the use of the system (especially operations and control mechanisms). A variation of this capability is the HELP command, which is a form of direct request for documentation on a specific element. The need for this capability is obvious given the frequent additions and deletions to the active elements in the system.

The users also need a way of depicting *potential* ROMC elements to guide their request for additions and deletions. Obviously, it is not feasible, or appropriate, to depict all the possible ROMC elements, but a listing of some, perhaps those defined by other users facing a similar problem, would be of valuable assistance.

For the DSS Generator, the builders need the same type of documentation capability to list and describe the dialog, data handling, and modeling capabilities which are a part of the Generator: for example, existing and potential dialog styles, data sources, and modeling subroutines. For DSS Tools, the documentation will be systems documentation prepared by toolsmiths and oriented to the builders. If tools are used directly and individually, the documentation will be of traditional form. If the DSS Generator is composed of tools integrated by an architecture of segmentable modules as we suggest in Chapter 10, the documentation will also be modular.

User Tutorials.   The iterative design approach may not require, but will certainly benefit from, a set of user tutorials which are also dynamic and built into the Specific DSS. Their function would be to help new users "catch up" with others in use of a system for group or organizational support, or to refresh and update a user who has not used the system for a while. If the tutorials use the techniques and principles of computer-aided instruction (CAI) they can be particularly effective. In Chapter 6 we describe a hybrid approach called the Interactive Training Manual which was used with GADS for user education.

Evaluation and Tracking.   Since evaluation is the primary guidance and control mechanism in interactive design, it is important that it, too, be supported with techniques and mechanisms built into the DSS. In Chapter 6 we discuss evaluation approaches and models in more detail; here we underscore the need for the technology to gather usage and performance data to support the evaluation process. The evaluation step serves as a systematic checkpoint to capture feedback on the SDSS and its use. One of the pioneering EMS systems, the EIES at the New Jersey Institute of Technology, uses a variety of data gathering approaches for evaluation [4]:

- User surveys in which users periodically respond, through the system, to questions from user consultants (builders).
- Participant observation, including the use of a user consultant file in which the user enters observations and notations during use of the system.
- Automatic monitoring which can be used to detect frequently used facilities and operations (especially in pairs or in combination) or infrequent activities.

Systematic data capture for evaluation allows tracking the progress of change in a system over time for single- or multiple-user systems. For the latter, it may reveal aggregate patterns to the builder that no one user can see.

SUMMARY

We have discussed many aspects of flexibility in this chapter. The conventional wisdom is that flexibility is needed in computer-based information systems to make them more viable and useful over time, and to reduce maintenance costs. It is possible, however, for information systems to have too much flexibility. Transactions processing systems and traditional reporting systems, for instance, have characteristics that place constraints on the value of flexibility. DSS, on the other hand, have characteristics that place a high premium on flexibility. In general, flexibility is required in DSS:

- To modify a small initial system iteratively so that it becomes a satisfactory system when the performance requirements cannot be defined in advance.
- To allow the system to change over time in response to changes in the tasks, users, and environment for which it provides support.

Meeting these requirements actually requires a spectrum of flexibility which can be defined across two dimensions: the level of technology and the time horizon for change. This taxonomy of flexibility is depicted visually in Figure 5-4 and summarized in Figure 5-7. A DSS that operates over time utilizing all levels of flexibility is an adaptive system—an "ideal" DSS.

The process by which flexibility is operationalized in DSS is iterative design. It is the process by which the Specific DSS is developed and modified over time. It can be described as a series of rapid cycles through the analysis/design/implementation/evaluation stages which are compressed and repeated. The development path of a Specific DSS begins with version 0, the minimal usable starting point, moves to version S, a satisfactory and relatively stable version, which then changes in response to changes in the user, task, and environment.

The iterative design process requires some specific support mechanisms to make it operable and effective. Included are:

- A definition of the roles and responsibilities of the people who participate in the development of DSS.
- A strong set of tools and/or a DSS Generator with ROMC and DDM capabilities.
- Communication mechanisms.

NOTATION	KEYWORD	PARTICIPANT	SYSTEM	TIME FRAME
F1	Solve	User	SDSS	Short range
F2	Modify	Builder–user	SDSS	Short and intermediate range
F3	Adapt	Builder–toolsmith	DSSG	Intermediate range
F4	Evolve	Toolsmith–builder	Tools	Long range

FIGURE 5-7   Taxonomy of Flexibility in DSS

- A dynamic documentation capability.
- A user-education mechanism, including tutorials.
- A set of data-gathering mechanisms for evaluation and tracking.

When these capabilities and mechanisms are built into the SDSS from the Generator or Tools, the iterative design process is a viable and continually dynamic approach for building DSS.

QUESTIONS AND PROBLEMS

REVIEW QUESTIONS

1. What are the characteristics of traditional information systems that make flexibility valuable? That limit the value of flexibility?
2. Answer Question 1 for DSS.
3. Identify four types of flexibility and describe each.
4. Construct a representation (a table, perhaps) showing the stages of the traditional SDLC, the problems inherent in each stage if it is used to build DSS, and how the iterative design approach helps reduce the problems.
5. Identify the steps in the iterative design process. Briefly describe each step.
6. What are version 0 and version S of the Specific DSS? What is the relationship between them?
7. Identify the mechanisms that support the iterative design approach. Explain why each one is needed and how it provides support.

EXERCISES

1. Construct a representation (a flowchart, perhaps) showing the steps in the iterative design approach and the relationships between them.
2. Construct a representation to depict the development path of a Specific DSS from version 0 through version S and beyond.

REFERENCES

1. COUGER, J. D., and F. R. MCFADDEN. *A First Course in Data Processing,* John Wiley & Sons, Inc., New York, 1977.

2. COURBON, J. C., J. GRAJEW, and J. TOLOVI, JR. "Design and Implementation of Decision Supporting Systems by an Evolutive Approach," Unpublished Working Paper, 1980.

3. GILDERSLEEVE, T. R. *Data Processing Project Management*, Van Nostrand Reinhold Co., New York, 1974.

4. HILTZ, S. R., and M. TUROFF. "Office Augmentation Systems: The Case for Evolutionary Design," *Proceedings, Fifteenth Hawaii International Conference on System Sciences*, Western Periodicals, North Hollywood, Calif., 1982.

5. KEEN, P. G. W. "Adaptive Design for DSS," *Database*, Vol. 12, Nos. 1–2, Fall 1980, pp. 15–25.

CHAPTER SIX

INTEGRATING DSS INTO THE ORGANIZATION

OUTLINE

INTRODUCTION: INTEGRATION PROBLEMS AND STRATEGIES

In Chapter 5 we described the iterative design process for developing a Specific DSS. For personal support, the user and the builder work together in a nearly continuous process to modify the DSS over time. For group support, the communication among builders and users must become more structured and formal, frequently to the extent that the steps in the systems development life cycle become discernible and the DSS moves through versions. For organizational support, there are typically many users, and the builders must take the responsibility for guiding the *integration* of the Specific DSS into the organization. By integration we mean (1) educating the users, (2) installing the DSS, and (3) evaluating the DSS. Obviously, these are not three separate sequential steps in the process of integrating a DSS into an organization.

In a DSS for personal support, integration is an informal, continual process. For group support, integration may be a planned part of iterative design. For organizational support, integration will be *required* when a DSS is installed for widespread use. When integration is needed, there are specific techniques that can be used. Before describing these techniques, it is important to make some general observations about the overall process of integration. As usual, some of the principles of traditional systems development prevail, but with some differences.

Fundamental requirements for developing any computer-based system are *user involvement* and *management involvement.* Often with DSS, users are managers, which simplifies the problem in that there are fewer people involved, but compounds the problem in that managers have less time to get involved and prefer to assign ("delegate") this responsibility to others. Evidence of the importance of user involvement in DSS development appears in the survey of Steven Alter [1], whose study of 56 DSS showed that there were fewer integration problems ("implementation" problems in Alter's terms) in DSS where users were involved in initializing or implementing the DSS. Alter's results suggest that user involvement is beneficial *before* the integration process begins. While this suggestion has been made for traditional systems, it is obviously mandatory for DSS.

A second observation regarding the integration process is that there are a variety of strategies that can be used as guidance. A derivation of a traditional strategy is some sort of contract (sometimes even written) between DSS builders and users, specifying who will do what and when. The contract can be strengthened by having the users pay for the DSS development and integration. Note that this strategy obtains user involvement in the form of payments *before* integration. Another strategy for integration is to view it as a process of social change. This strategy is generally related to the Lewin–Schein theory of social change [11, 14], which involves:

- Creating an organizational setting that will be receptive to the DSS ("unfreezing")
- Directing organizational changes to prepare for the DSS ("moving")
- Reinforcing the use of the DSS ("refreezing")

Keen and Scott Morton [9] argue for a "clinical" integration strategy that is based on an attempt to diagnose problems during integration and then to prescribe solutions. This strategy is based on the observations that there is little experience with DSS and that each DSS is sufficiently different that the integration strategy should be more like clinical psychology than engineering. The clinical approach is amplified by Alter [1], who identifies classes of integration problems (diagnosis) and situations (prescriptions). Unfortunately, Alter's data did not permit him to determine which prescriptions seem to work for particular diagnoses. Even so, Alter's list of problem situations is a useful guideline for the integration process. Figure 6-1 gives four categories of problems with sample symptoms that can be used to diag-

---

TECHNICAL PROBLEMS

- Response times
- Availability
- Accessibility

- Inadequate function
- Excess function
- Too difficult to operate

DATA PROBLEMS

- Inaccurate
- Out of date
- Inappropriate units
- No index

- Too much is required
- Too much is available
- Not enough is available

DECISION MISMATCH PROBLEMS

- Does not solve a real problem
- Cannot decide if it helps or not
- Cannot use it to do things my way
- Did not adapt to changes

PEOPLE PROBLEMS

- Too hard to use
- Too hard to learn
- Too many mistakes
- Unpredictable

- Too hard to understand
- Cannot get help
- Never works properly

FIGURE 6-1   Integration Problems (from Alter [1])

1. Cooperative effort
     Prescribed for: technical, data, decision mismatch
     User involvement: initiation, development, integration
2. Service to user
     Prescribed for: technical, data, decision mismatch
     User involvement: initiation, integration
3. Kit for user
     Prescribed for: technical, data
     User involvement: development, integration
4. Sell to user
     Prescribed for: decision mismatch, people
     User involvement: integration
5. Impose on user
     Prescribed for: decision mismatch, people
     User involvement: development

FIGURE 6-2   Integration Strategies (from Alter [1])

nose the problem. Figure 6-2 lists five integration strategies. We have characterized these strategies on two dimensions:

1. The integration problems for which they seem most appropriate
2. The degree of user involvement in DSS initiation, development, and integration

The labels for the strategies indicate their underlying assumptions.

1. *Cooperative effort*: Try to get users and builders together for the entire process.
2. *Service to user*: Technical experts serve the user.
3. *Kit for user*: Technical experts teach users how to do it themselves.
4. *Sell to user*: Technical experts know what is best.
5. *Impose on user*: Top management knows what is best.

The labels and the numbering scheme were chosen to indicate our preferences for each strategy. The clinical approach, however, suggests that each strategy has its place, depending on the problems and the patient.

A final observation on integrating DSS into the organization relates to organizational politics. There are many reasons for developing a DSS, and often improving decision making is not the major reason. Other reasons include:

1. To change the decision-making process
2. To change organizational goals
3. To establish a power base (a select group of DSS users)
4. To get attention
5. To challenge the "old line" (status quo)

It is important to realize that the reasons for developing a DSS affect the integration process. For example, the installation of a DSS designed to "get attention" will be much different than for a DSS that is intended to change a decision-making process.

Although the degree of user involvement, the general implementation strategies, and the organizational politics differ among organizations and among DSS, an integration plan can be developed. The plan is a guide for the integration process and consists of three elements: education, installation, and evaluation.

USER EDUCATION

User education clearly is a process that begins before a DSS gets built and continues throughout the lifetime of the DSS. Preliminary phases of education begin with introduction to DSS concepts, soliciting user involvement, identifying applications, and developing a plan for building DSS. During design and development, user education involves discussions of data requirements and sources, choice of functions, and dialog alternatives. During installation of the DSS, user education involves training on how to operate the DSS. Finally, during ongoing use of the DSS, user education involves teaching the users how to solve problems with the DSS, how to adapt the DSS to new problems, and how to use special "features" of the DSS. Figure 6-3 summarizes these four phases of education. Remember that because DSS often are used irregularly, are frequently modified, and their users often change, the phases of user education are iterative.

In each of the four phases there are several education techniques from which to choose. Choice of technique depends on the phase of education, as well as on the number, skill, and DSS experience of the users. Because DSS is a new concept, and because users generally are professionals who do not have the time or inclination for training, there is very little research or reported experience on DSS user education. From the case studies and academic literature on DSS, six education techniques can be identified.

The technique that seems to be the most effective, the most common, and the most expensive is one-on-one or tutorial technique. With this technique, each user is individually taught by an instructor or colleague. There are usually few instructional materials, and the material is covered in an order determined by the interests of the student (i.e., the user). The tutorial technique has been used in all phases of DSS user education.

A second technique is to use courses, lectures, or professional development seminars. Usually, the instructor is an internal or external "expert" in DSS. There are instructional materials, and the instructor determines the contents. Like the tutorial technique, this technique has been used in all phases of DSS user education.

PHASE	CONTENT
1. Preliminary	DSS concepts, user involvement, application, planning
2. Design/development	Data requirements/sources, functions, dialog
3. Installation	Operation
4. Ongoing use	Problem solving, adapting, special features

FIGURE 6-3   Phases in User Education

Program instruction (PI) and its automated counterpart, computer-assisted instruction (CAI), have been used for a very small number of DSS. In both techniques the instructor prepares lessons which consist of three parts: content, questions, and answer/next lesson pairs. The content describes the material, the questions attempt to determine whether the student has understood the material, and the answer/next pairs determine what happens next given the answer to each question. The materials for the course are the PI booklet or the CAI system. The course content is strictly controlled by the PI or CAI system, although in some cases the student can control the sequences of the material.

A combination of tutorial and PI/CAI called Interactive Training Manual (ITM) was proposed by Barbara Grace [7]. An ITM is a Specific DSS and a guidebook, which are used together. The guidebook contains lessons and the Specific DSS provides the examples and the exercises. Both the guidebook and SDSS are oriented toward example problems. The examples may be intended to help students learn how to operate the DSS (e.g., what buttons to push) or how to solve problems effectively with the DSS. Grace's results with ITM technique are extremely encouraging. The technique seems to be as effective as the tutorial technique, to offer the economies of scale-of-the-course technique, to be no more expensive than either tutors or courses, and to offer the personalization and privacy (anonymity) of the PI/CAI technique.

Two other educational techniques have also been used. One of these involves having a resident expert whom users can consult. This technique is a passive version of the tutorial technique in that education is user initiated. The rationale for this method is that DSS users are more likely to ask when they need to know than to attend a course or consult a book or system. If the resident expert is the DSS itself, the DSS is said to contain a "training" or "guidance" or "help" component. Most DSS contain primitive "help" components which give error messages when the user makes mistakes, or provide short explanations of the commands. A "layered" help component lets the user proceed through successive layers of instructional material, each involving more detail. The "bottom" level may be a CAI system.

A good example of a built-in education component is the Interactive User Guidance System (IUGS) of IDAMS [6]. The IDAMS IUGS helps the user select which DSS commands will be useful for particular characteristics of the data, the analyses (models), and the desired output. Experiences with this "on-line" technique indicate that there are three capabilities which all users seem to require of such a technique:

1. The ability to turn it off once they know how to use the DSS
2. The ability to issue DSS commands while using the on-line education (without extraneous steps either to exit or reenter the education component)
3. The ability to get paper copies of the material to serve as reminders and references, or to avoid having to use the on-line technique

Figure 6-4 summarizes these six user-education techniques.

INSTALLATION

Our limited definition of installation is *making the DSS ready for use.* Installation must be preceded by the traditional testing of the software, and review and approval by the user groups. That is, the installation process assumes that the DSS operates correctly (technical testing) and that it appears to operate appropriately (acceptance testing). Attempting installation before technical and acceptance tests increases the risk of failure of the DSS.

During installation, builders and users must work closely together. The builder's role is to perform the installation steps, and the user's role is to introduce the DSS into the decision-making environment. If the user group has not been responsible for management of the DSS project before the installation phase, management control should shift to a manager in a user group at this time.

As noted in Chapter 5, a formalized and structured version of the iterative design process (prototyping) is a valuable approach to installing large DSS. In fact, most of the DSS literature currently advises that the most successful installation technique is prototyping. There are several reasons. First, a prototype usually gets the DSS into use as early as possible. Early use can provide assistance to the decision makers and feedback to the builders. Second, prototyping is considerably cheaper than a "full-build" approach, which delays installation until the DSS is complete. Third, prototyping is a convenient way of keeping the DSS simple, which is valuable to both builders and users. Finally, prototyping lowers risk and expectations. There are two approaches to prototyping: the throwaway prototype and the evolving prototype. Most DSS builders proclaim that they are developing a throwaway (to lower their risk and their users' expectations). If the users like the prototype, the evolving prototype is hard to avoid, because the users cannot see any reasons to throw it away. The throwaway prototype is an acknowledged experiment, designed to create user interest, develop builder skills, and

TECHNIQUE	EDUCATION PHASE WHERE MOST USED	MATERIAL	EMPHASIS	EFFECTIVENESS COMPARED TO TUTORIAL TECHNIQUE
TUTORIAL	All	Verbal	Personal contact	Equal
COURSE/ SEMINAR	Preliminary design/ development	Written and/ or verbal	Expert instruction	Less
PI/CAI	Installation, ongoing use	Written or computer-based	Individual rates of instruction	Less
ITM	Installation, ongoing use	Written and computer-based	Hands-on experience	Equal
LOCAL EXPERT	All	Verbal	Education on demand	Equal
DSS HELP COMPONENT	Installation, ongoing use	Computer-based	On-line education	Less

FIGURE 6-4 **User-Education Techniques**

reduce risk and investment. It is supported by the "software engineering" approach to installation [3] and by the "social change" approach to installation [9].

If the throwaway prototype is useful, it can continue to be used while a second-generation DSS is built. The pressure for additional functions or data, improvements in the user interface or performance, or expansion of the user groups often force the builders to modify the throwaway rather than build a replacement. This prototype evolution can work if the builders are clever or if the prototype was designed to evolve (e.g., if the prototype was built using a DSS Generator). If one of these two conditions is not the case, then trying to evolve a prototype almost certainly will lead to increasing the complexity of the DSS while decreasing performance and increasing costs. It is usually much cheaper to "freeze" the prototype, let it continue to be used, and if the additional capabilities can be justified, let the builders develop a replacement.

Prototyping is not the only installation strategy. As the DSS team (builders and users) gains experience, and as DSS Generators become more available, prototyping may not be necessary. Organizational considerations, such as overselling of the DSS, high development costs, and exposure of the managers who supported the DSS may make prototyping infeasible. In cases where prototyping cannot be used, the installation strategy can be one of the following:

- The DSS as an alternative (parallel installation).
- The DSS as a requirement (forced installation).
- The DSS as a requirement for now (trial installation).

Of the three, parallel installation seems the most likely to succeed if there are a few interested (and talented) users. These supportive users generally will convince the others to use the DSS, hopefully because the supportive users can demonstrate the advantages of using the DSS.

Once an installation strategy has been chosen, the installation team proceeds through a series of steps that seem to be relatively independent of the installation strategy, the organization, the users, or the DSS. The steps are:

1. *Gathering the data*: collecting the data needed for the DSS
2. *Preparing the data*: validating, converting, and reducing the data
3. *Loading the data base*: creating the data base that is used by the DSS
4. *Priming the models*: initializing the parameters of the models in the DSS
5. *Tailoring the dialog*: customizing the representations and control provided by the dialog component of the DSS
6. *Creating examples*: installing sample reports and alternative solutions for a typical decision, or executing examples for a model
7. *Introducing the DSS*: giving demonstrations

These steps illustrate that installation is a separate process from user education, but that installation and user education must be coordinated. Installation should not proceed without the preliminary or design/development phases of user education, and should occur (a short time) before the startup and ongoing use phases of user education. The greatest danger in installation is that user education has created too high or too early an expectation among users.

Figure 6-5 summarizes the installation prerequisites, strategies, and steps.

EVALUATION

Evaluations of DSS, if they occur, have not been widely reported. In general, if users like the DSS, a short "confirming" evaluation might be done. If the users do not like the DSS, an evaluation may be done to find out why. Evaluation is an important, if difficult and often overlooked, part of the

PREREQUISITES

1. Technical test
2. Acceptance test

STRATEGIES

1. Throwaway prototype
2. Evolving prototype
3. Parallel installation
4. Forced installation
5. Trial installation

STEPS

1. Gather data
2. Prepare data
3. Load database
4. Prime models
5. Tailor user interface
6. Create examples
7. Give demonstrations

FIGURE 6-5 Installation Prerequisites, Strategies, and Steps

process of integrating DSS into the organization. Not only does evaluation help decide which DSS to undertake and which to continue, but DSS evaluation also can help quantify the impact of decision-making processes on organizational goals (e.g., does better decision making really affect profits?). Like user education, DSS evaluation should begin before the technical phases (analysis, design, development, testing, and installation) and should continue beyond the life of the DSS. If evaluation is simply a postaudit of the DSS, it is likely not to be done, and if done is likely to be a "confirmation" rather than a useful source of information.

In this chapter we devote considerably more attention to evaluation than to education and installation. Evaluation is no more important than the other two. It is less well understood, less often done, and can take advantage of more specific techniques than either education or installation. Our description of the evaluation process is divided into three sections: what to measure, how to measure, and a general model for evaluation.

What to Measure

Figure 6-6 gives examples of possible measures that can be used in evaluating the impact of DSS. We divide these measures into four categories.

- Productivity measures are used to evaluate the impact of the DSS on decisions.
- Process measures are used to evaluate the impact of the DSS on decision making.
- Perception measures are used to evaluate the impact of the DSS on decision makers.
- Product measures are used to evaluate the technical merit of the DSS.

Where the measures involve a judgment (e.g., all the perception measures), a three-, five-, or seven-point scale usually is used to try to quantify the measure. For example, a three-point scale might be

_____ poor   _____ adequate   _____ excellent

Obviously, such measures are not as precise or reliable as measures with detailed scales such as times and counts, and are not as useful for statistical summaries such as averages.

How to Measure

Any evaluation can be described in terms of two systems: (1) an initiating system (the DSS) whose impact is to be evaluated, and (2) a target system (the decision, the organization, the product) on which impact is to be measured. Each evaluation conjecture describes the expected impact of an initiating system on a target system.

The initiating and target systems can be all or parts of four basic systems.

1. The DSS
2. The user
3. The environment, organizational or external
4. The task or problem

These are the four parts of the decision-making system depicted in Figure 2-2. A precise definition of each of these systems is probably impossible, and is unnecessary as long as the basic distinctions are clear. Some of the elements of each system will overlap; for example, DSS users will be employees of the organizational environment. Initiating and target systems can be various inter and intra combinations of elements of the four basic systems.

There are several factors that may be considered in specifying an initiating system. The initiating system will usually be all or specific parts of the DSS. However, it may be necessary to specify which version is being evaluated as the DSS is modified and corrected. Changes in versions may not affect evaluation measurements, but analysis is easier when each measurement covers only one version. The initiating system often consists of the

---

PRODUCTIVITY MEASURES

1. Time to reach a decision
2. Cost of making a decision
3. Results of the decision
4. Cost of implementing the decision

PROCESS MEASURES

1. Number of alternatives examined
2. Number of analyses done
3. Number of participants in the decision making
4. Time horizon of the decision
5. Amount of data used
6. Time spent in each phase of decision making
7. Time lines of the decision

PERCEPTION MEASURES

1. Control of the decision-making process
2. Usefulness of the DSS
3. Ease of use
4. Understanding of the problem
5. Ease of "selling" the decision
6. Conviction that the decision is correct

PRODUCT MEASURES

1. Response time
2. Availability
3. Mean time to failure
4. Development costs
5. Operating costs
6. Maintenance costs
7. Education costs
8. Data acquisition costs

FIGURE 6-6   Examples of Measures for DSS Evaluation

DSS plus elements from the other basic systems. For example, in evaluating the impact of a DSS on services, there may be an impact from elements of the environment (e.g., the impact of the courts on education services). Occasionally, it may be useful to select an initiating system other than the information system. For example, one might evaluate the impact of federal agencies on the development of a DSS for municipal financial management.

The most common target systems will be all parts of the organizational environment, but elements of the external environment, such as customers and events, are also important target systems. The target system, like the initiating system, may overlap the four basic systems. Possible target systems that overlap are: services/clients, services/events, and employees/events.

Eight methods that can be used to measure and evaluate the impact of DSS are discussed in this section. These methods are not mutually exclusive nor do they represent all possible methods for DSS evaluation. They do, however, represent a range of methods that are system and hypothesis independent. That is, none requires a specific type of DSS, and none is restricted to investigation of a particular impact. More important, each of the eight methods can be identified by the techniques it employs, and each is a systematic method for evaluating DSS impact. Given the complexity of the evaluation task, these qualities seem essential. The following paragraphs briefly describe each method, list its apparent advantages and disadvantages, and present examples of its use. Figure 6-7 is a summary comparison of the methods.

Event Logging.   In an event logging evaluation, events that might indicate DSS impact are recorded. An example is keeping a log of customer complaints before and after implementation of a customer service DSS. Event logging is the least structured of the methods to be discussed, and it has the least well defined set of techniques. The methodology for event logging is a combination of historiography and journalism. The basic technique is the recording of events that relate to the effects being investigated. The events may be actions, opinions, newspaper articles, items from memos, dates, and so on. Judgment is required in selecting the events to be recorded, and the set of possible relevant events is not predefinable. The recording may be on a continuous or a before/after basis. The evaluation is simply an analysis of the recorded events.

Event logging is most useful when quantitative measures cannot be used, when a time series of effects is of interest, and when multiple effects are being considered. Event logging can also provide valuable insight for designers and users of similar systems, and can be a useful background for other evaluations. Event logging has a wide range of applicability, is relatively simple to perform, does not require special data collection techniques, and can be performed on a continuing basis. However, it usually results in large volumes of data which may be difficult to interpret, and it is difficult to guarantee the completeness and accuracy of the data.

Although event logging is a simple method, it has been used infrequently. McLean and Riesing [12] give a short evaluation of a DSS based on event logging.

Attitude Survey.   The attitude survey is a method that attempts to measure opinions through a questionnaire administered to a set of individu-

MODEL	EVENT LOGGING	ATTITUDE SURVEY	COGNITIVE TESTING	RATING AND WEIGHTING	SYSTEM MEASUREMENT	SYSTEM ANALYSIS	COST-BENEFIT ANALYSIS	VALUE ANALYSIS
Objective	To log events relating to impact on citizen services	To determine impact on citizen attitudes on services	To determine impact on municipal officials' decision processes	To determine impact through service ratings	To test the null hypothesis of no difference in measurements on services	To determine impact on methods of service delivery	To determine impact on costs and benefits of services	To determine whether or not to continue to use the DSS
Measures	Events relating to services	Questions on services	Role Repetoire Tests	Ratings	Times, quantities, possibly others	Aspects of services (e.g., method of delivery)	Dollar value of services	Dollar value of services, DSS costs
Treatments and Experimental units	Before and after DSS; Services	Before and after DSS; Citizens	Before and after DSS; Decision makers	Before and after DSS; Parameters of service	Before and after DSS; Services	Before and after DSS; Services	Before and after DSS; Cost and benefit items	Prototype DSS; Cost and benefit items
Plan for assigning treatments to units	Use same services before and after (i.e., block on services)	Block on services	Test before and after DSS use	Block on services and evaluators	Block on services	Block on services	Only one department include additional services	Treatment; assign to all units
Plan for selecting units	Judgmental selection	Random selection	Department managers in all direct service departments	Judgmental selection	Either all services or random selection	Judgmental selection	Judgmental or random selection	Judgmental
Analysis criteria and techniques	Qualitative comparison of logged events	Chi-square comparison of response frequencies	Comparison of test scores	Compare overall scores (sums of) rating times weight	Wilcoxon signed ranks comparison for each measure	Qualitative comparison of standard descriptions	Compare cost-benefit ratios	Are benefits obtained within cost threshold?

FIGURE 6-7 Comparison of Eight Methods for DSS Evaluation in Terms of the General Model (in the context of evaluating the impact of a Municipal DSS on citizen services)

als. The questionnaire may be mailed out or administered via interviews. Questions cover a wide variety of attitudes, and usually provide multiple-choice, short statement, or open-ended answer formats. There is a large body of psychological and behavioral research which can be used in designing and analyzing the questionnaires. For example, questionnaires have been developed for measuring perception of working environment, motivation, and interpersonal contacts. For best results the questionnaires are administered at various intervals during the development and use of the DSS and the results are compared. There are four major problems that may arise in attitude surveys.

1. In developing a questionnaire to measure attitudes, one may be trying to quantify that which is not quantifiable and the subsequent analysis may be misleading.
2. Questionnaire respondents may interpret questions differently than intended, and answers to some questions may influence answers to others. Thus unintended impacts may be measured, or a single impact may be interpreted as more than one.
3. Administering questionnaires may be an inconvenience to individuals and expensive (in terms of hours lost by respondents and hours spent by interviewers).
4. The method does not identify the causes of any measured changes.

Because of these problems it is best to use questionnaires and analysis techniques validated by others or by pretests, and if possible, to facilitate data collection by sampling. An attitude survey is most useful when the target system consists primarily of people and when perception measures are being used. The evaluation of the San Jose Police Department's use of GADS [4] and Alter's DSS study [1] both used attitude surveys.

Cognitive Testing. Cognitive testing utilizes methods developed by social psychologists. It is a variation of the attitude survey based on having explicit theories of behavior and more formal evaluation procedures (the tests). In cognitive testing, structured interviews or "games" are used to determine behavior patterns, preferences, processes, or understanding. The cognitive test seems to be a better technique than the attitude survey for understanding decision-making processes, and about the same for perception measures. The theories behind this method are still under development, and the results of the tests are often difficult to interpret. Although the techniques are likely to improve, cognitive testing evaluation will have to be done by experts. The use of this method for DSS evaluation was pioneered by Charles Stabell, whose Ph.D. thesis is the most complete, if not the only, example of the use of cognitive testing to evaluate a DSS [15]. Stabell utilized a variation of a cognitive test, called the Role Repertoire Test [10], to measure individual differences in decision-making processes.

Rating and Weighting. Rating and weighting is a highly structured method for a composite numerical evaluation. The methodology involves developing a set of parameters related to the system and effects being evaluated, weighting these parameters in terms of relative importance, and having one or more individuals rate the system on each parameter. For example, department managers could be asked to rate a DSS on accuracy, timeliness, and useability of displays using a scale of 1 to 10, and to assign a relative importance (weight) to each of the three factors. The summation of the ratings times the corresponding weights gives an evaluation score. The scores from each individual may be averaged or totaled.

The rating and weighting method may involve several evaluations and a comparison, or a single evaluation. However, because ratings, and sometimes the weights, are ordinal numbers (i.e., they can be ranked, but their differences are meaningless), the summation of ratings times weights is undefined theoretically. Moreover, in comparing two scores, only if all ratings for one system are less than those for the other, and the same evaluators rate each system, do the scores necessarily give an indisputable direction of difference. Therefore, in analyzing results of rating and weighting, the evaluator must remember that the numbers are not precise and may not be accurate. If the ratings and weights are reliable, this method is the easiest to interpret. If not, the method will be misleading.

System Measurement. This method attempts to quantify effects through measurements of the performance of the target system, and therefore it is similar to performance evaluation. In fact, if the target system is the DSS, the evaluation should use product measures for the DSS. Measuring the time to locate a suspect before and after implementation of a DSS for a police department is an example of a system measurement evaluation. The measurements may be collected automatically by the DSS or other sensors, through questionnaires, interviews, or observations, or extracted from documents. The method of evaluation is usually a before/after comparison of measurements. The analysis of the measurements often utilizes statistical techniques, the data collection is straightforward and often employs sampling, and the results are usually easy to interpret. Unfortunately, the method has a narrow range of applicability because it requires that the affected elements of the target system have performance characteristics that can be quantified. However, if this requirement is satisfied, system measurement is the most reliable evaluation method. Grace's study of the impact of a DSS training method is an example of system measurement [7].

System Analysis. Although the system analysis method may include some system measurement, it is essentially a formalized, qualitative technique for describing the impact on multiple aspects of the target system. The techniques for system analysis evaluation are those used in the analysis that precedes the development of any system. The target system is described in terms of procedures, information flows, data stored, personnel activities, data used in reports and decisions, and so on, depending upon the impact being investigated. Interviews, document review, and observation are the data collection techniques; flowcharts, organizational charts, input–output matrices, and decision tables are among the tools that can be used in data collection. The evaluation may consist of a single description or of a comparison of descriptions. The method has a wide range of applicability and it encompasses qualitative and quantitative measures and a variety of well-known techniques. It is the best technique for evaluating system impact on procedures, organizational structures, and other administrative factors in a target system. Its biggest advantage is that baseline data can be gathered during the analysis that precedes the DSS design. It does not, however, provide a numeric measure of system impact, and the results are often difficult to interpret.

It is easy to posit potential uses of system analysis. For example, the method could be used to evaluate the impact of a DSS on the preparation of ad hoc reports. Specific documents would be identified through interviews and direct review of departmental activities. Requirements for data used to prepare reports would be documented and these requirements compared with the content and retrieval capability of the DSS. The method could also be used to evaluate the impact of a DSS on budget preparation. The before/after comparison would involve attending budget meetings and analysis of budget requests and outcomes. A good example of a system analysis evaluation is Scott Morton's investigation of the impact of a DSS on the decision making of three middle-level managers [16]. The experiment included detailed analysis of decision processes in the areas of marketing, production, and inventory before and after the introduction of the information system. The experiment not only indicates the potential benefits of interactive systems, but also the usefulness of the system analysis method in case study evaluations.

Cost/Benefit Analysis.   Cost/benefit evaluation may utilize some of the data collection techniques of system analysis and system measurement, but it is a separate method because it has a specific focus and specific analysis techniques. Cost/benefit analysis produces evaluations in terms of dollars, and has been used for many years in evaluating private and public investments. It is more often used in feasibility studies for DSS than in evaluations. Cost/benefit impact evaluation would follow the traditional approach of estimating or measuring costs and benefits. The only costs that should be included are those that relate to the aspects of the target system for which benefits are being compiled. That is, if the target system is only one process or department in an organization, only those costs (and benefits) of the DSS relating to that process or department should be included in the analysis. There are several possible analysis procedures. The simplest is a year-by-year comparison of the costs and benefits or of the cost/benefit ratio. This analysis can be enhanced by comparing cost/benefit ratios or amounts before and after the DSS implementation. Costs and benefits from more than one year can be converted into a single cost/benefit measure using a ratio of present values, net cash flow, or rate of return. These three techniques require that future costs and benefits be discounted, and they are enhanced if they compare present values, cash flow, or rate of return with and without the DSS (or with alternative DSS).

Cost/benefit evaluations will probably provide the most meaningful results to management and they are based on some well-developed economic theories. The usual problems of delineating direct and indirect costs and benefits, of measuring benefits, and of choice of discount rate will be encountered. Cost/benefit impact evaluation may be particularly difficult because the benefits and costs of a DSS may be social (e.g., better services, loss of privacy), because the system may appreciate rather than depreciate over time due to the accumulation of data and experience, and because of the difficulty of allocating computer system costs among users. Because of these problems, the method may reduce to a comparison of direct costs. As in the evaluation of any investment, the cost/benefit method is the only way to evaluate economic impact, and it should not be ignored or limited only to direct costs and benefits.

A good example of a cost/benefit evaluation of a DSS is Sutton's evaluation of the impact of GADS on an IBM branch office [17]. A portion of this study is given as a case example at the end of this chapter.

Value Analysis. Peter Keen recently proposed an evaluation technique which he called value analysis [8]. The approach is similar to cost/benefit analysis, with three important differences. First, the emphasis is on benefits first and costs second. This emphasis is based on the assumption that it is the benefits that are of primary interest to decision makers and that the calculations of cost/benefit ratios are not necessary if the benefits meet some threshold and the costs are within some acceptable limit. Second, the method attempts to reduce risk by requiring prototyping as part of the evaluation method. The assumption here is that the prototype is a low-risk, relatively inexpensive way to obtain relatively accurate evaluation data. Third, the method evaluates DSS as an R&D effort rather than as a capital investment. An R&D evaluation tends to encourage innovation rather than return on investment.

Keen describes value analysis as a series of four steps.

1.   Establish the operational list of benefits that the DSS must achieve to be acceptable.
2.   Establish the maximum cost that one is willing to pay to achieve the benefits.

3. Develop a prototype DSS.
4. Assess the benefits and the costs.

The advantages of the value analysis approach are that it is simple and integrated with an installation approach (prototyping). The main disadvantage is that it is a limited form of evaluation, which may not include all the measures that are relevant. Value analysis also is a much less rigorous method than either the cost/benefit or system analysis techniques. Although not reported in the DSS literature, value analysis seems very close to the intuitive approach that many managers use to evaluate DSS.

Combining Methods. The choice of evaluation method will depend on the DSS and the impacts being investigated, and on the evaluator and the environment in which the evaluation is performed. Because of the variety and complexity of the potential effects and because there are problems with all evaluation methods, a combination of methods will probably result in the best evaluation. The usefulness of the event log in explaining changes in attitudes has already been mentioned. An attitude survey and a cost/benefit analysis is another attractive combination because the methods measure different impacts. System measurement, system analysis, and cost/benefit analysis use similar data collection techniques and therefore can be combined easily. Regardless of which combination of methods is chosen, the breadth that the combination provides to the evaluation is worth the effort.

A General Model for Evaluation

The discussions of evaluation methods and measures were structured to illustrate that DSS evaluations should be considered as planned experiments designed to test one or more hypotheses. Thus the model for planned experiments developed by statisticians for agricultural, manufacturing, and other investigations can serve as a general model for impact evaluations. Cochran and Cox [5] include the following in this model: statement of objectives, choice of treatments and experimental units, plan for assigning treatments to experimental units, plan for selecting the experimental units, and choice of analysis criteria and techniques. In this section, we discuss each of these aspects.

The *statement of objectives* describes the purpose of the evaluation experiment and what is being evaluated (i.e., the initiating and target systems). It also includes relevant background information, such as a description of the environment in which the evaluation is being performed. Often the statement of objectives can be presented as a hypothesis; the objective of the evaluation is to test the hypothesis. The hypothesis may be open-ended— that a DSS will improve decision making. The hypothesis may be specific—

that a DSS will provide a 10 percent rate of return on investment. In general, the more specific the statement of objectives, the easier it will be to design and interpret the evaluation experiments based on the objectives.

The *choice of measures* depends on the method and objectives of the experiment, and on factors such as previously used measures, ease of collecting data for the measures, general agreement among evaluators, and demonstration that a measure is correlated with the variables (factors) of interest. Even after all these criteria are applied, there are usually several measures that can be used. The design and analysis of evaluation experiments will be facilitated if the measures chosen satisfy three conditions. First, the measures should be well defined; that is, there should be an identifiable algorithm for computing their values, which does not depend on the agent (human or mechanical) computing those values. Second, it should be possible to identify the factors that the evaluator assumes affect the measure, and to estimate the distribution of the error in the measurement resulting from the inability to identify all the factors. Third, the measures should be at least ordinal scale, and preferably interval scale. For reasons to be presented later, measures satisfying these three conditions will be called statistical measures.

The *choice of treatments and experimental units* will also follow directly from the statement of objectives. The treatment is the initiating system to be evaluated. The experimental units are the elements of the target system that are to be measured (i.e., the elements on which an impact is expected). In the choice of treatments and experimental units it is often useful to include control treatments and units. A control treatment is a system other than the one whose impact is being measured. When a new system is being evaluated, the previous system is a useful control treatment. Control units are elements of the target system on which no impact is expected, but which are similar to the experimental units being measured. If a DSS is designed to serve only a few departments in an organization and the experimental units are employees, it might be useful to select as control units employees in unserved departments (the control treatment is the existing information system in the unserved departments). In evaluating the impact of a DSS on executive decision making in a life insurance company, it might be useful to select executives from a life insurance company without a DSS as control units (the control treatment is the "null" DSS in this company). Control treatments and experimental units are so named because they help control for the external factors problem.

Once the treatments and experimental units are identified, the *plan for assigning the treatments* can be determined. This plan specifies which units will be measured for each treatment. Because most evaluations will analyze only one or two treatments and because there usually will be only a small, reusable set of experimental units, the most common plan will be to measure each unit for each treatment. If this plan is not feasible, the assignment should be random in order to reduce bias. There will be evaluations where certain units are of particular interest, and in such cases a subjective plan is appropriate. It may often be useful to "block" (i.e., group) experimental units according to common, nontreatment factors assumed to affect the measure(s) in an experiment. This is another method for controlling the external factors problem. For example, in measuring impact on employees, it might be useful to block on education level, department, or position. The plan for assigning treatments to experimental units is often called the design. The four "classic" designs are completely randomized (no blocking), randomized block (one-way blocking), Latin-square (two-way blocking), and factorial (*n*-way blocking); these are described in texts on experimental statistics (e.g., Mendenhall [13]).

The *sample selection plan* specifies how the experimental units will be chosen and how many there will be. As already stated, in many impact evaluation experiments all the units will be measured. If this is not feasible, the choice of units should be random or should be based on particular interest in certain units. There are a number of techniques for predetermining sample sizes for random sampling. Most of these require the assumptions that the measure being used is normally distributed and that the experimental units were randomly selected. Mendenhall [13] explains some sampling techniques. The techniques that seem most appropriate for use in DSS evaluation are simple random sampling, systematic sampling, and cluster sampling. If random sampling cannot be used, one may choose as large a sample as possible, or choose a sample of typical units (as in benchmarking). The as-large-as-possible strategy is recommended if there is no other basis for selecting the sample. Choosing typical units is an appropriate plan if there is no need to generalize from the results of the experiment beyond samples for which the one chosen is typical, or if the experimental plan does not include statistical analysis of results. The as-large-as-possible and typical unit plans for sample selection may provide accurate results. However, in comparison to randomized techniques, both the theory of experimental design and experience with its use suggest that for a given level of accuracy the as-large-as-possible plan will result in higher cost, and that for a given sampling cost the typical unit plan may lead to less accuracy.

The *choice of analysis criteria and techniques* specifies how the data will be analyzed. There are two important analysis criteria. The first is the aspect of the measurements to be analyzed. Depending on the measure and the experiment, these may be quantitative (e.g., standard scores, totals, means, frequencies, distributions), or they may be qualitative (e.g., general trends, similar procedures). More than one aspect may be chosen. The importance of this criterion is that it influences the choice of the analysis technique. The second important analysis criterion is the desired level of accuracy. The accuracy criterion may be defined as the probability of rejecting the null hypothesis (from the statement of objectives) if it is really true, as a desired confidence interval for the mean of the measurements, as a probability of the observed values occurring, or as a percent of variation in the measurements to be explained by the analysis. The accuracy criteria may also be judgmental, such as a consensus opinion or reasonable certainty. The analysis techniques used will depend on the evaluation method, the choice of measures, and the analysis criteria. Cost/benefit analyses, some attitude surveys, and rating and weighting approaches have specific analysis techniques associated with the approach. Some techniques are designed for analyzing specific aspects of measurements, such as means or frequencies. For statistical measures, statistical analyses can be used; among those which may be applicable are descriptive statistics, parametric and nonparametric comparisons, parametric and nonparametric correlations, factor analysis, and regression analysis.

The model outlined in this section applies to evaluations using all the methods described previously. There will, of course, be variations among the methods in the degree of formalism associated with each element of the model. In fact, the differences among the methods are essentially differences in the choices they offer for the elements of the model. Using the general model, Figure 6-7 illustrates the differences among the methods as applied to an experiment to evaluate the impact of a municipal DSS system on services to citizens. For each method there are choices for each element of the model other than those listed.

An Example.   As an example of the use of the model for DSS evaluations, consider the design of a statistical evaluation of the impact of a DSS on the preparation of a personnel allocation plan (summarized in Figure 6-8). The objective is to test the hypothesis that the DSS does not affect plan preparation time. The measure is the time (person-hours) to prepare the plan, the treatments are the planning procedures before and after implementation of the DSS, and the experimental units are the departments that must prepare allocation plans. Suppose that it is decided to use the system measurement method and to measure preparation times under each treatment. Because this is difficult and potentially bothersome to employees, it is decided to use only 10 of 26 departments. A random sample of 10 is selected. The analysis criterion is a comparison of mean plan preparation times, with a significance level of 0.05 (95 percent confidence of accepting the evaluation hypothesis if it is true). The plan for assigning treatments to experimental units is to block on department (i.e., to measure times in the same departments before and after system implementation). Assuming that the plan preparation times are normally distributed, with the same variance for each treatment, the analysis technique would be a paired test (with nine degrees of freedom) of the difference in times (see [13] for a discussion of this test). If the assumptions cannot be made, the Wilcoxon signed ranks test could be used for the analysis.

METHOD:	System measurement
OBJECTIVE:	Test the hypothesis that the DSS does not affect plan preparation time
MEASURE:	Plan preparation time
TREATMENTS:	Plan preparation procedures before and after the DSS is implemented
EXPERIMENTAL UNITS:	Departments in the organization
PLAN FOR ASSIGNING TREATMENT TO UNITS:	Measure all units for each treatment
SAMPLE SELECTION PLAN:	Random sample of 10
ANALYSIS CRITERIA AND TECHNIQUES:	95 percent chance of accepting hypothesis if true using paired test (or Wilcoxon signed ranks test)

DATA (HYPOTHETICAL)

DEPT.	BEFORE (PERSON-HOURS)	AFTER (PERSON-HOURS)
1	200	188
2	147	160
3	190	140
4	250	220
5	237	245
6	175	178
7	168	140
8	210	190
9	182	188
10	157	150

ANALYSIS RESULTS

PAIRED t TEST:	($t = -1.378$) Cannot reject hypothesis (at 0.05 level)
WILCOXON TEST:	($T = 13$) Cannot reject hypothesis (at 0.05 level)
CONCLUSION:	There is insufficient proof that the DSS had significant impact on preparation for the personnel allocation plan. That is, the measured changes may be due to external factors rather than (or in addition to) the DSS system.

FIGURE 6-8   Evaluation of the Impact of a DSS on Personnel Plan Preparation Time

SUMMARY

A review of the figures in this chapter summarizes the process of integrating DSS into the organization. Integration consists of three processes: user education, installation, and evaluation. Each process can be performed using a variety of techniques described in this chapter. The integration processes continue throughout the lifetime of a DSS and are part of iterative design.

The three components of DSS integration are not isolated from each other, and the planning for integration should consider the three together. For example, the "prestudy" for an attitude survey evaluation must be considered as part of the preliminary phase of user education, and attitude survey evaluation is probably more appropriate for an evolving prototype than for a throwaway prototype. For organizations that are just beginning to build DSS, our recommendation for an approach to integration is:

- *User education*: local expert or tutorial technique
- *Installation*: evolving prototype
- *Evaluation*: value analysis

For organizations that are building their second or further DSS, our recommendation for integration is:

- *User education*: local expert and ITM
- *Installation*: evolving prototypes based on DSS Generators
- *Evaluation*: combination of methods, including cost/benefit analysis or system analysis

The interrelationships among the components of integration can be seen in John Bennett's description of the "integrating agent" roles in installation [2]. Bennett identifies four roles:

1. An exergist, who explains the concepts and objectives for the DSS (*education*)
2. A confidant, who provides support, encourages users, and is aware of impacts (*education and evaluation*)
3. A crusader, who can demonstrate and sell the DSS (*installation*)
4. A teacher, who can tailor the training to the user and who can tailor the system to individual needs (*education and installation*)

Bennett emphasizes the importance of the integrating agent in increasing the probability of successful integration of a DSS, and experience to date with DSS confirms this conclusion.

The integration process is thus intended to increase the probability of success of the DSS. Put another way, the integration process is intended to reduce the risk of failure. Alter's study of DSS identified eight risk factors which, if present, increase the probability of DSS failure [1]. The purpose of

RISK FACTOR	INTEGRATION PROCESS THAT CAN HELP REDUCE RISK
1. Nonexistent or unwilling user	Education, evaluation
2. Multiple users or implementers	Education, installation
3. Disappearing users, implementers, or maintainers	Education, installation, evaluation
4 Inability to specify purpose or usage pattern	Education, evaluation
5. Inability to predict and cushion impact	Evaluation, education
6. Loss or lack of support	Education, installation, evaluation
7. Lack of experience with DSS	Education, installation, evaluation
8. Technical problems and cost effectiveness	Installation, evaluation

FIGURE 6-9   DSS Risk Factors and Integration Processes

the integration process is to minimize these risks. We conclude this chapter with Figure 6-9, which lists Alter's risk factors together with the integration processes that can help reduce each risk. The fact that each risk is addressed by two or more of the integration processes reemphasizes the interrelationships among these processes.

QUESTIONS AND PROBLEMS

REVIEW QUESTIONS

1. Describe the importance of having a plan for integrating DSS into the organization.
2. What are some of the problems that are likely to occur? What are some general strategies that can be used to avoid these problems?
3. Compare six methods for DSS user education.
4. What is the relationship between prototyping and the iterative design process?
5. Why is prototyping generally thought to be a good installation strategy for DSS?
6. What are the steps in installation?
7. What different types of measures can be used to evaluate DSS?
8. Compare the eight methods for DSS evaluation using the general model for evaluation given in this chapter.

DISCUSSION QUESTIONS

1. DSS should be judged on the same basis as any other information system—with cold, hard, quantifiable benefits compared to costs. But DSS deal with intangible, hard-to-measure benefits which have significant value, so the evaluation must be more intuitive. Which position do you support? Why?

EXERCISES

1. Develop a flowchart for an installation plan for a Specific DSS.
2. Develop a user education plan for a Specific DSS.
3. Develop an interactive training manual for a Specific DSS.
4. Develop an evaluation plan for a Specific DSS.

REFERENCES

1. ALTER, S. L. *Decision Support Systems: Current Practices and Continuing Challenges*, Addison-Wesley Publishing Company, Inc., Reading, Mass., 1980.
2. BENNETT, J. L. "Integrating Users and Decision Support Systems," in *Proceedings of the Sixth and Seventh Annual Conferences of the Society for Management Information Systems*, J. D. White (ed.), University of Michigan Press, Ann Arbor, Mich., 1976, pp. 77–86.
3. BROOKS, F. P., Jr. *The Mythical Man Month*, Addison-Wesley Publishing Company, Inc., Reading, Mass., 1975.
4. CARLSON, E. D., and J. A. SUTTON. "A Case Study of Non-programmer, Interactive Problem-Solving," *IBM Research Report RJ1382*, IBM Research Division, San Jose, Calif., 1974.
5. COCHRAN, W., and G. COX. *Experimental Design*, John Wiley & Sons, Inc., New York, 1957.
6. ERBE, R., et al. "Integrated Data Analysis and Management for the Problem Solving Environment," *Information Systems*, Vol. 5, 1980, pp. 273–285.
7. GRACE, B. F. "Training Users of a Decision Support System," *Data Base*, Vol. 8, No. 3, Winter 1977, pp. 30–36.
8. KEEN, P. G. W. "Value Analysis: Justifying Decision Support Systems," *Management Information System Quarterly*, Vol. 5, No. 1, March 1981, pp. 1–16.
9. KEEN, P. G. W., and M. S. SCOTT MORTON. *Decision Support System: An Organizational Perspective*, Addison-Wesley Publishing Company, Inc., Reading, Mass., 1978.
10. KELLY, G. A. *The Psychology of Personal Constructs*, W. W. Norton & Company, Inc., 1955.
11. LEWIN, K. "Group Decision and Social Change," in *Readings in Social Psychology*, T. M. Newcomb and E. L. Hartley (eds.), Holt, New York, 1947, pp. 330–344.
12. MCLEAN, E. R., and T. F. RIESING. "MAPP: A DSS for Financial Planning," *Data Base*, Vol. 3, No. 3, Winter 1977, pp. 9–14.

13.   MENDEHALL, W.   *Introduction to Linear Models and the Design and Analysis of Experiments*, Wadsworth Publishing Company, Inc., Belmont, Calif., 1968.
14.   SHEIN, E. H.   "Management Development as a Process of Influence," *Industrial Management Review*, Vol. 2, No. 2, Spring 1961, pp. 59–77.
15.   STABELL, C. B.   "Individual Differences in Managerial Decision Making Processes: A Study of Conversational Computer Usage," Ph.D. dissertation, MIT, 1974.
16.   SCOTT MORTON, M. S.   *Management Decision System: Computer Based Support for Decision Making*, Harvard University Press, Cambridge, Mass., 1971.
17.   SUTTON, J. A.   "Evaluation of a Decision Support System: A Case Study with the Office Products Division of IBM," *IBM Research Report RJ2214*, IBM Research Division, San Jose, Calif., 1978.

CASE EXAMPLE

INSTALLING GADS

In the GADS case example for Chapter 1, we listed 17 applications of GADS. Each of these involved installing GADS in a new organization. Before each installation, the builders always loaded a sample data base (map plus data) and gave the potential users a demonstration. The loading step was a form of technical testing, and the demonstration was a preliminary acceptance test. If the users decided to try GADS, then a Specific DSS (version of GADS) was prepared following the steps given in Figure 6-10. Not all installations of GADS followed the same steps, or used the same order as shown in the figure. The steps were usually iterative, due to the iterative nature of the overall process (see Chapter 5).

The GADS installation philosophy was of a constantly evolving prototype. The choice of this approach was largely because of the experimental nature of GADS. However, with each additional application it became apparent that the evolving prototype approach was especially useful where a DSS was to be used by multiple organizations. Organizational differences, combined with individual differences among decision makers, prohibited any of the other installation approaches, as did the fact that the builders and the users were always from different organizations. The major modifications to GADS over the six year period of its most intensive use (1970-1976) were primarily in the dialog component, in an attempt to make GADS easier to use and to tailor it for different user groups.

The installation steps shown in Figure 6-10 indicate that data base preparation required the most work in installation. If the source data was not available, then gathering the data was always the most expensive and longest single step. Omitting data gathering, GADS was usually installed in

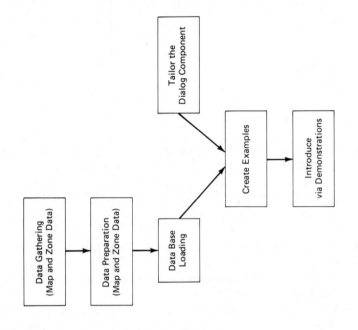

FIGURE 6-10 GADS Installation Steps

1–2 months. When the data and the map were already in a form suitable for GADS, then installation usually could be completed in about one week.

The final step in installation, giving a demonstration, was always planned to use actual data for the organization, and the demonstration always related to a problem or decision known to be of interest to the potential users. This demonstration strategy proved to be extremely successful. During the demonstration, potential users often became actual users as they asked the demonstrator questions not about GADS, but about the data or about how a certain alternative would look.

Figure 6-11 shows a summary of the installation costs covering five GADS applications. The data are summarized as percentages in five installation steps:

1. data gathering
2. data preparation
3. data base loading
4. tailoring the dialog component
5. creating examples/introducing GADS

The summaries are for the application with the highest, lowest, and average total installation costs. Figure 6-11 confirms the indication of Figure 6-10 that data preparation was the most significant part of installation. This significance follows from the fact that most GADS users did not have an existing data base on which to build. The fact that the tailoring costs were such a low percentage of installation costs indicates both the similarity of the applications and the adaptability of GADS to support new decisions and decision makers.

INSTALLATION STEP	% OF INSTALLATION COSTS		
	HIGHEST COST APPLICATION	AVERAGE OF 5 APPLICATIONS	LOWEST COST APPLICATION
Data Gathering	16	6	23
Data Preparation	41	39	41
Data Base Loading	15	16	0
Tailoring the Dialog Component	8	8	0
Creating Examples/ Introducing	20	31	36
TOTAL	100%	100%	100%

FIGURE 6-11 Relative Costs of Installation Steps for GADS (5 applications)

A CHAPTER FROM THE GADS
INTERACTIVE TRAINING MANUAL

Barbara Grace developed a version of GADS and a manual to interactively teach decision makers to use the system for problem solving. The system and manual were tested in a controlled experiment [7] and were used extensively to train GADS users. Lesson 2 of the manual is included here to illustrate the method. This lesson covers displaying data on maps and performing simple map manipulations. Before reading this lesson, readers are encouraged to review the case example in Chapter 2. The scenario in that example illustrates the use of the functions covered in this lesson.

LESSON 2

In this lesson you will learn to relate data to a map, which is one of the most important capabilities of the GADS system. You will learn how to display maps, enlarge maps, and create data displays.

If you have just finished Lesson 1, you should now have the GADS main menu displayed on the screen.

2.0 How to Display a Map

Since all GADS problems have a geographical flavor, let us look first at the San Jose map as it is stored in the computer.

POSITION THE CROSS HAIRS
THROUGH THE WORD MAPS,
DEPRESS THE CH KEY,

and you will see this display:

```
                    ZONE-VALUES    STATEMENTS    SSMODE          FIND ZONE
ZONESYMB  1  SUBMAP  EXPAND  SHRINK  NORMAL  CLEAR  RETURN
OVERLAY MAP 0
```

You will notice some action words, called commands, located at the bottom of the display. Some of these commands will take effect immediately when you cross-hair the command names, and others will only cause the computer to save your instructions for later use. For example, OVERLAY MAP will draw a map as soon as you cross-hair, whereas EXPAND will make no immediate change to your current display. It will merely cause the computer to remember that you want the map expanded the next time you draw it. Notice the line, OVERLAY MAP 0. Map 0 is the basic building block map, depicting all 273 zones. To display the map,

CROSS-HAIR (CH) THE WORDS
OVERLAY MAP

The system should now be drawing the San Jose map. Notice that one of the command word says ZONESYMB. The system provides space for 20 sets of symbols, called ZONESYMBs; each set contains symbols, one for each zone. One set may represent ranges of TOTCTIME (total consumed time) for a given day, one might represent ranges of TOTAL (total number of calls for service) for all days, and so on. In Lesson 4 we learn how to create meaningful symbols. Your instructor has saved a set of *'s in ZONESYMB 1. If we put some symbols on the map, we can point to individual basic zones by cross-hairing the symbols in the zones of interest.

CROSS-HAIR THE WORD ZONESYM

and the computer should put a "*" in each of the 273 zones.

2.1   How to Expand or Enlarge a Map

It is often valuable to expand a map about a specific zone. Look at the paper map of San Jose, locate the San Jose airport on the paper map, and then see if you can find it on the computer map.

POSITION THE CROSS HAIRS
THROUGH THE "*" IN THE
AIRPORT ZONE AND HIT
THE CH KEY

Notice that the system will supply the zone number in the upper right section of the screen, in the next available position below the heading ZONES, as pictured here:

MAPS

ZONES
79

We want to expand the map about the airport. Cross-hairing EXPAND will tell the computer that we wish to enlarge the map by about 40. Each time we CH EXPAND, the computer simply increases the enlargement factor. You will not see the results until you CLEAR the screen and redraw the map. Let us try to tell the computer that we want to enlarge four times:

    CH (CROSS-HAIR) THE
    WORD EXPAND

Notice that the computer rewrites the word EXPAND to signal that it undertands you. Now,

    CH EXPAND 3 MORE TIMES,

You may see the results of the expansion by doing the following:

    CH THE WORD CLEAR, AND THEN
    CH THE WORDS: OVERLAY MAP

You should see a map centered about the San Jose airport looking very much like this:

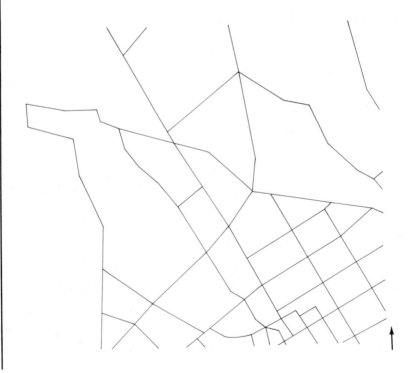

If you have a hard-copy facility, ask your instructor how to use it, and

TAKE A PICTURE OF
YOUR MAP DISPLAY

2.2 How to Display Data Values for One Zone and One or Two Units (days)

GADS gives you the capability to relate data to the map. There are many ways of doing this in the GADS system. One way is by use of a subfunction of MAPS called ZONE-VALUES. You will notice that this is one of the commands available in the lower portion of the screen. Look at the structural diagram, Appendix G. Notice that from the main menu, we went to MAPS. ZONE-VALUES is one level below MAPS and two levels below the main menu. It will provide data for the zone number, which is noted in the last position below the title ZONES in the upper right section of the screen. When we cleared the display, the system erased the airport zone number (79) from the screen, so let us get it back. We can do this either by entering the zone number in the next available position or we can put the *'s on the map and point to the airport zone. Let us do the latter for practice.

CH THE WORD ZONESYMB

After the system finishes displaying the "*'s",

CH THE "*" IN THE AIRPORT ZONE

Notice that the zone number is now noted in the upper right portion of the screen. To display data for zone 79,

CH THE WORD ZONE-VALUES

You should see the following display:

```
┌─────────┐ ┌───────┐                    ┌────┐
│ RETURN  │ │ PRINT │        ZONE        │ 79 │
└─────────┘ └───────┘       ┌──────┐┌───┐└────┘
                            │ PAGE ││ 1 │
                            └──────┘└───┘
                                        ┌────┐              ┌────┐
                    UNIT    │ -1 │              UNIT    │ -2 │    DIFFERENCE
                                        └────┘              └────┘
        LABEL

        TOTROU          1.                      1.                      0.

        TOT1            0.                      0.                      0.
        TOT2            0.                      0.                      0.
        TOT3            1.                      0.                     -1.
        TOT4            1.                      0.                     -1.
        TOT5            0.                      1.                      1.
        TOTAL           2.                      1.                     -1.

        INP1            0.                      0.                      0.
        INP2            0.                      0.                      0.
        INP3            0.                      0.                      0.
        INP4            1.                      0.                     -1.
        INP5            0.                      0.                      0.
        TOTINP          1.                      2.                     -1.

        CTIME1          0.                      0.                      0.
        CTIME2          0.                      0.                      0.
        CTIME3         57.                      0.                    -57.
        CTIME4         28.                      0.                    -28.
        CTIME5          0.                    107.                    107.
        TOTCTIME       85.                    107.                     22.

        MULTI1          0.                      0.                      0.
        MULTI2          0.                      0.                      0.
        MULTI3          0.                      0.                      0.
        MULTI4          0.                      0.                      0.
        MULTI5          0.                      0.                      0.
        TOTMULTI        0.                      0.                      0.

        WORKA           1.                      0.                     -1.
        WORKB           1.                      0.                     -1.
        WORKC           0.                      0.                      0.
```

This table allows you to look at the values of all data for two different days, as well as the difference between the two days. Notice that in the copy of the display, solid-lined boxes are drawn around command words (words which, when cross-haired, will cause certain actions, such as RETURN, PRINT, and PAGE). Dashed-lined boxes are drawn around numbers or words that the user can change; for example, "−1," "−2," the page number, "1," and the zone number, "79." Let us suppose that we are interested in finding data values for zone 79 for the two days, Sunday 1/30/73 and Tuesday 6/20/72. Refer to Appendix E to see if you can find the unit numbers for these two days. We will need to change the "−1" and "−2" to the proper unit numbers, "32" and "45," respectively. To key in a change, it is necessary to obtain the cursor next to the number we wish to change. We do this by cross-hairing the word or number to be changed. Now,

CROSS-HAIR THE NUMBER, "−1"

A cursor should appear, indicating that the computer is ready to receive data from you. Now key in

32

In a similar fashion,

CHANGE "−2" TO "45"

Now, to see the results of the display,

CH THE WORD PAGE

Refer to Appendix F, which gives you the conceptual picture of all user data. You see that the data on the display represent a row from Table 32 and a row from Table 45. In other words, ZONE-VALUES gives us the values for all variables for one or two units (days) and only one zone: in this case, zone 79. Now write the total routine calls for service for 1/30/72 in the space provided below.

ANS: _____

Write the TOTCTIME for all day 6/20/72 below.

ANS: _____

If you answered "1" and "12," you understand the ZONE-VALUES table very well. To see the rest of the data for zone 79,

CHANGE THE PAGE NO. "1" TO "2"
AND CH THE WORD PAGE

Now, let us review what we have done. We have enlarged the map about a zone and have displayed all data variables for a specific zone.

When we enlarge the map about a zone, we do the following:

1. Display zone symbols by cross-hairing the word ZONESYMB.
2. Cross-hair the zone symbol in the zone of interest.
3. Cross-hair the word EXPAND the number of times we desire.
4. Cross-hair CLEAR.
5. Cross-hair OVERLAY MAP.

To change a number or word on a display, we do the following:

1. Cross-hair the word or number to be changed.
2. After the system displays the cursor, key in the new number.

To obtain data for a specific zone, we

1. Display zone symbols by cross-hairing the word ZONESYMB.
2. Cross-hair the zone symbol in the zone of interest.
3. Cross-hair the command word ZONE-VALUES.
4. Change the unit numbers to the days of interest.
5. Cross-hair the word PAGE to see the results.

2.3 How to Return to the Main Menu

Now, refer to the GADS structural diagram in Figure 6-12. Notice that from the GADS main menu we have gone to MAPS and then we have gone to a subfunction of MAP display: ZONE-VALUES. Every time we cross-hair RETURN, we move up one box in the system structure. Therefore, one RE-TURN would move us to MAPS and another would get us back to the GADS main menu. You can see that this diagram helps answer the question: "Where am I?" Now,

CROSS-HAIR THE WORD RETURN

and you will see the map display function.

CROSS-HAIR THE WORD RETURN AGAIN

and you will be at the GADS main menu.

2.4 How to Exit GADS and Logoff

In the main menu,

CH THE WORD EXIT

On the next display,

CH THE LINE "EXIT REALLY"

The system will say: STEPLIB1 NOW UNALLOCATED, followed by "READY." You might recall that when you logged on, the computer also said "READY." That is because you are still logged on the computer and at this point you could, if you wished, call the GADS program again, by saying "EXEC EGADS." This time, however, we will logoff, by saying (of all things!)

LOGOFF

The system will say: xxxxxxxxxx LOGGED OFF TSO AT time ON data.

TURN THE POWER OFF THE TERMINAL

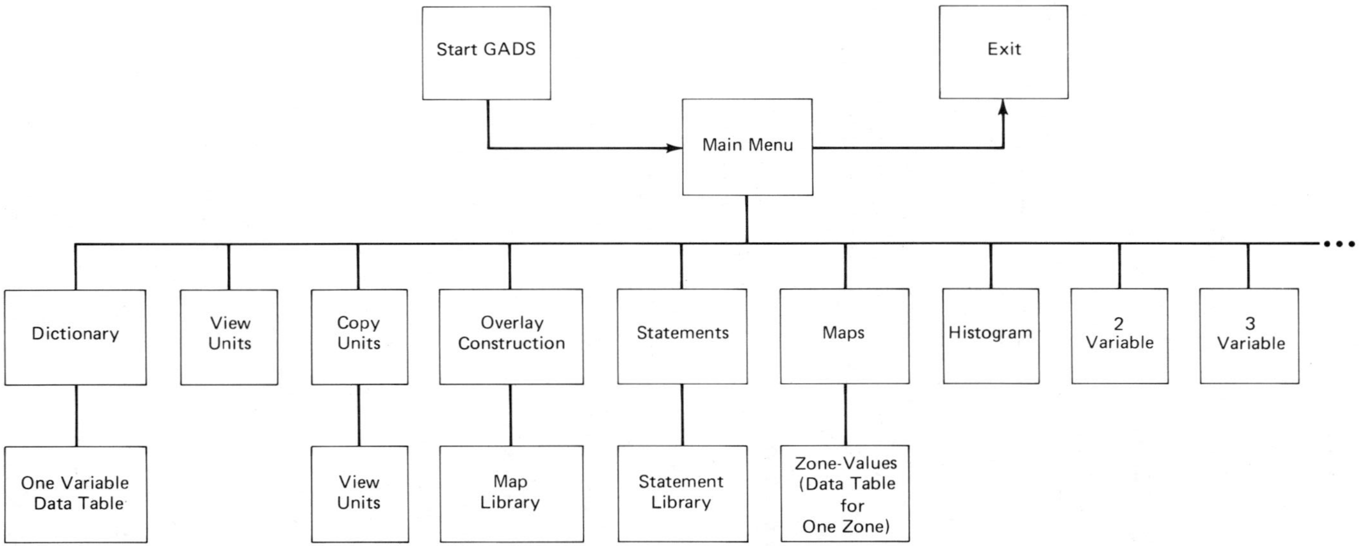

FIGURE 6-12 GADS Structural Diagram

If you wish to take a break, do so.
When you are ready to proceed,

Do a LOGON using APPENDIX A,
Start GADS, using APPENDIX B
(TAKE THE INITIALIZE OPTION AGAIN)

LESSON 2 REVIEW

In Lesson 2 you have learned to display maps, use ZONE-VALUES to display all data values for one zone and one or two days, and enlarge maps about a desired zone. You have learned to change a field (name or number) on a display, how to return to the main menu from anywhere in the system, and how to EXIT GADS and LOGOFF. Appendixes G, H, I, J, K, L, and M summarize these for easy reference.

Following are some review exercises and some extension exercises. Do as many of the review exercises as you wish. Then you may try the extension exercise, which will allow you to learn more about GADS, mostly by your own exploration and discovery.

REVIEW EXERCISE ONE

Choose any zone (perhaps where you live), and do the following:

1. Enlarge the map about this zone.
2. Make a hard copy of the map if you have a hard-copy unit.
3. For this zone, find
   a. Total calls for service (CFS)
   b. Total consumed time
   c. Total multiple-unit CFS
   for all day Wednesday 2/16/72.

Write your answers in the spaces provided below.

Your zone number   _____
Total CFS   _____
Total consumed time   _____
Total multiple-unit CFS   _____

REVIEW EXERCISE TWO

Choose any other zone (perhaps where you work) and find:

   a. In-progress CFS from 0301 to 0800 (3:01 to 8 a.m.)
   b. In-progress CFS from 1301 to 1800 (1:01 to 6 p.m.)
   c. In-progress CFS all day
   for the sum of all day (Unit 61).

Write your answers below.

In-progress CFS from 0301 to 0800   _____
In-progress CFS from 1301 to 1800   _____
In-progress CFS all day   _____

EVALUATION OF GADS IN AN IBM
OFFICE PRODUCTS DIVISION (OPD)
BRANCH OFFICE (FROM [17])

Background

In an OPD branch office, it is necessary periodically to solve the problem of the allocation of each OPD machine to be serviced to a specific customer engineer (CE). This decision presently is made by constructing one or more territories for a CE, each composed of one or more basic geographic areas called zones. This decision is characterized by its lack of structure (i.e., there is no set procedure for achieving a solution) and by requirements for the consideration of data unknown to the computer (e.g., travel time, personnel issues). The need to redefine territories may be triggered by changes in inventory, personnel issues, customer requests, and so on. A given territory change may affect any subset of the zones for which a branch office is responsible.

OPD sells a variety of products, and a given CE may be trained to repair any subset of those products. Further, the ability of a CE to repair a product may vary by product type. Hence the territory served by any CE generally varies by product type. These differences mean that CEs are not interchangeable.

The DSS (a version of GADS) supported CE territory allocation in Santa Clara County, California (most, but not all, of the territory covered by the San Jose branch office). Santa Clara County has been divided into several hundred zones by OPD for purposes of territory allocation. These zones are aggregated into territories for field managers (there were four field managers in the study area and a fifth was added during the course of the study). The field manager territories are further decomposed into CE territories by the appropriate field manager. The goal of this decision is to compose territories for each product type from these zones subject to the objectives and constraints perceived by the field manager.

In addition to the CE territory allocation decision, we anticipated that the field managers would find other uses for the DSS. The other uses observed were:

1. *Zone location*: The DSS was used to find the geographic location of customers and/or zones.
2. *Map correction*: The DSS computerized map was used to update maps in the branch office and to create tables identifying subzones within zones.
3. *Customer lists and status of installed inventory*: The DSS was used to produce specialized listings of customers (e.g., those with Series 3 copiers) and to ascertain the timeliness of information on the Installed Machine Inventory file.
4. *Personnel planning*: The DSS was used to ascertain personnel and training requirements both at the field manager and branch office levels.

5. *Field manager territory allocation*: The DSS was used to create a territory for a new field manager and to create initial CE territories in the field manager's territory.

The case study began in February 1976. The DSS was installed at the branch office during the first week of August 1976. The intervening six months were used (1) to observe decision making by the field managers before the introduction of GADS and (2) to prepare GADS for use by OPD. Preparing GADS involved (1) entering a computer-readable version of the OPD zone map, (2) preparing GADS to use OPD zone names (numbers), (3) making several (non-OPD-specific) functional changes in the system (e.g., to allow the direct display of data on a map), and (4) writing two special-purpose programs to prepare (existing) Installed Machine Inventory (IMI) and current CE territory files for entry into the system. These two special-purpose programs were run monthly to update the data base. Upon installation of GADS, each of the four field managers who would be using the system was given about four hours of training in its use. (In retrospect, we believe about eight hours of training would have been better, enabling more sophisticated system use more quickly.)

Following system installation, we continued to observe decisions made by the field managers. This observation (one or more observers present at nearly every session) was coupled with structured interviews and questionnaires administered both before and after each decision. Informal meetings with the field managers also contributed to our understanding of their use of GADS.

As results of the case study, we were interested in examining the fixed and variable costs of this application and the associated benefits. Benefits were broken into three categories: (1) productivity changes, (2) process changes (differences in how decisions were made), and (3) perception changes (how users felt about the decision).

Costs

A summary of the costs of providing the OPD GADS to an OPD branch office is shown in Figure 6-13. This summary assumes a two-year life for the DSS (a conservative estimate, we believe), and 20 branch offices with an equal or larger number of CEs as compared to the study area within the San Jose branch office (again, a conservative estimate).

The cost of the base GADS system has been estimated at $100,000 (10K lines of code at 25 lines/day = 2 person-years; cost estimated at $50,000 per person-year). To date, 17 different applications have been served by GADS. Figure 6-13 shows three alternative methods for allocating the cost. Option A shows the actual case for OPD (wherein costs are sunk), option B shows the costs allocated evenly among the 17 applications served, and option C shows the costs as if the entire cost of the DSS were borne by

| | ASSUMPTION | | |
	A	B	C
Fixed costs of software			
(allocated to each branch office)			
Base system	$ 0	$ 300	$ 5,000
OPD modifications	0	2,450	2,450
Subtotal	0	2,750	7,450
Nonrecurring costs for			
each branch office			
Map entry	4,000	4,000	4,000
Training	1,000	1,000	1,000
Subtotal	5,000	5,000	5,000
Variable costs (per branch)			
Computer usage	7,200	7,200	7,200
Terminal rental	8,400	8,400	8,400
Data base maintenance	2,400	2,400	2,400
Subtotal	$18,000	$18,000	$18,000
Total cost for two years	$23,000	$25,750	$30,450

ASSUMPTIONS

All costs are invariant with branch office size. Although this may not be strictly true, it is a reasonable estimate, and the same assumption is made in the analysis of benefits. Also, it is assumed that there are 20 branch offices the same size or larger than the test area.

A Assumes that fixed costs are sunk (actual case for OPD).

B Assumes that base system costs are allocated across all applications of base system.

C Assumes that full costs of base system are allocated to this application.

FIGURE 6-13   Costs

this application. It should be noted that $35,000 for non-OPD-specific DSS improvements of GADS could also be amortized across any future applications using GADS.

The fixed costs for the OPD application (i.e., the costs for preparing the system for use by OPD and writing the special-purpose data reformatting programs) totaled about 11 person-months and about $3000 in computer use. Using a fully allocated cost of $50,000 per person-year for programming, the fixed cost was approximately $49,000. Of this, approximately $14,000 represented OPD specific work and $35,000 represented general extensions to GADS. The latter costs would be nonrecurring for any other similar applications. In addition, there was a nonrecurring cost of about 1 person-month ($4000) for entering the zone map and a training cost of about $1000. This training cost is the estimated value of personnel time for field managers and trainers.

The operational costs associated with the OPD use of GADS were (1) about 15 hours per month (average) terminal connect time (billed at approximately $300 per month); (2) terminal rental of $250 to $350 per month (including hard-copy unit), depending on the terminal; and (3) about 1/2 person-day/month to maintain the data base. Data base maintenance would be more efficient with a larger number of branch offices, as that process could be largely automated.

Benefits

We had hoped to observe changes in the productivity of the customer engineers. Unfortunately, during the course of the study it became obvious that there would be many alternative explanations for productivity changes (e.g., changes in expected service times as set by OPD headquarters) and that we would be unable to distinguish whether observed productivity improvements were due to the DSS or other factors.

However, changes in the productivity of the field managers were both dramatic and easily observable. These changes are summarized in Figure 6-14 and included:

1. *Reduction in the percentage and amount of time spent gathering data*: Observations prior to the use of the DSS indicated that 40 to 60 percent of a field manager's time during decision making was spent actually retrieving given pieces of data once the data required had been identified. This data-gathering time was reduced to near zero with the DSS.

2. *Reduction in the time required to reach solution*: Observed decisions required from 4 to 40 hours of terminal time and 4 to 150 hours of field manager time (in each case the longest time was observed when a new field manager was assigned to the office), and the field managers estimated that this represented time savings of a factor of 2 or 3. The differences between terminal time and field manager time are due primarily to having up to four field managers around the terminal at once.

Decision frequency was less than had been expected (about one territory allocation decision per 2 months per field manager), but time savings on large decisions still created dramatic productivity increases (the estimates of the field managers involved ranged from 150 to 300 person-hours saved on the new field manager territory decision).

Using a conservative estimate (based on the decisions observed) of 40 field-manager hours per month made available for other uses by the DSS, and an estimated fully allocated cost of $38 per hour for a field manager (this estimate is the higher of two published rates for customer engineer time),

| | ESTIMATE | |
	LOW	HIGH
Productivity improvements		
(1 branch for 10 months)		
CE territory allocation	$ 15,200	$ 15,200
($38/hour x 40 hours/month x 10 months)		
FM territory allocation	5,700	11,400
Map correction	1,600	1,600
	$ 22,500	$ 28,200
24-month extrapolation	$ 54,000	$ 67,680
24-month net benefit (1 branch)*	$ 23,550	$ 44,680
24-month net benefit (20 branches)†	$471,000	$893,600

ASSUMPTIONS

All   Benefits are invariant with branch size; this is a conservative estimate.

Low This is the lowest field manager estimate.

High This is the highest field manager estimate.

*Low net benefit is low 24-month benefit extrapolation minus cost assumption C. High net benefit is high 24-month benefit extrapolation minus cost assumption A.

†For the OPD case, the cost estimate is that shown as A in Table 1, and the net benefit range is $620,000 to $893,600.

FIGURE 6-14   Benefits

we estimate savings of about $1520 per month for the San Jose branch office from routine territory allocation decisions. The new field manager allocation decision resulted in savings of $5700 to $11,400 (depending on the estimate used).

The map correction use of the DSS was done by administrative personnel and required about two days to complete a job estimated to take at least two weeks with previously existing methods. Using a lower estimated fully allocated cost of $25 per hour for these personnel, about $1600 was saved by this use. We presume that the other unanticipated uses of the DSS also had value to the branch office, but we presently have no estimate of that value.

Thus, from the 10 months that GADS was in place at the San Jose branch office, we estimate productivity improvements worth $22,500 to $28,200. This estimate includes CE territory allocation and the two most significant of the five other uses of GADS. Using straight-line extrapolation for the estimated two-year software life, these improvements would be worth $54,000 to $67,680.

Observations on Decision-Maker Processes

A variety of observations were made of the way in which the field managers used GADS. Although no dollar value is directly associated with these process changes, several of these changes may indicate that "better" solutions were achieved. Among these observations are:

1. Less time was spent gathering data.
2. More data were applied in making decisions.
3. More appropriate data were used [i.e., actual data of interest were used instead of more readily available (but less desirable) surrogate measures].
4. More alternative approaches were generated and evaluated using the DSS than before the DSS was introduced.
5. Enhanced ability to view data for subzones (zones within zones) caused increased use of that information.
6. The error rate in calculations was substantially reduced (territory allocation involves a large number of arithmetic calculations, and observations before introduction of the DSS indicated a very high error rate in these calculations).

User Perceptions

Field manager perceptions of GADS were quite favorable. Observations of these perceptions are (subjectively) summarized below:

1. The field managers' perception of GADS's net worth to them started off very high (before use and during training), declined somewhat during early periods of use (while they were not sure how to use the system), and became very high again when they had become familiar with the system. This observation suggests that a more intensive training period would be appropriate.
2. The field managers perceived that the system enabled them to arrive at solutions of a quality previously unattainable even with unlimited time available in which to reach a decision.
3. The field managers perceived that achieving solutions took one-third to one-half of the time required using previous methods (this perception was supported by observation).
4. The CEs were generally not involved in DSS use. The majority of CEs saw and/or received hard-copy outputs used to implement decisions. Several CEs saw the system in operation and at least one CE used the DSS to construct an alternative territory for himself (which was subsequently agreed to by his field manager). However, CE perceptions of the DSS were vague.
5. The CE branch manager was not directly involved in system use.

Conclusions

From our case study we estimate that the DSS would result in a net dollar benefit to OPD of $620,000 to $893,000 spread over two years. Since in this particular case the DSS would also be directly applicable to the analogous sales representative allocation decisions, we believe that approximately equal additional gross benefits would be available at small additional cost. Evidence suggests that this DSS application improves the decision-making process and is perceived as useful by the field managers.

Thus the OPD DSS case study provides evidence that DSS can be economically justified. There is also evidence that the frequency and magnitude of CE and field manager allocation decisions within OPD will increase significantly in the future, increasing the net expected value of such a system. The evidence suggests other benefits from such a system, both from other uses of the function available and from the higher quality of solutions.

PART THREE
THE TECHNOLOGY COMPONENTS FOR DSS

Part Three deals with the three major technology components required to build DSS. The approach used for structuring the technology is the dialog management, data management, and model management structure as explained in the framework of Part One. This paradigm has proven valuable in organizing the functions and capabilities that must be provided by the technology to develop and build effective DSS. Although long-range development in DSS technology may modify or invalidate this paradigm, it is the most useful approach at the present time.

Each of the three areas has been the subject of intense study and development in recent years, but by basically different groups of professionals. Dialog issues have been studied by people interested in man-machine interface; data management was (and is) perhaps the most studied area of computer science; decision and analytic models have evolved from two decades of work in management science and operation research, and an even longer history in statistical analysis.

We make no attempt to cover or even summarize the rich heritage and literature base of research, development, and experience in these three areas. Rather, we draw on key concepts from this background to focus on what is necessary for building and using DSS. Chapter 7 outlines the hardware and software capabilities for dialog management, and focuses on the concept of "dialog styles" to support a variety of decision making environments. The chapter concludes with a suggested software design for the dialog management component of DSS. Chapter 8 summarizes alternative approaches to the structure of data in a data base management context and stresses the key role that data management must play in DSS. Chapter 9 deals with decision making and analysis models which comprise an important corporate resource—the model base. It discusses the way models must be used in DSS, the relationships with other components that will be required, and how these relationships are changing.

Chapter 10 integrates the previous three chapters by focusing on several alternative architectures of DSS for combining the three technical components. Four architectures, with an illustration of each based on an existing system, show alternative approaches for building an integrated DSS software system. In summary, Part Three provides a detailed look at the three major technical components that will be required in DSS, the capabilities and functions which each must provide, and suggestions for how they can be provided in building DSS. It is the most technical part of the book, and speaks most directly to the hardware-software design aspects of building DSS that will be confronted by builders, technical supporters, and toolsmiths.

CHAPTER SEVEN
DIALOG MANAGEMENT

OUTLINE

INTRODUCTION

As we have pointed out in Parts 1 and 2, DSS users are discretionary users. Their use may be frequent or infrequent, routine or ad hoc, interactive or batch mode, "hands-on" or via an assistant. Whatever the form of use, DSS usage involves a dialog between the user and the DSS. Even if a DSS provides extremely powerful functions, it may not be used if the dialog is unacceptable. Even when the decision makers use a DSS via an assistant, the dialog must provide a meaningful framework within which information is presented and inputs are given.

The dialog component of a DSS is the software and hardware that provides the user interface for a DSS. In terms of the ROMC requirements for DSS dicusssed in Chapter 4, the dialog component:

1. Produces the output *representations*
2. Enables user inputs that invoke and provide parameters for the *operations*
3. Enables user inputs that invoke and provide parameters for the *memory aids*
4. Provides the *control mechanisms* that enable the user to combine outputs and inputs into processes (dialogs)

The dialog component is that part of a DSS which the builders and toolsmiths build to meet the representation and control mechanism requirements identified during the systems analysis for the DSS. The dialog component presents the DSS outputs to the users and collects the user inputs to the DSS.

This chapter is intended to provide a guide for building the dialog component of a DSS. It presents a description and examples of alternative dialog styles, hardware devices, and software packages and suggests a design for the dialog component. Dialog styles describe the nature of the interface between the system and the user, while design techniques are the methods used to design the dialog component. Hardware devices and software packages are the technologies available for constructing the dialog component. The design we suggest can be built from software packages to support a variety of hardware devices. Because there are no absolute rules for developing a human–computer dialog, examples and comparisons illustrate the economic, technological, and usability trade-offs that will be required. Although the topics covered are relevant to the design of any user–computer dialog [16], the examples and trade-offs make this chapter specific to DSS. The chapter is not intended to provide complete coverage of all the technical details necessary to build the dialog component for a DSS. These technical details will change over time and among DSS. We do, however, identify the issues and alternatives that will need to be considered, and suggest ways of evaluating alternatives.

It will become obvious in reading this chapter that there are very few data comparing alternative dialogs or clarifying basic issues (e.g., are color graphics really useful?). Even for such fundamental questions as "What query language should I use?", there are very few data on which to base a choice [17]. Therefore, this chapter provides guidelines, but some unanswered questions will inevitably remain.

EXAMPLES OF DIALOG STYLES

The examples given in this section certainly do not cover all possible dialogs, nor do they necessarily represent the best dialog styles. The examples are taken from DSS which have been used. The examples are classified according to the "style" of the dialog that takes place between the user and the DSS. All of the DSS cited in the examples are interactive, but the designs can also be used in batch DSS.

Question–Answer Dialogs

A dialog style that is very common in DSS employing line-at-a-time terminals is the *question–answer* (Q/A) design. Figure 7-1 shows a Q/A dia-

```
--------PATIENT-248--------
1)   Patient's name: (first-last)
**   C.R.
2)   Sex:
**   MALE
3)   Age:
**   52
4)   Have you been able to obtain positive microbiological information about
     a possible infection of C.R.?
**   YES

        --------INFECTION-1--------
5)   What is the infection?
**      ENDARTERITIS (.6)
6)   Please give the date and approximate time when signs or symptoms of
     the endarteritis (INFECTION-1) first appeared.  (mo/da/yr time)
**   21 JULY 1975
The most recent culture yielding positive microbiological information
about the endarteritis (INFECTION-1) will be referred to as:

        --------CULTURE-1--------
7)   From what site was the specimen for CULTURE-1 taken?
**      BLOOD
```

Questions from MYCIN preceeded by: 1), 2),...
User answers are typed in following: **

FIGURE 7-1   Q/A Dialog from MYCIN [7]

log from the MYCIN system [7]. With Q/A dialogs, the DSS asks the user a question (possibly multiple choice), the user answers the question, and so on, until the DSS produces the answers needed to support the decision. As shown in the MYCIN example, a Q/A dialog may use "natural" language, and may determine the next question based on the answer(s) to the previous question(s). If the DSS cannot "understand" an answer, or needs additional information, clarification questions may be asked. In some DSS the user can redirect the questioning by giving answers such as "SKIP QUESTION" or "BEGIN WITH QUESTION 25."

Q/A dialogs tend to be most successful for inexperienced or infrequent users who are unfamiliar with the problem to be solved [9]. Q/A dialogs tend to be least successful for sophisticated or frequent users, who get tired of proceeding through the questions. To accommodate both frequent and infrequent users, a Q/A dialog may provide more than one mode of use (e.g., full sentence mode and abbreviation mode) or may have default answers. The Q/A dialog leads to awkward usage patterns if, during a dialog, users need to modify answers to previous questions.

Command Language Dialogs

A second dialog style is to develop a command language for invoking DSS functions. The usual format of command dialog involves verb–noun pairs (e.g., PLOT SALES) with short spellings (e.g., six to eight characters) for the nouns and verbs. Figure 7-2 gives an example of a command language dialog [12]. The implied verb is "print" and the output commands are a set of nouns. Several existing DSS use this style of dialog [3]. For simple applications, a command language is easily learned, but it will probably need to be relearned by infrequent users. For complicated applications, a command language can easily become a programming language, thereby requiring more skill to use. It is, however, possible to develop a "layered" command language. In a layered language there are simple commands for simple or frequently used functions, and these commands can be combined with other, more complicated commands for complex or infrequently used functions.

Menu Dialogs

A dialog style that is popular for DSS that utilize (CRT) terminals is the menu dialog. Instead of having to type commands, a menu dialog lets the user select from a menu of alternatives, such as report names or computation commands. Selection is accomplished with a keyboard or a "picking" device such as a light pen. Figure 7-3 illustrates a menu interface from Trend Analysis [13]. The menu lets the user select the type of reports to be displayed by the DSS.

The menu dialog seems to be quite effective for inexperienced or infrequent users who are familiar with the problem to be solved. For DSS that provide a large number of functions, menu dialogs often require many menu items, and in such cases the menus should be structured. Restaurant menus are examples of structuring by grouping (entrees, desserts, wines, etc.). Another structuring technique is to use hierarchies of menus.

Input Form/Output Form Dialogs

Input form/output form dialogs provide input forms in which the user enters commands and data, and output forms on which the DSS produces responses. After viewing an output form, the user can fill in another input form to continue the dialog. If the system determines which input form is

COMMANDS:

```
'INPUT VALUES'
CASH_INFLOW
CASH_OUTFLOW
AMOUNT,   CHAR = '-'

'NET PRESENT VALUE', NET_PRES_VAL,LEVEL=2,TOTAL=NO
'CUMULATIVE PRES.VAL.',CUMPV,LEVEL=2,TOTAL=NO
```

RESULTING OUTPUT:

INPUT VALUES				
CASH_INFLOW	18.00	31.00	43.00	92.00
CASH_OUTFLOW	3.00	6.00	8.00	17.00
AMOUNT	15.00	25.00	35.00	75.00
NET PRESENT VALUE	13.64	20.66	26.29	
CUMULATIVE PRES.VAL.	13.64	34.30	60.59	

Implied verb in commands is "PRINT"

FIGURE 7-2   Command Language Dialog from PLANCODE [12]

next, this dialog style parallels the Q/A style, with input forms corresponding to a set of questions, and output forms corresponding to a set of answers. Figure 7-4 shows an input form and an output form from Query-by-Example [22].

Input form/output form dialogs can be very successful if there is a correspondence between the input/output forms in the DSS and paper forms or thought patterns which are familiar to the users. For example, an input form can correspond to an existing checklist, or it can be arranged to group items that a decision maker is likely to think about together.

Input-in-Context-of-Output Dialogs

An extension of the input form/output form dialog is to combine input and output forms so that user inputs are always given in the context of the previous output from the DSS. In this dialog style, the DSS presents an output (e.g., a table or a graph or a list) within which the user may fill in or select inputs that will either modify the current output or result in a different output. For example, a skeletal report giving sample or standard data can be used as an input form if the user can write new data names or selection criteria on the report for subsequent use as inputs to the DSS. More sophisticated versions of this type of design combine menus of commands that can

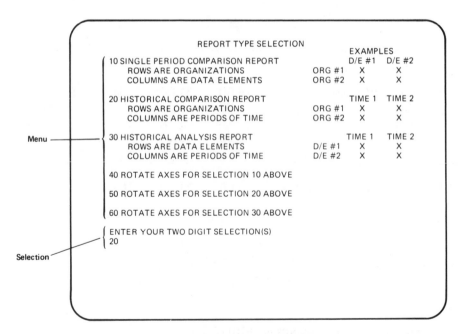

FIGURE 7-3   Menu Dialog from Trend Analysis 370 [13]

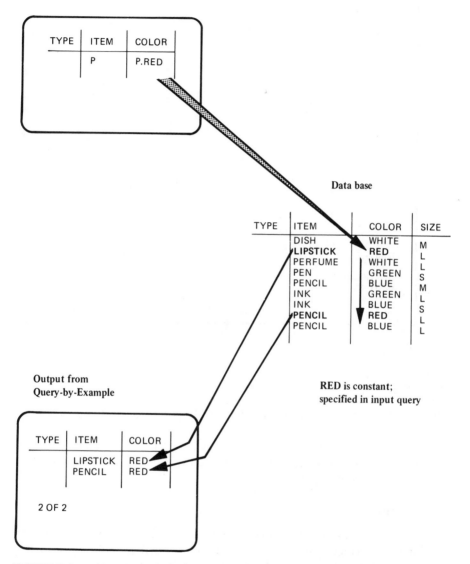

FIGURE 7-4   Input Form/Output Form Dialog from Query by Example [22]

be used to create and modify an output form. Figure 7-5 gives an example from GADS where many inputs are given in the context of previous DSS outputs [5]. The output is a scatterplot and the inputs for any scatterplot are given beneath the output. The inputs are the variable names (TBASE, CEIDENT) and the *xy* axis scales (0–200, 100–610). An output/input con-

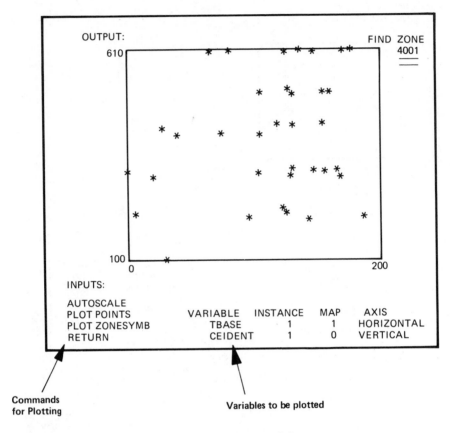

FIGURE 7-5   **Input-in-Context Dialog from GADS [5]**

text dialog can provide a "high-function" user interface which supports complex decisions. Using a system based on this design, however, is likely to require a few hours of training [10].

Combinations

It is likely that the dialog component for a Specific DSS will combine one or more dialog styles. For example, a Q/A dialog could be used in a "help" or "tutorial" feature of a DSS, with command or menu dialogs being used for routine interactions. In such a DSS, the HELP command would invoke a Q/A dialog to assist the user in accomplishing a task. The multiple-choice answers could be the possible commands that the user could have selected from the menus to accomplish the same task. Thus the Q/A dialog can help train the user. Another possible combination is to use menus for command selection in a command language dialog or to use menus for inputs in an input-in-context dialog.

Trade-offs

If alternative dialog styles are considered, trade-offs are involved in selecting among the alternatives. Whether or not the designers recognize or enumerate the trade-offs, they are made. These trade-offs affect the usability of the DSS as well as its cost. Reducing hardware or development costs often is the predominant consideration in making trade-offs. Better measures of the cost of poor dialog design are needed to help better compare reduced development or hardware costs with the costs of poor usability. Training time, number of errors, number of potential users, and time to do a given task are examples of such measures.

A list of trade-offs is a useful guide for evaluating alternatives. For each DSS the list will involve trade-offs unique to the users, application, and organizational environment for the DSS. For example, Donovan and Madnick illustrate the differences that "types of decision" make in the design of DSS [8]. Figure 7-6 gives a list of some of the trade-offs that need to be considered in designing the user interface, and Figure 7-7 compares Q/A

VARIABLES	EXAMPLES OF ALTERNATIVES
Hardware	
1. output media	line-at-a-time, full-screen graphics
2. input media	keyboards, pointing device, voice recognition
Software	
3. available programs	graphics subroutines, natural language parsers
4. amount of code to write	device drivers, control logic, simple subroutine calls
User	
5. interaction style	batch, slow-speed, high-speed
6. training constraints	will accept, must minimize
7. control style	"hands-on," tell someone else
8. familiarity with problem	low, high
9. familiarity with computer	low, high
Decision Making	
10. type of decision	Ad hoc, Institutional[8]
11. number of participants	few, many

FIGURE 7-6   Trade-off Variables in Dialog Design

TRADE-OFF VARIABLE	Q/A	INPUT IN CONTEXT
Hardware		
1. output media	line-at-a-time terminal	full-screen CRT
2. input media	keyboard	keyboard and/or pointing device
Software		
3. available programs	computer-assisted instruction packages	graphics subroutine packages
4. amount of code to write	large	large
User		
5. interaction style	slow speed	high speed
6. training constraints	low training time	high training time
7. control style	"help-me"	"do-it-myself"
8. familiarity with problem	low	high
9. familiarity with computer	low	some
Decision Making		
10. type of decision	Institutional, infrequent	Ad hoc, frequent
11. number of participants	one	several

FIGURE 7-7   Sample Comparison of Alternative Dialog Styles

designs with input-in-context designs using the list in Figure 7-6. Note that the list is not necessarily complete and that the comparison is qualitative.

DIALOG DESIGN TECHNIQUES

Regardless of the dialog styles that are chosen for a DSS, the builders must implement the output and input formats that will be used in the dialogs. At this time it is useful to establish dialog conventions which can be used to guide the dialog design. For example, a convention could be that only one dialog style would be used for the DSS. Other conventions might cover error message formats, restricting error messages to certain locations in the output formats, restricting input formats (e.g., all commands will be alphabetic, eight characters, and mnemonic), and requiring feedback (e.g., each user input in a interactive system will be acknowledged by the system). These conventions can serve as standards to which the dialog should conform. A useful technique is to allow exceptions to the conventions only if the dialog design has first been completed using the conventions and a good reason can be given as to why this design is not satisfactory. For example, a convention may not be followed because it is too expensive to implement, or it conflicts with another convention, or it will severely degrade performance.

Once a set of output and input formats has been developed, the next step in the design of the dialog component should be a "usability walk-through." For a usability walk-through, a sample set of output and input formats is developed on paper or as part of a prototype system. A review group, containing some potential users, then "walks-through" (simulates the steps needed for) sample decision-making tasks using the sample formats. Every output and every user input should be checked. The walk-through gives the builders (and potential users) a first chance to get a feeling for what it will be like to use the DSS *before* any implementation. A walk-through is even more effective if real data are prepared for use in the sample outputs, if actual inputs are required to get the output, and if a real decision-making situation (even a past decision) is used. The walk-through should generate numerous suggestions. These are checked against the conventions, trade-offs are assessed, and the dialog design is revised. Additional walk-throughs may be necessary.

An important, but usually overlooked, part of designing the dialog component is to establish measures that can be used to evaluate the design. The choice of measures should be based on the types of users and tasks that the DSS is to support. For example, for infrequent users, "sign-on" time is an important measure. These measures are valuable in making design trade-offs, and they can help the design team to decide if modifications to the user interface are necessary. The measures should be checked with the users because the users will often have suggestions on what usability criteria are important to them. Examples of measures that could be used are:

- Training time
- Number of input errors per session
- Time to relearn after a week (month, etc.) away from the system
- Time to select the correct inputs
- Time to enter the correct inputs
- Number of alternative choices at each user decision point

After the dialog component implemented, of course, there will be one obvious measure. Is the DSS used or not? For more detailed evaluations, experiments can be designed as described in Chapter 6.

HARDWARE SUPPORT FOR DIALOG MANAGEMENT

Hardware affects the functionality and the usability of the dialog component. Although the choice of hardware may be made before, during, or after the design of the dialog software, in many cases the hardware choice is specified by what is already available within the organization. In this case the hardware becomes a constraint in building the dialog component. For batch-mode DSS, the relevant hardware includes the output device (usually a printer) and the input media (e.g., cards, forms, etc.). For interactive DSS, the relevant hardware is the terminal and its associated input and output devices (e.g., keyboards, light pens, audio units, and tablets).

The variety and price/performance of the relevant hardware for the dialog component of DSS are changing rapidly. For example, the price of an eight-color, medium-resolution (512 × 512 picture elements) graphics terminal decreased by a factor of 3 (to about $15,000) between 1974 and 1978. The number of vendors of these terminals increased by at least the same factor (to at least 9). Builders will thus face an increasing number of hardware alternatives for the dialog component.

In choosing among hardware alternatives there are a number of parameters to consider [2]. Figure 7-8 lists some of these parameters and gives sample values for the parameters that would be "typical" of those required by batch and interactive DSS. The values for batch DSS assume a printer for output and keypunched input, while the values for interactive DSS assume a CRT (cathode ray tube) terminal. If the CRT has an associated printer, its characteristics should approximate those of the output parameters for batch DSS. A more detailed discussion of these parameters, as applied to graphics terminals, is given in Ref. 2. The parameters in Figure 7-8 are divided into four groups. The parameters in group 1 characterize output capabilities (representations), and group 2 refers to input capabilities (control mechanisms). Group 3 is a set of parameters relating to how the hardware is programmed. Group 4 includes performance, price, and packaging parameters.

The sample values given in Figure 7-8 are not nearly as important as the parameters. In choosing the hardware for a DSS, the designers should develop "required" values for each parameter based on the design and "provide" values for each parameter for each hardware alternative. The parameters thus serve as a framework for comparing hardware alternatives based on design requirements. For example, a DSS that displays computer-stored photographs (e.g., satellite pictures) would require an output resolution of about 100 points per inch to display the photographs. Such a requirement would greatly reduce the number of hardware alternatives that could be considered.

SOFTWARE SUPPORT FOR DIALOG MANAGEMENT

The largest costs in developing the software for a DSS probably will be the development and maintenance of the software that implements the dialog

EXAMPLE VALUES

PARAMETER	BATCH DSS	INTERACTIVE DSS
Group 1 (output)		
composed of:	text, lines	text, lines, audio
size/page:	8 ½ × 11 inches	19 inch diagonal
resolution:	100-200 points/inch	50-100 points/inch
volume/page:	over 1000 characters or 1000 vectors	over 500 characters and 100 vectors
refreshed:	daily	many times/second
must last:	several months	several seconds
Group 2 (input)		
devices:	forms	pick (e.g., light pen) keyboard, switches ,audio
text:	several hundred characters, at least 2 fonts, at least 2 sizes	same
graphics:	none	two-dimensional drawings
colors (shades):	2	2-8
Group 3 (programming)		
interface to computer:	standard communication codes	same
interface to program:	high-level language	same
Group 4 (product quality)		
performance:	600 lines/minute output, 400 characters/minute input	9600 bits/second communications, refresh 60 times/second
price:	$600,000 shared	$10,000/terminal
package:	remotable, low noise, fit in small room, standard power and operating environment	remotable, portable, low noise, no glare, fit on desktop, standard power and operating environment

FIGURE 7-8   Parameters for Choosing Hardware for the DSS Dialog Component

component. As an example, about 60 percent of the code written for the GADS is code for the dialog component, and about 75 percent of the changes made to GADS over a four-year period were changes to this code.

Software packages are collections of programs that can be used as part of, or to implement, other programs. For the dialog component, the most useful software packages are those which support output and input commands for the hardware devices selected for use in the DSS. This section focuses on such packages, and the terms "output" (or "write") and "input" (or "read") refer to communication to and from the user. The reason for using these packages is to reduce the implementation costs. Software packages are available from a variety of computer vendors, software vendors, and government agencies. Most of the packages are restricted to use with a small set of hardware, so the hardware choices for the dialog component usually will reduce the choice of software packages (or vice versa). A few software packages are free, some can be leased with rates ranging from about $100 to over $1000/per month, and some can be purchased for around $1000 to around $20,000. Because of high development costs and small markets, the prices of the software packages for DSS are unlikely to decrease as rapidly as hardware costs. The number of available software packages, however, should increase.

Types of Software Packages

The types of software packages for the dialog component are characterized more by the languages that are used to invoke the packages than by any significant differences in function.

The predominant type of software that could be acquired to help implement the dialog component is a *subroutine package*. Subroutine packages are sets of programs that are accessed via CALLS from a high-level programming language, such as FORTRAN or COBOL. CALL statements usually require the programmer to know a second, small language (that of the CALL statements) in addition to the language used to implement the other parts of the DSS. As parameters to the CALLS the programmer gives the data to be written or read, and a series of attributes telling how the data are to be written or read (e.g., format or position). The subroutine name and parameters are the only details the programmer needs to know. The internals of how the subroutine works should not be of concern. Subroutine packages can be quite flexible, so that almost any dialog style (which can be designed for the hardware which the package supports) can be implemented using the packages. A report from an ACM SIGGRAPH Committee compares 10 packages designed to support graphics terminals and/or plotters [21].

A second type of software package is *a programming language with high-level constructs* (e.g., more than WRITE and READ commands) for data output and input. The high-level constructs simplify programming of the output and input formats, and the interpretation of the inputs. Such languages are not common today, but are likely to become more common as programming languages reflect advances in hardware. Programming language constructs for supporting dialogs allow the code for the dialog component to be written in the same language used for the other components of the DSS. There are no CALL statements required as in subroutine packages.

Because high-level constructs in a programming language are consistent with the language, they often are easier to understand than subroutine calls. Because high-level constructs are integrated into the language and can be compiled directly into the program, they tend to produce a more efficient implementation than subroutine calls. LaFuente designed a set of such constructs as an extension of the programming language PASCAL [14]. Although the extensions were not implemented, they are indicative of what can be done to improve the support that the commonly used high-level languages (COBOL, FORTRAN, etc.) provide for programming the user interface.

Data definition languages describe the outputs and inputs for the dialog component as data rather than as subroutines or statements in a programming language. The data definitions are invoked by a subroutine call, similar to subroutine packages. However, there is only one call to the data definition interface per output or input "frame" in the user interface, whereas a subroutine package requires several calls. In addition, calls to the data definition package give the device and format names plus parameters for the formats, whereas the calls to a subroutine package specify the entire formats. Data definition languages help specify the attributes to be used in writing or reading the data that are passed as part of the call. Historically, data definition packages have supported fewer devices than subroutine packages, and they have required more skill to use than high-level constructs in a programming language. However, there are no technical reasons why these differences need to exist. Because the data definitions are stored separately from the program, they are easy to modify and reuse. In addition, data definition packages may be more efficient than either subroutine packages or high-level constructs because they are tailored for specific devices and because they tend to be "lower-level" languages. IBM's Message Formatting Services (MFS) is an example of a data definition package [11].

A final type of software package is a *dialog component of a DSS Generator*. A DSS Generator may provide functions to define new reports, to modify the formats of reports provided by the DSS, or to create new input formats (e.g., inputs to a new forecasting routine that has been added to the DSS). This type of package usually provides fewer functions and control structures than the other three types of software packages (because it is developed for specific sets of DSS applications). This restriction, however, often makes it easier to program using this type of package. In fact, the major examples of "users" developing a DSS involve use of a DSS Generator for creating new dialog components. PLANCODE is an example of a software package that provides output definition capabilities [12].

Figure 7-9 gives examples of program segments in a hypothetical language for each of the four types of software packages. The examples show code segments used to produce a table comparing up to five balance-sheet items for up to three different companies. The inputs are the names of the

(a) Subroutine package

```
CALL INTEXT (DATANAMES(5), Length(10), CHARACTER,
             ROW(l0), COL(30));
CALL INTEXT (COMPANYNAMES(3), LENGTH(25), CHARACTER,
             ROW(l2), COL(30));
CALL ERASE;
CALL DRAWTABLE (DATANAMES, COMPANYNAMES,
             HEADINGS = YES, LOWER LEFT = (24,l),
             UPPER RIGHT = (1,70);
```

(b) Constructs in a programming language

```
DECLARE TABLE
             COLUMNS = DATANAMES(l-5),
             ROWS = COMPANYNĀMES(l-3),
             LOWER = 24, l,
             UPPER = l, 70,
             HEADINGS = YES;
DECLARE INPUT-AREA
             DATANAMES(5) CHAR(l0) ROW(l0) COL(30),
             COMPANYNAMES(3) CHAR(25) ROW(l2) COL(30));
    .
    .
    .
READ INPUT
DISPLAY TABLE;
```

(c) Data definition package

TABLE	FORMAT
FIELD 1	LTH10, POS(1,1)
.	
.	
.	
FIELD 24	LTH5, POS(24,66)
TABLE	END
INPUT	FORMAT
FIELD 1	LTHl0, POS(l0,30)
.	
.	
.	
FIELD 8	
INPUT	END

(d) DSS Generator

```
DATA = SALES77, S
COMPANIES = IBM,
TABLE DATA FOR C
```

FIGURE 7-9   Examples of Languages for Building the Dialog Component

balance-sheet items and the names of the companies. The exact meaning of each program segment is not given here because the figure is intended to illustrate the syntactic differences among the types of software packages.

Figure 7-9(a) shows subroutine calls to read data from a display terminal (INTEXT), to clear the display screen on the terminal (ERASE), and to draw the tabular output (DRAWTABLE). In Figure 7-9(b), the table is described (DECLARE TABLE), the input fields are described (DECLARE INPUT-AREA), the input is read, and the table is displayed. Figure 7-9(c) shows an output data definition (TABLE FORMAT) and an input data definition (INPUT FORMAT). These descriptions would be stored in a file and could be requested by name in a program that wanted to write or read that particular format. The identity of names in the output and input formats is intentional and required if the input fields are to be associated with specific output fields. In Figure 7-9(d) the inputs are specified (DATA=, COM-PANIES=) and the output is requested (TABLE DATA) using a command language interface to a DSS Generator. Note that the formats of the input and output data are not specified. If the DSS builder is not willing to take the default formats for inputs and outputs in the Generator, specifying new formats, if allowed, usually is in a language similar to one of the other three types of software packages. An important advantage of the Generator for building the dialog component is the availability of these default formats.

Criteria for Choosing among Software Packages

Figure 7-10 lists some criteria that could be used in selecting a software package. In addition, the table indicates the authors' ranking of the four

CRITERION	SUBROUTINE PACKAGES	LANGUAGE CONSTRUCTS	FORMATTING LANGUAGES	DSS GENERATOR
Hardware				
1. devices supported	1	3	2	4
2. hardware independence	1	3	2	4
Software				
3. interface to existing	2	1	3	4
programming language	4	1	3	2
4. interface to data base	4	1	2	3
Functionality				
5. number of output representations possible	1	2	3	4
6. transformation (e.g., scaling) of output representation	1	2	3	4
7. number of input formats supported	2	1 (all are weak here)	3	4
8. support for specifying responses to inputs	4	2	3	1
Costs				
9. acquisition costs	1	4	3	2
10. installation costs	2	3	4	1
11. execution costs	3	2	1	4
12. ease of programming	3	2	4	1

FIGURE 7-10   Criteria for Choosing Among Software Packages for the Dialog Component of a DSS

types of software packages with respect to each criteria. A ranking of 1 indicates that existing software packages of this type currently are the best of the four types (in the authors' opinion) with respect to the criterion; a ranking of 2 is next best; and so on. In the criteria related to costs, a 1 indicates lowest cost. DSS builders should do their own ranking of the software packages that are being considered.

The first two criteria relate to hardware/software interaction. If the software package is limited to a small set of hardware, the set of user interfaces that can be described will be limited accordingly. Criteria 3 and 4 are important if the software package will be used in connection with other software packages in order to implement the DSS. Criteria 5 through 8 indicate what dialog designs will be possible with the software package. For example, if the package only supports display of a single line of text at a time, a contextual dialog design cannot be implemented. Similarly, a package that does not provide support for "parsing" of text input will be of limited value for a question–answer design. The last four criteria in Figure 7-10 deal with the costs of acquistion and use of the package.

DESIGN OF THE DIALOG
COMPONENT FOR DSS

A design for the dialog component is shown in Figure 7-11. There are eight modules. The three modules (1–3) on the left of the figure transform commands and data from other components of the DSS (i.e., modeling and data base) and create commands to the user interface hardware (e.g., a terminal for creating the output representations). The three modules (5–7) on the right of the figure transform user inputs into commands and data for the other DSS components. The module (4) at the bottom of the figure sends and receives data from the user interface hardware, and the module (8) in the middle manages (stores and retrieves) any local data for the dialog component.

The design in Figure 7-11 does not imply any hardware configuration for the DSS. The user interface hardware could be a terminal connected to a host computer on which the DSS executes. Or the user interface hardware could contain enough processor and memory capacity to execute the entire DSS or to execute the dialog component of the DSS. The design also is not dependent on the dialog style(s) chosen for the DSS. Q/A dialogs would have very short data and control flow from output construction back to response construction. Input-in-context dialogs would involve more complex output and response construction. The following paragraphs describe the design shown in Figure 7-11. Other designs are possible, but will have to provide the same set of functions.

The output formatter (1) translates commands and data (parameters)

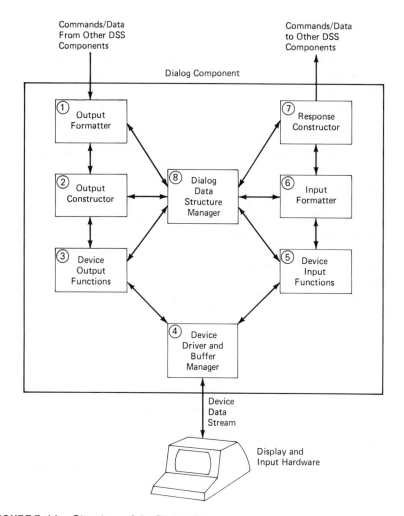

Commands/Data From Other DSS Components

Commands/Data to Other DSS Components

Dialog Component

① Output Formatter

⑦ Response Constructor

② Output Constructor

⑧ Dialog Data Structure Manager

⑥ Input Formatter

③ Device Output Functions

⑤ Device Input Functions

④ Device Driver and Buffer Manager

Device Data Stream

Display and Input Hardware

FIGURE 7-11   **Structure of the Dialog Component**

from the other components into a data structure that contains a description of the output representation. That is, the output formatter translates output commands and data such as those shown in Figure 7-9 into a data structure representing outputs such as those shown in Figures 7-1 through 7-5. The data structure contains values (e.g., text strings) and attributes (e.g., color, position, size) which describe how the values are to be displayed. The values and attributes should be device independent; that is, they should not be specific to any particular user interface hardware. Device independence permits the dialog component to support a variety of hardware.

The output constructor (2) takes the data structure built by the output formatter and generates commands (e.g., subroutine calls) to the device output functions (3). In other words, the output constructor translates the dialog data structure into commands to create an output representation on one or more devices. The output constructor should also be device independent in that the commands it generates for the device output functions should not be specific to any device.

The device output functions generate device-specific commands to create outputs on one or more specific devices. The device driver (4) sends the commands to the device, waits for user inputs, or requests user inputs if the output message is an interrupt rather than commands to generate a representation. When user inputs are received, the device driver buffers them and sends them to the device input functions. The device input functions (5) translate device specific inputs into device independent inputs.

The input formatter (6) translates the users input into a set of action–object pairs. The action describes the user's input action (e.g., typed on the keyboard, pointed at an item on a menu). The object designates which object in the output representation that was affected by the action (e.g., new value for name field, or menu item 26).

The response constructor (7) uses a set of action–object pairs to create commands and data for the other components of the DSS. For example, the response constructor might invoke the data base component to update the field in the data base which corresponds to the field in the output representation into which the user had just typed a new value.

The data structure manager (8) stores and retrieves data used by the dialog component, such as the data structure that describes the output representation. Other data might include "predefined" output representations and previous user inputs (e.g., for backtracking, reentry, or recovery). For details on data structures for the dialog component, see [4, 15].

The dialog component may need to support partitioning the user interface hardware into multiple windows [1] (also called viewports [21]). Multiple windows are used to support multiple contexts for decision making [2]. To support multiple windows, the dialog component must keep track of which part of the hardware is associated with which context. This is usually done either by partitioning the hardware in a static manner with a dialog component for each partition, or by dynamic partitioning, in which case the dialog data structures are segmented to indicate which context they represent. In dynamic partitioning the data structure for each representation contains a context (window) identifier that can be used by the input formatter and response constructor to determine which other DSS components are to be invoked when the user actions affect the representation.

In summary, the dialog component of the DSS thus must provide the following functions:

1. Create a data structure containing values and attributes which describe the output representations (output formatter)

2. Invoke device functions to create the representations (output constructor)
3. Create device orders for the specific hardware being used (device output functions)
4. Send/receive device orders to/from the device (device driver)
5. Translate device specific inputs into device-independent inputs (device input functions)
6. Create action–object pairs describing the input (input formatter)
7. Send commands/data to other components of the DSS (response constructor)
8. Store output and input data (data structure manager)

The communication among the modules shown in Figure 7-11 could be subroutine calls, coroutine calls or message passing, depending on the operating system(s), programming language(s), and hardware configuration being used for the DSS.

An implementation of the design shown in Figure 7-11 can be called a Dialog Generation and Management System (DGMS) [2]. The output modules of a DGMS (modules 1, 2, 3, 4, 8 in Figure 7-11) provide functions for implementing representations used in a Specific DSS. The input modules (4, 5, 6, 7, 8 in Figure 7-11) provide functions for implementing control mechanisms in a Specific DSS. Thus a DGMS is clearly part of a DSS Generator.

SUMMARY

A well-designed dialog component does not guarantee the success of a DSS, but it is a necessary ingredient. Although there is little research which indicates the relative importance of the dialog component with respect to the many other factors that influence the success of the DSS, two facts do indicate its importance. The first is that the code for the dialog component is often the largest percentage of the total code in a DSS and the code most often modified [20]. The second is that communication is known to be an important ingredient in effective decision making, and the dialog component of a DSS is the means through which the users communicate with the DSS. In describing one of the first DSS, Scott Morton emphasized the importance of the dialog component [18], and research on DSS has indicated that attention to the dialog component can enable a variety of decision makers to use a single DSS [6,19].

To design a dialog component that supports effective communication between the decision maker and the DSS, design must begin with an analysis of the decision makers and of the decision-making processes that the DSS is to support. This analysis should focus on the representations (outputs) that are, or are intended to be used, and on the control mechanisms (inputs) that are used to invoke operations involving those representations. Following the analysis, the dialog component can be designed using one or more dialog styles. Although choice of dialog style depends on hardware and software constraints, the goal should be to provide effective representations and understandable control mechanisms. Once the dialog has been designed, a usability walk-through can help designers evaluate effectiveness and understandability. At this stage in the development process, the dialog design can be used to establish the criteria for selecting among hardware devices and software packages. Often, however, external constraints such as availability and costs will limit the alternatives or will require revisions in the dialog. These revisions should be checked by another usability walk-through.

If acceptable trade-offs can be made among the technology (hardware and software), the economics (cost and availability), and the usability of the design (training times, error rates, user acceptance), the dialog component can be designed and implemented. Implementation costs will be reduced and the implementation will be more likely to conform to the dialog design if dialog conventions are established. The design and implementation of the dialog component should be based on a set of output and input handling modules.

To evaluate the dialogs during walk-through, implementation, testing, and installation, ease-of-use measures are needed. These measures should focus on performance (time or number of errors), process (how decisions are made), and perceptions (what users say). Evaluation is needed throughout development of the dialog component because the earlier that errors in the dialog are detected, the cheaper they are to fix.

In the future, better hardware and different (although often not better) software can be expected to be available for use in developing the dialog component for DSS. Color display terminals and printers capable of producing extremely high quality outputs and easier-to-use input devices (e.g., voice input) will be the most noticable hardware improvements. Software will become available for these devices, but implementing the dialog component is likely to remain difficult unless a Dialog Generation and Management System (DGMS) is provided as part of the DSS Generator.

As the number of DSS increases, there will be more information available on successes and failures in design of the dialog component of DSS. Because the design of the dialogs is likely to remain more an engineering discipline than a science, these experimental data will be extremely valuable in reducing costs and increasing the effectiveness of the dialog component of DSS.

QUESTIONS AND PROBLEMS

REVIEW QUESTIONS

1. Identify and briefly describe five dialog styles that can be used in DSS.
2. What are the trade-offs that should be considered in deciding which dialog style(s) to use in a DSS?
3. What are dialog conventions?
4. What is a usability walk-through?
5. How can you decide if there are usability problems with the dialog component of a DSS?
6. What are some of the parameters to consider in selecting the hardware for the user interface for DSS?
7. Identify four types of software packages that can be used to implement the dialog component of DSS.
8. Identify and briefly describe the eight major functions of the dialog component of a DSS.
9. What is a Dialog Generation and Management System?

DISCUSSION QUESTIONS

1. Dialog conventions are helpful to the builder because they simplify the dialog building effort, but they also constrain users who need flexibility. Discuss.
2. A usability walk-through is unnecessary if the iterative design approach is used, because problems will turn up during use and can be solved as you go. Discuss.

EXERCISES

1. Identify a Specific DSS, perhaps one that you are familiar with through the exercises in a previous chapter.
   (a) Select the appropriate dialog style(s) and explain your choice.
   (b) Define the specifications of the hardware required and explain why you chose them.

REFERENCES

1. BUNEMAN, O. P., et al. "Display Facilities for DSS Support: the DAISY Approach," *Data Base*, Vol. 8, No. 3, Winter 1977, pp. 46–50.
2. CARLSON, E. D. "Graphics Terminal Requirements for the 1970's," *Computer*, Vol. 9, No. 8, August 1976, pp. 37–45.
3. CARLSON, E. D. (ed.). Proceedings of a Conference on Decision Support Systems, *Data Base*, Vol. 8, No. 3, Winter 1977.
4. CARLSON, E. D., and W. METZ. "Integrating Dialog Management and Data Base Management," *Information Processing 80*, North-Holland Publish-

ing Company, Amsterdam, 1980, pp. 463–468.

5. CARLSON, E. D., et al. "The Design and Evaluation of an Interactive Geo-Data Analysis and Display System," *Proceedings of the IFIP Congress 74*, North-Holland Publishing Company, Amsterdam, 1974, pp. 1057–1061.

6. CARLSON, E. D., et al. "Case Studies of End User Requirements for Interactive Problem Solving," *Management Information System Quarterly*, Vol. 1, No. 1, March 1977, pp. 51–63.

7. DAVIS, R. "A DSS for Diagnosis and Therapy," *Data Base*, Vol. 8, No. 3, Winter 1977, pp. 58–72.

8. DONOVAN, J. J., and S. E. MADNICK. "Institutional and Ad Hoc DSS and Their Effective Use," *Data Base*, Vol. 8, No. 3, Winter 1977, pp. 79–88.

9. EASON, K. D. "Understanding the Naive Computer User," *The Computer Journal*, Vol. 19, No. 1, February 1976, pp. 3–7.

10. GRACE, B. F. "Training Users of a Decision Support System," *Data Base*, Vol. 8, No. 3, Winter 1977, pp. 30–36.

11. IBM CORPORATION. *IMS/VS Message Formatting Services User's Guide*, SH20-9053.

12. IBM CORPORATION. *PLANCODE General Information Manual*, GH19-1103.

13. IBM CORPORATION. *Trend Analysis/370 General Information Manual*, GH20-1961.

14. LAFUENTE, J., and D. GRIES. "Language Facilities for Programming User-Computer Dialogues," *IBM J. Res. Dev.*, Vol. 22, No. 2, March 1978, pp. 145–158.

15. LISKOV, B., et al. "Abstraction Mechanisms in CLU," *Communications of the ACM*, Vol. 20, No. 8, August 1977, pp. 564–576.

16. MARTIN, J. *Design of Man–Computer Dialogues*, Prentice-Hall, Inc., Englewood Cliffs, N.J., 1973.

17. REISNER, P. "Human Factors Studies of Data Base Query Languages: A Survey and Assessment," *Computing Surveys*, Vol. 4, No. 1, 1981.

18. SCOTT MORTON, M. S. *Management Decision Systems*, Graduate School of Business Administration, Harvard University, Boston, 1971.

19. SUTTON, J. A. "Evaluation of a Decision Support System: A Case Study with the Office Products Division of IBM," *IBM Research Report No. RJ2214*, IBM Research Division, San Jose, Calif., March 1978.

20. SUTTON, J. A., and R. H. SPRAGUE, JR. "A Study of Display Generation and Management in Interactive Business Applications," in *Display Generation and Management Systems (DGMS) for Interactive Business Applications*, E. D. Carlson, et al. (eds.), Friedr. Vieweg & Sohn, Braunschweig Wiesbaden, West Germany, 1981.

21. Status Report of the Graphics Standards Planning Committee, *Computer Graphics*, Vol. 13, No. 3, August 1979.

22. ZLOOF, M. M. "Query by Example," *Proceedings of the National Computer Conference 1975*, AFIPS Press, Montvale, N.J., 1975, pp. 431–437.

CHAPTER EIGHT

DATA BASE MANAGEMENT

OUTLINE

INTRODUCTION

A *data base* is generally defined as a collection of (computer-stored) data, and a *data base management system* (DBMS) is generally defined as a collection of computer programs used to create, maintain, access, update, and protect one or more data bases. Data base management is, of course, a topic that is relevant to most applications of computers, including DSS. In fact, data base management was probably the most important research area in computer science in the 1970s. Because it is still the topic of many papers, books, and conferences, no attempt is made in this chapter to provide a data base management tutorial or survey. However, because lack of data and inadequate DBMS are often cited as reasons for the failure of MIS, data base management is an especially important component of a DSS. In distinguishing data from data base, the key word is "maintains." Data such as intermediate calculations, messages, and queue numbers (e.g., in a bakery) are purely transient, but are not maintained and therefore not part of the data base. A data base, then, contains data that are maintained by an organization and, therefore, can be presumed to be of value to that organization. Although a data base need not be maintained on a computer (by a DBMS), an increasing percentage of organizational data bases are computerized. We will restrict our discussions of data base management for DSS to computerized data bases, although many of the principles are valid for any data base used in decision making.

We will begin with a discussion of why a data base and a DBMS are important prerequisites for a DSS and how DBMS are important tools for building a DSS. We then illustrate five data models that can be used for the DSS data base component, and describe the functions of DBMS which are useful for DSS. After the overview of data base management, we turn to data base requirements for DSS. Based on these requirements, we present a design for the DSS data base component. Finally, we discuss the role of data base query languages as part of DSS.

IMPORTANCE OF DATA BASE
MANAGEMENT TO DSS

Data base management is important for building a DSS in two ways. First, data bases and DBMS are an important prerequisite to a DSS because building a DSS without existing data bases and associated DBMS will be extremely difficult. Second, as we have pointed out earlier in this book, data base management is one of the three major components of a DSS. A DBMS is an important tool for building a DSS, and a poor data base management component can cause the failure of a DSS.

As a Prerequisite

Every organization maintains a collection of data that is used for the planning, control, and operation of that organization. We will call this the *internal* data base. Most organizations also use *external* data—data gathered and maintained by another organization. Internal and external data bases are important prerequisites for DSS because these data bases will contain some of the data relevant to the decisions supported by the DSS. Without these data bases, the DSS will have to include functions for the collection and maintenance of the relevant data. Data collection and maintenance will probably involve different users (and possibly different organizations) from those using the DSS for decision making. If a DSS has to support data collection and maintenance, the DSS design may be complicated and the DSS performance may be reduced. DSS support for data collection and maintenance may introduce security constraints (e.g., limited access) on the DSS which otherwise would not have been necessary. When the DSS provides the data collection and maintenance functions, data sharing among DSS may be difficult because of the data structures chosen or because of the desire to limit access to data which are particular to each DSS. If data sharing is difficult, maintenance of redundant data is likely. Thus, having a data base prior to building a DSS:

1. Simplifies collection and maintenance of (some of) the data used by the DSS
2. Limits the set of functions and users that the DSS needs to support
3. Simplifies the design of the DSS
4. Eliminates potential conflicting performance and security requirements (data update versus data retrieval)
5. Increases the chances of data sharing among DSS

The "bottom line" of having a data base before building DSS is that the cost of building DSS will be reduced and the accuracy of the data for use in DSS will be increased.

An illustration of these advantages of data base as a prerequisite for DSS can be given from the history of GADS [12] in terms of installation costs and decision makers' time. In applications of GADS where the data base had to be created before using GADS, over 50 percent of the costs of installing GADS were for the data collection. In applications where the data base existed prior to using GADS, interfacing GADS to the data base (i.e., getting the relevant data out of the data base and into GADS) was less than 10 percent of the installation costs. In the applications where the data base had to be created, the decision makers spent about 10 percent of their time validating or correcting the data. In cases where the data base existed prior to GADS use, less than 1 percent of the decision maker's time was spent in data validation or correction. This experience indicates that if the appropriate data base exists prior to use of a DSS, the costs of installing the DSS will be reduced, and the users of the DSS will spend less time performing data base management tasks rather than decision-making tasks.

If the data base itself is an important prerequisite, so is the data base management system, because a DBMS provides the functions that make a data base useful. The DBMS provides for the maintenance and control of the data base, and simplifies programming of the interface between the DSS and the data base. A DBMS may also provide a dictionary that describes the data stored in the data base, and thus may be useful in deciding what data to use in the DSS.

In summary, the advantages of data base and DBMS as a prerequisite to DSS are:

1. Reduced costs of building and using the DSS
2. Increased data control and sharing
3. Reduced data redundancy

These advantages are similar to the advantages of data base management in general [7].

As a Component

The second reason for the importance of data base management for DSS is the value of data base management as a component of DSS. Data base management supports the memory requirements of DSS. A data base can be used to store not only the internal and external data that are used in the DSS, but also the workspace, libraries of results, links among data, and triggers. In addition, a DBMS may be used to support dialog management and model management. We return to this key role of data base management in Chapter 10.

Data base management is an important component of a DSS because of the diversity of data that is required. A data base is a mechanism for integrating a variety of internal and external data. These data may or may not be in existing data bases, and probably will have to be manipulated (e.g., aggregated) and/or converted (i.e., through storage structure and format changes) for use in the DSS. Often there will be multiple sources of the same data, so the data will need to be made consistent. Data integration, conversion, and consistency checking can be simplified by use of a DBMS. Using a DBMS for these functions involves developing a data base design that can be shared by the applications that create and maintain the data base, and by the DSS that use the data base. Often, this task is assigned to a group or an individual known as the data base administrator (DBA). Because of the variety of data sources used by DSS and because of the differences between data base requirements for DSS and for other applications, DSS generally have data bases which are built from other data bases. This does not mean that separate data base management systems are required, or that a data base system with several data bases is not integrated.

We have argued that data base management is both an important prerequisite and an important component for DSS. The question remains: What specific data base management functions are needed to build a DSS? To answer this question, we must first discuss data models, data base management systems, and data base management requirements for DSS.

DATA MODELS FOR DSS

What Is a Data Model?

In building the data base management component for a DSS, there will be an implicit or explicit choice of one or more data models. A data "model" is a method of representing, organizing, storing, and handling data in a computer. A data model has three parts [6].

1. A collection of data structures. Lists, tables, relations, hierarchies, and networks are examples of data structures.
2. A collection of operations that can be applied (usually by the DBMS) to the data structures. Retrieval, update, combination, and summation are examples of these operations.
3. A collection of integrity rules that define the "legal" states (set of values) or changes of state (operations on values) for the data structures. Constraining all data values to be in dollars and less than 1 million is an example of an integrity constraint.

The data model for a DSS should not be confused with the modeling component of DSS. Although the data base management component may be used by the modeling component, the data model is a model of data storage and of operations on storage, whereas the modeling component contains models of decision processes.

Some of the data base literature describes different "levels" of data models. For example, Date [7] discusses the "external model," the "conceptual model," and the "internal model." The external model is used in the application program and thus is closest to the users. The conceptual model is an integrating or global model that encompasses several external models for different applications. The internal model describes how the conceptual model is represented in storage. Figure 8-1 shows the relationships among the three levels of data model. The relationships between levels are called *mappings*. Mappings describe the transformations needed to obtain one model from another. For example, the user may see a table that requires a mapping to a tabular, external data model. The tabular external model may be derived from a set of relations in a conceptual model, and these relations may be represented in the data base as a set of lists stored on a disk.

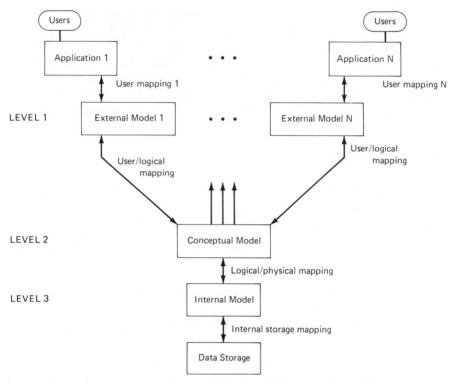

FIGURE 8-1   Three Levels of Data Models Adapted from Date [7]

In discussing data models for DSS, we will be concerned primarily with the external model, since this model is the most important to the DSS users. The conceptual model is important because it is the model for an integrated data base which provides data for use in several Specific DSS. In other words, the conceptual model is appropriate for a DSS Generator, while the external model is most appropriate for Specific DSS. The data model, through its data structures, operations, and integrity constraints, influences the representations and operations for the DSS as well as the user's understanding of the memory functions of the DSS. A simple and consistent data model can often be a strong unifying and simplifying factor for helping users understand a DSS.

Most existing DSS use one (or more) of five data models [2]. These are the record model, the relational model, the hierarchic (tree) model, the network (graph) model, and the rule model. In providing a brief description of each of these models we will use a simple example. The example is a hypothetical data base consisting of data on customers (e.g., of a bank), loans (to customers), payments (on loans), and guidelines for customer credit rating and loan classifications. Such a data base might be used in a DSS designed to support decisions on loan applications.

No matter what data model is used, it describes a set of *objects*. These objects can be either values or relationships among values. Examples of values are customer name and loan number; an example of a relationship is the fact that customer ABC has loan 123. In general, values are represented in a data model by *fields*, and relationships are represented by collections of fields called *records* or by values in *linking fields*. The definition of a data model can now be made more precise.

1. The data structures define the fields and records allowed in the data base.
2. The operations define the allowed manipulations of those fields and records.
3. The integrity constraints define what fields and record constraints must be preserved by the operations.

From these basic concepts we can now proceed to descibe the five data models that have been used in DSS, with examples given in Figure 8-2.

The Record Model

The record model is perhaps the oldest and most common data model. It has the most varied data structures and the least well-defined (and agreed upon) operations and integrity constraints. It is very common in DSS using time series data. As illustrated in Figure 8-2a, the data structure for the record model is a set of records. Each record consists of a set of fields. If there is more than one "type" of record, one field usually contains a value that indicates what other fields are in the record. In Figure 8-2a there are four types of records. In addition to the type field, the *customer* records contain fields describing the customer name, assets, liabilities, and credit rating. Similarly, the *loan* records contain fields describing the loan number, the name of the customer, the percentage interest rate, the loan amount, and the loan class. The *payment* records contain fields describing the loan number, the payment amount, and the date of payment. The *guideline* records contain fields describing asset/liability ratios, number of loans, and the credit rating and loan classification for specified asset/liability ratios and number of loans. Thus the data structures for the record model consist of fields combined into records, and the data base is a collection of these records.

The operations commonly associated with the record data base model are: (1) creating an instance of a record, (2) updating a field in an existing instance of a record, (3) deleting an instance of a record, and (4) selecting a record. The integrity constraints for the record model usually include at least three. First, each record must contain a field whose value is unique among all records (of that type). This field is called the *key* field. Multifield keys are sometimes used. In Figure 8-2a the "loan #" field in the loan record is an example of a key field. The second common constraint is that new record

CUSTOMER RECORDS

Field Names:	RECORD TYPE	CUSTOMER NAME	ASSETS	LIABILITIES	CREDIT RATING
Example Values:	crecord	ABC Corp	100000	25000	B

LOAN RECORDS

Field Names:	RECORD TYPE	LOAN #	CUSTOMER NAME	INTEREST RATE	LOAN AMOUNT	LOAN CLASS
Example Values:	lrecord	123	ABC Corp	12.25	102000	2

PAYMENT RECORDS

Field Names:	RECORD TYPE	LOAN #	PAYMENT AMOUNT	DATE
Example Values:	precord	123	1089	62581

LOAN GUIDELINE RECORDS

Field Names:	RECORD TYPE	A/L RATIO	NUMBER OF LOANS	CREDIT RATING	LOAN CLASS
Example Values:	lgrecord	2	4	B	2

FIGURE 8-2a   Example of the Record Model of Data

types cannot be added, and the third common constraint is that every field must contain a value.

The Relational Model

The relational model [5] is often thought of as a model that limits the data structures of the record model, provides a mathematical basis for (set) operations on records, and defines integrity constraints that require the operations to leave the data base in "consistent" states. There is a formal definition of the relational model [5], but we will use an informal definition here. The data structures in the relational model consist only of relations. A *relation* is a set of fields that are "related." Each instance of a relation consists of a set of tuples, or records. Each relation can be thought of as a table and each row in the table is a tuple. Each column in each row is a field; the columns are often called *attributes*. Another important aspect of the data structures for the relational model is that each field (attribute) has a domain that defines the set of allowed values for that field. Many fields can have the same domain, for example, the domain of positive integers. In Figure 8-2b there are four relations (customers, loans, payments, and guidelines). In the customer relation there are four attributes (name, assets, liabilities, and rat-

CUSTOMER RELATION

NAME	ASSETS	LIABILITIES	CREDIT RATING
ABC	100	25	B
XYZ	25	100	C

LOAN RELATION

LOAN #	NAME	INTEREST RATE	LOAN AMOUNT	LOAN CLASS
123	ABC	12.25	102000	2
456	WDQ	13.00	50000	3

PAYMENT RELATION

LOAN #	PAYMENT AMOUNT	DATE
123	1089	62581
456	2961	62581

LOAN GUIDELINES RELATION

A/L RATIO	NUMBER OF LOANS	CREDIT RATING	LOAN CLASS
2	4	B	2
2	10	B	3

FIGURE 8-2b   Example of the Relational Model of Data

ing). The assets and liabilities attributes are drawn from the domain of positive integers in dollars. Note that the difference in *structure* between the record model (Figure 8-2a) and the relational model (Figure 8-2b) is minimal. In the relational model the relationships among fields in a relation are represented by the name of the relation. In the record model, relationships are represented by a field in the record.

The important differences between the relational model and the record (or any other model), however, are the *operations* and *constraints* usually associated with the relational model. The common relational operations are: (1) insertion (add a tuple), (2) updating (the value of a field in a tuple), (3) deleting (a tuple), (4) creating (a relation), (5) deleting (a relation), (6) selecting (a tuple from a relation), (7) joining (combining two relations based on common values in fields with the same domain), and (8) projection (selecting a subset of the fields in a relation). The mathematical basis for these operations and their precise definition are beyond the scope of this chapter, but the important characteristics are:

- The operations in the relational model operate on entire relations (sets of tuples) rather than on individual records.
- The operations do not depend on the order of the fields or of the records. That is, they are independent of the data structures other than the relation itself.
- The operations form an *algebra*, which is a set of operations defined mathematically rather than by convention.

The usual integrity constraints of the relational model specify that each tuple in a relation must contain a unique set of values. However, no single field need contain a unique (key) value for a relation. In addition, relational theory specifies a number of other constraints that lead to "normal forms" for a relation [7]. These constraints guarantee that certain relationships among fields in a relation (called functional dependencies) are preserved by the operations. For example, the normal form constraints of the relational model would guarantee that deleting a loan record in Figure 8-2b would not cause loss of information on names of customers (since this information is stored in the customer relation). Contrast this with the record model, where there is no constraint on dependencies among field values. Thus in Figure 8-2a we could have combined the customer and loan records (repeating the customer data in each for each loan record). If a customer had only one loan, and this loan record was deleted (e.g., the loan was paid off), the customer information would be lost.

The Hierarchic Model

Figure 8-2c shows the sample data base with hierarchical data structures. There are two data structures. The first is a two-level tree. The "root" level of this tree is the loan record. There would be one loan record for every loan. One descendent from the root is the customer record. There would be one customer record for each loan record. A second descendent record is the payment record. There would be multiple payment records for each loan record. In a hierarchic data base there may be several descendent record types at any level, and for any record there may be several instances of any descendent. The second data structure in Figure 8-2c is a single-level tree with only a "root," which is the guidelines record.

There are three main differences between the hierarchical structure in Figure 8-2c and the relational structure in Figure 8-2b. First, the structures in the hierarchic model represent information that is captured in fields in the relational model. That is, the relationship between customers and loans is represented in the structure of the hierarchy in Figure 8-2c and in a specific field (customer name) in Figure 8-2b. A similar observation holds for the relationship between loan and payment records. Second, in the hierarchic model certain records must exist before others can exist. In particular, every data structure must have a root record (e.g., loan); no instance of a descendent record (e.g., payment) can exist without an instance of its parent record (e.g., loan). Third, if a particular customer had several loans, the asset, lia-

ROOT (LOAN) LEVEL:

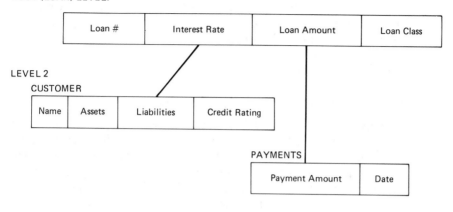

LEVEL 2
    CUSTOMER

LOAN GUIDELINES

A/L Ratio	Number of Loans	Credit Rating	Loan Class

FIGURE 8-2c   **Example of the Hierarchic Model of Data**

bility, and credit rating data would be repeated in a customer descendent record for each loan record. In the relational model, the customer data would be stored only once (in the customer relation) regardless of the number of loans to this customer.

The operations usually associated with the hierarchic model are: (1) create instance (of a record), (2) delete instance, (3) update field within record, (4) retrieve next instance within same level, (5) retrieve next descendent record, and (6) retrieve parent record. Unlike the relational model, the structural information is specified in the operations (e.g., next, level, descendent, parent). For this reason, the hierarchic model is a "navigational" model because the operations help "navigate" through the data structures.

The constraints for the hierarchic model are the constraints on root and descendent records mentioned earlier. In addition, each instance of a record within a level is usually required to have a unique (key) field. Further, no record can be a descendent of more than one parent record (otherwise, the data structure would not be a strict hierarchy). The hierarchic model does not have the strong mathematical properties of the relational model. This may lead to undesirable properties of the model for deletion, insertion, and updating. For example, deleting a root deletes all descendents, and a descendent cannot be added without a root. In Figure 8-2c deleting a loan could delete all the customer data, and a new customer record cannot be added if there is no loan record. If a customer has several loans, updating the customer record requires that the entire data base be searched to change all instances of the customer record. Although it is possible to define hierarchical data structures or additional constraints to avoid some of these problems, in general the hierarchic model is not as well constrained as the relational model.

The Network Model

The network model is similar to, but more general than, the hierarchic model. As shown in Figure 8-2d, a network consists of sets of records and "links" among the records. The records are as in the hierarchic model, but the links are explicit (named) representations of relationships. Unlike the hierarchic model, a record can participate in several relationships. Comparing Figure 8-2c and d, we see that the network model has two main structural differences from the hierarchic model. First, some fields in the hierarchic model are replaced by relationships in the network model. For example, the rating field from the customer record in the hierarchic example is replaced by a relationship in the network example. Second, the relationships are explicit and may be two-way. Thus we have the "has loan" and "to customer" relationships, which make it possible to access both loan and customer data directly or via a relationship. In the hierarchic example, customer data can be accessed only via loan data.

The operations and constraints in the network model are very similar to those in the hierarchic model. The main differences are that the relation-

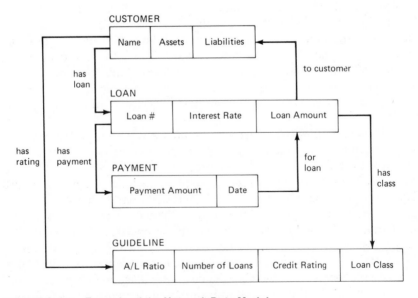

FIGURE 8-2d   Example of the Network Data Model

ships in the network model can be many-to-many (a weaker constraint than in the hierarchic model), and thus the operations generally support "navigation" (for add, insert, delete, update, and retrieve) through a two-way linked structure. The insert, delete, and update problems discussed for the hierarchic model may also occur in the network model, and the relationships (links) must be maintained for the data base to remain consistent. An additional problem is that any search (for update, retrieval, deletion, and addition) can start at several places, and thus there is additional complexity in specifying the operations.

The Rule Model

The fifth data model that has been used in DSS we call the rule model. This model is seldom used in traditional information systems, but is common in artificial intelligence systems, where the model is called production rules. The rule data model is most common in so-called "knowledge-based" DSS, where part of decision making involves making inferences based on the data. Not surprisingly, the rule model describes data using a set of rules. These rules may be considered as a set of data definitions, some of which may be conditional. In Figure 8-2e there are four sets of rules. The first set defines customers, the second defines loans, the third defines payments, and the fourth defines definitions for credit rating and loan class. All but the payment rules are conditional.

CUSTOMER RULES

Rule Pattern: if name = x, then assets = y, liabilities = z, etc.
    Example: if name = ABC, then assets = 100000, liabilities = 25000

LOAN RULES

Rule Pattern: if loan # = x, then cname = y, amount = z, etc.
    Example: if loan # = 123, then cname = ABC, amount = 102000

PAYMENT RULES

Rule Pattern: loan # = x, payment = y, date = z
    Example: loan # = 123, payment = 1089, date = 62581

GUIDELINE RULES

Rule Pattern: if A/L $\geq$ and # loans $\leq$ y, then credit rating = z and loan
            class = w
    Example: if A/L $\geq$ 2 and # loans $\leq$ 4, then credit rating = B and loan
            class = 2

FIGURE 8-2e   Example of the Rule Model of Data

Note the similarity between the rules in Figure 8-2e and the records in Figure 8-2a. In general, rules involving only equality ($=$) in their definitions are very similar in structure to the record model. For example, the customer rule and the customer record (Figure 8-2e and a) have the name field as the key (independent) field with assets, liabilities, and so on, as the dependent fields. For rules involving conditions, such as the guideline rules in Figure 8-2e, the correspondence to the record model is less specific. For data with complicated, computational relationships, the rule model is the most appropriate. For example, the data definition:

> if customer $=$ X and loan amount $=$ Y and (last payment date $-$ today's date) > 30 then payment $=$ payment $+ 10\%$ else payment $=$ payment $- 1\%$

can be represented in the other data models, but the conditional dependencies are implicit, rather than explicit as in the rule model.

Like the other models, the operations on the rule data model include: (1) create (a set of rules), (2) update, (3) delete, and (4) retrieve (select a rule). Operations that are unique to the rule model involve using the rules. The three most powerful of these "using" operations are *compute* (from rules), *deduce* (from rules), and *explain* (from rules). For the example in Figure 8-2e, a compute operation would be: *compute* credit rating for customer ABC. The DBMS for the rule system would determine that to compute credit rating, the definitional rules for assets, liabilities, and loans are needed, and that given a set of values (i.e., definitions), a credit rating rule (definition) can be selected from the guideline rules. Similarly, a *deduce* operation could determine the set of allowed credit ratings for a customer with a specific number of loans. An *explain* operation could list the rules that define why a customer has a specific credit rating.

The integrity constraints for the rule model generally restrict the set of rules so that (1) no data are defined twice, (2) the definitions are not circular (no data depend on themselves), and (3) the definitions are complete (there is a definition for all data in the data base).

Choosing a Data Model

The five examples in Figure 8-2a–e illustrate that there is a rough "equivalence" among the data base models in terms of what information can be represented in each. For a given set of data (objects) there is a representation in any of the five models. The differences among the models will be whether the relationships are explicit or implicit, what operations are possible given the representation, and what constraints are placed on the representation. In choosing a data model for a DSS, the choice thus should be based not so much on the representation of the data, but on the operations and integrity constraints.

A particular DSS, of course, can use more than one data model, and may impose restrictions on the data structures, operations, and constraints in addition to those that are inherent in the model. For example, a DSS might choose the hierarchic model, but restrict the data structures to binary trees with exactly two descendents for each record that has descendents. The most common variation on the data models for DSS will be in the operations, because a Specific DSS may require particular operations that are not part of the data model. For the example of Figure 8-2, an operation used in a decision on giving a loan might be to retrieve total loans by customer by year of due date. The aggregation operation (total by customer and by year of due date) might not be part of the data model (not provided by the DBMS), and therefore be provided by the DSS.

The choice of data model depends on the users, the decisions, and on the capabilities of the DBMS that could be used. In making the choice, the references shown in the following table may be useful:

DATA MODEL	GENERAL REFERENCE	DSS WHICH USES THIS MODEL
Record	Wiederhold [18]	SIMPLAN [13]
Relational	Date [7]	REGIS [10]
Hierarchic	Date [7]	AAIMS [11]
Network	Date [7]	GPLAN [9]
Rule	Shortliffe [16]	MYCIN [8]

DATA BASE MANAGEMENT SYSTEMS AND DSS

The data base model and a DBMS determine the data structures, operations, and integrity constraints that will be available to a DSS. A DBMS usually supports only one data model, and provides operations used to create, maintain, and access one or more data bases that conform to this model. The operations provided by a DBMS can be divided into the following categories: (1) dictionary, (2) creation, (3) deletion, (4) update, (5) query (retrieval), (6) views, (7) protection, (8) sharing, (9) recovery, and (10) optimization. In this section we summarize these operations. More detailed descriptions can be found in [4], [7], and [18]. The dictionary, creation, deletion, update, and query operations may be used by both DSS builders and DSS users. The other operations are used primarily by the builders or toolsmiths.

The *dictionary* operations are used to catalog the data in the data base. Like a library's card catalog, the data base dictionary supports adding new entries, deleting entries, retrieving information on the entries, and maintaining multiple indices (e.g., data name, date created, responsible organization). Figure 8-3a shows a dictionary for the example of Figure 8-2, assuming the relational model (Figure 8-2b). The dictionary operations are most useful when they are integrated with the other functions. For example, deleting an item from the dictionary should result in deleting it from the data base.

The *creation* and *deletion* operations support addition and subtraction of objects in the data base. The data base model defines what type of creation and deletion operations are permitted, although a DBMS may not strictly adhere to the definition. Figure 8-3b shows a (relational) creation operation for a loan record and Figure 8-3c shows a deletion operation.

The *update* operations permit values to be replaced in the data base. Such operations obviously are important for data accuracy and timeliness. Figure 8-3d shows a loan payment update operation.

The *query* operations actually form the basis for the creation, deletion, and update operations, and these operations often are included in the definition of a query language. The query language supported by a data model is one of the important differences among models; the query operations of a particular DBMS are usually what distinguish it most from other DBMS. Figure 8-3e gives simple relational queries against the data base from Figure 8-2b. Queries are used to select and manipulate records and fields from the data base. In the final section of this chapter we describe in more detail the

FIELD NAME	INTEGER RELATION	NUMBER OF VALUES	DOMAINS
Name	Customer	14	character
Name	Loan	400	character
Assets	Customer	14	integer
Liabilities	Customer	14	integer
Credit Rating	Customer	14	character
Credit Rating	Guidelines	8	character
Loan #	Loan	400	integer
Loan #	Payment	3000	integer
Interest Rate	Loan	410	percent
Loan Amount	Loan	400	dollars
Loan Class	Loan	5	integer
Loan Class	Guidelines	12	integer
Payment Amount	Payment	400	dollars
Date	Payment	365	date
A/L Ratio	Guidelines	10	decimal
Number of Loans	Guidelines	18	integer

FIGURE 8-3a   Example of a Data Dictionary

Create Loan where Loan # = 456,
Name = WDQ, Interest Rate = 13.00,
Amount = 50000, Class = 3

FIGURE 8-3b   Example of a Create Operation

Delete Loan where Loan # = 456

FIGURE 8-3c   Example of a Delete Operation

Update Payment where Loan # = 456,
Payment = 2961, Date = 62581
Set Payment = 2916

FIGURE 8-3d   Example of an Update Operation

(1) Select Loan #, Name, Amount from Loan where Loan Class = 2

(2) Select Loan #, Name, Amount from Loan where Loan Class =
Select Loan Class from Guidelines where Credit Rating = B

(3) Select Amount from Loan where Name = Select Name from Customer where Name = ABC, Order by Name, Sum Amount by Name

FIGURE 8-3e   Examples of Query Operations

```
DEFINE View Carlson ___View as
   Select Name, Assets, Liabilities
   from Customer
```

FIGURE 8-3f   Example of a View Operation

use of query operations in a DSS, and illustrate query operations which are useful for DSS, but are beyond those provided by most DBMS.

View operations determine if a user is allowed to access customized data structures (data bases, records, or fields). A view customizes a data base by defining a subset, aggregation, or other combination. A view is never stored in the data base and thus is only part of the external or conceptual data model. Views are often implemented using the query language. That is, a view can be defined as a query that is always prefixed to every other query using that view. Figure 8-3f defines a view of the customer relation that does not contain the credit rating. Hence anyone using the view could not access credit rating.

A DBMS will offer a variety of *protection* operations. The most common is some form of usage authorization. Password schemes are used to check whether a particular user (person and/or program) is allowed to access the data base. Access control may be used to restrict usage of other DBMS operations. That is, a user may be authorized to retrieve from but not update a data base. Access control may be at the data base, group of records, record, group of fields, field, or field value level. That is, a user may be able to retrieve any customer data (data base level) but may not be able to update a credit rating with a value greater than 2 (field value level). Other protection operations may include checking data for consistency or accuracy (validation), and checking data against standards. Figure 8-3g shows a simple protection scheme for our sample customer data base.

The *sharing* operations of a DBMS determine how many users can access the data base simultaneously. A DBMS may permit no sharing, or sharing at the data base, record, or field levels. If sharing is allowed, then the DBMS should also provide locking functions to prevent users from accessing inconsistent data and preventing "deadlock" (preventing each other from proceeding). System R, a relational DBMS, defines three levels of locking [1]. Level 1 locking allows one to retrieve (but not update) data that is currently being updated by another user. Level 2 locking does not allow access to a record unless no other user is updating that record. This assures any user that the current value is "the latest value." Level 3 locking ensures that every retrieval of a record during a user-defined transaction (period of

USER	RELATION	ACCESS
Carlson	Customer	Read (Carlson - view)
Carlson	Loan	Read
Carlson	Payments	None
Carlson	Guidelines	None
Sprague	Customer	Read, Write
Sprague	Loan	Read, Write
Sprague	Payments	Read
Sprague	Guidelines	Read
Thompson	Customer	Read, Write, Delete
Thompson	Loan	Read, Write, Delete
Thompson	Payments	Read, Write
Thompson	Guidelines	Read, Write

FIGURE 8-3g   Example of an Access (Protection) Scheme

the lock) yields the same values (i.e., no other user can update the record during the transaction).

Recovery operations are used to provide the ability to restore the data base to a consistent state after either a hardware (disk) failure or after a software (program) failure. To be able to recover, the DBMS must checkpoint (save) the data base and must log (journal) changes between checkpoints on a separate file (usually tape). In the case of a failure, the data base can be recovered by applying the sequence of operations in the log (create, update, and delete) to the most recent checkpoint.

The final category of operations is *optimization*, which is really an internal DBMS operation that can be applied to other operations. These operations are used to increase the performance of other operations. Automatic file reorganization based on usage statistics, access path optimization, and operation batching are three optimizations. File reorganization involves changing the physical arrangement of records on the disk, and possibly changing the structure of the data base. To permit these reorganizations, the programs that use the data base should not depend on the data structure. This data independence is one reason for the separation of the external, conceptual, and internal models of data. Access path optimization involves choosing the order in which records are selected (from the disk) and minimizing the number of records that have to be searched. Operation batching involves combining sets of operations (queries and updates) that access a common data base. Other optimizations include precompilation of queries/updates, storing frequently used operations and results, and maintaining indices that can be used to improve access times [1].

The key characteristics of a DBMS for use in a DSS include the operations provided, the costs, and the suitability of the data model for the DSS. In this section we have summarized the operations generally provided by DBMS. The costs include the costs of obtaining the DBMS plus the costs of using it (programming and operation). The suitability of the data model can be determined by identifying the data base requirements, which are discussed in the next section. Specific examples of the use of data base management systems in DSS can be found in [2] and [14].

DATA BASE REQUIREMENTS FOR DSS

To understand the data base requirements for DSS, we can draw on studies/theories of decision making in general, and on studies of existing DSS. The former source of requirements is more normative (what should be), whereas the second source is more descriptive (what is and has been). Because of the differences among theories of decision making (e.g., bounded rationally versus optimization), because of differences in requirements among DSS, and because our understanding of decision making and of DSS is limited and still growing, a comprehensive list of data base requirements for DSS is not possible. We can indicate requirements that seem to be common to more than one DSS or common to more than one study/theory of decision making. However, we do not claim that this is an exhaustive list.

Support for Memories.   As discussed in Chapter 4, we can expect a DSS to require data base support for four kinds of memory aids: workspaces for intermediate results, libraries for saving workspaces, links (indices) among data, and triggers to remind decision makers of operations to be performed or of data that should be considered.

Data Reduction.   Almost every study of decision making and DSS indicates that decision making involves reducing/abstracting from large amounts of data. Data reduction involves subsetting, combination, and aggregation of records and fields in a data base.

Varying Levels of Detail.   Although data reduction is common, this requirement does not imply that all data should be aggregates. Often an aggregate value will cause the decision maker to want to examine the detailed data that were used to create the aggregate (e.g., "Why is this budget item so high?").

Varying Amounts of Data.   As indicated in the case studies of GADS, the amount of data used during decision making varies over time [3]. The amounts also vary among decisions and decision makers. An important finding is that large volumes of data are potentially relevant to a decision, but only small volumes are actually used during decision making (see Figure 8-4).

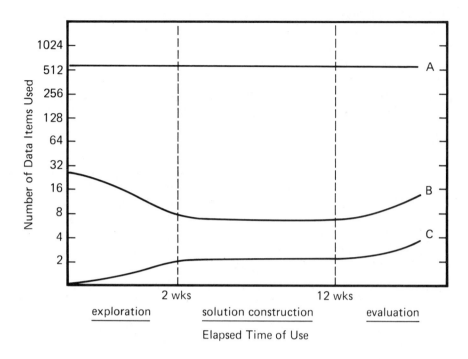

Curve A : Total data available
Curve B : Average amount of data used per session
Curve C : Average amount of data used consistantly
in consecutive sessions

FIGURE 8-4   Data Usage Patterns from GADS Case Studies [3]

Multiple Sources. The data used in decision making are likely to come from both external and internal sources, and even the internal data may come from different parts of an organization. The more "planning oriented" the decision, the more varied the sources of data.

Catalog of Sources. Because a variety of sources are used, and because part of decision making is "intelligence" gathering, a catalog of data sources is a valuable aid which a DSS can provide.

Wide Time Frame. Usually, DSS are intended to help solve a problem which requires looking at data from the past and projecting data for the future. The traditional use of computers generally involves data from only two time frames: the previous data (old master file) and the current data (transactions to produce new master file). For DSS, several "old master files" and alternative projections of "new master files" are likely to be needed.

Public and Private Data Bases. Many decisions involve sharing of data, either among decision makers or among operational and DSS applications (i.e., DSS use data maintained by other applications). However, many decision makers also want to base decisions on "their way of looking at things," and many decisions require that data be protected from use by others.

Varying Degrees of Accuracy. Because aggregate data are often used in decision making, absolute accuracy may not be required. That is, if two aggregates differ by 50 percent, a 1 percent error in each is not likely to affect a decision based on the two values. However, if decision makers discover errors in the data base, their level of confidence in the DSS may be reduced, and they may spend most of their time looking for additional errors or correcting errors rather than making decisions. The most recent data also may not be required, especially in DSS where decisions are based on time series data which cover several years.

Set Operations. Decision making often involves operations on sets such as time series data or sets of event records.

Random Access. Decision makers generally do not proceed through a set of data in a sequential or other predetermined order. Rather, insights or questions based on one set of data tend to lead to the desire to access data that the decision maker did not expect to need or data that are not related to the data currently being used in terms of storage location or access keys.

Support for Relationships and Views. Decision-making insights often come from looking at data in new ways (views) or from establishing relationships among data.

Performance. The key aspect of data base performance for DSS is its impact on response times. However, good response times are relative to the time frame of the decision and the time constraints and expectations of the decision makers. The increasing popularity of interactive DSS indicates that data base performance is likely to become an important requirement.

Interface to Other DSS Components. Because data base management is only one component of a DSS, it will need to be integrated with the dialog and model management components. Such an interface will always be possible. The questions are: How long will it take and how much will it cost?

End-User Interface. Because DSS users will tend to have low programming skills, the data base management component of the DSS should interface to the user at the external level rather than at the internal level. That is, the DSS user should be free from having to know details of how data are stored and how operations on the data base are implemented.

This (possibly incomplete) list of requirements indicates why the relational model of data and relational DBMS are increasingly popular for use in DSS. The relational approach is generally claimed to have five main advantages [15]: ease of understanding, set operations, increased independence of data programs, theoretical foundation for operation and integrity constraints, and close coupling between data base and data dictionary. Each of these advantages corresponds to one or more data base requirements for DSS. In spite of these assertions, studies comparing relational and other data models and their affiliated DBMS have not verified the five claimed advantages of the relational approach. There are still many data base experts who, while acknowledging the importance of the relational approach, argue convincingly in favor of one of the other approaches in terms of ease of use, power of the operations and data structures, or performance. There certainly have been successful DSS which did not use a relational data base.

A DESIGN FOR THE DATA BASE COMPONENT OF DSS

In this section we build on the discussion of data models, DBMS, and data base requirements for DSS to propose a design for the data base component of DSS. The proposal is best characterized as a two-level data base connected by a data extraction component. This approach has been used successfully in many existing DSS, so we believe it is justified both in theory and in practice. An overview of the design is shown in Figure 8-5 and more details are given in Figure 8-6. We will call this the data extraction design, because of the key role data extraction plays in interfacing the two levels of the DSS data base and because the approach does not depend on any particular data model.

Data Extraction Approach

The data extraction design is based on the premise that neither a large integrated data base nor an isolated, special-purpose data base will support the data base requirements for DSS. With a special-purpose data base, if the users want different data or more details, new computer programs are required and a significant delay in decision making is incurred. A special-purpose subset, derived from a source data base maintained as part of the

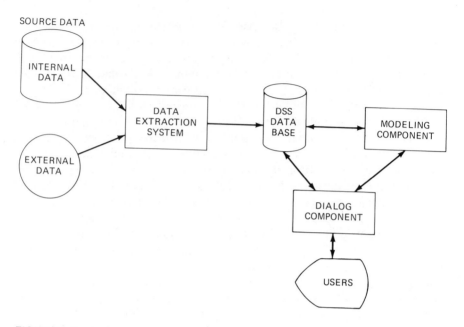

FIGURE 8-5 An Overview of Data Extraction

normal operations of an organization, is difficult to change and the data structures are different from those used in the source data base. In most organizations the source data base will contain a variety of file structures and access methods. If this is the case, a special-purpose data base must be interfaced with the relevant files, or these files must be converted to the data formats required by the DSS. Adding new files or changing the formats of existing files in the source data base then requires reprogramming of the DSS or conversion programs.

Using a single, "integrated" data base management system to support DSS may reduce the interfacing, conversion, and reprogramming efforts, but will add processing and data storage overhead which degrades the performance of DSS. In addition, the variety of data sources for DSS usually precludes a single integrated data base.

Data extraction is a technique for interfacing a variety of source data bases with a DSS data base. The technique involves aggregating and subsetting from source data bases to form an extracted data base which is used by the modeling and dialog components of the DSS. The CODASYL Systems Committee identified a data extraction capability in many DBMS [4]. This capability is essentially report generation and includes functions for using selected subsets from one or more files to generate reports or new files. The data extraction design for DSS extends the CODASYL concept to a two-level data management scheme which combines source data base management functions such as maintenance and protection with interactive functions for exploring and analyzing subsets of the source data base and for generating data bases for use by the DSS dialog and modeling components. Data extraction is a data base design for DSS and not an access method, file organization, or data model. The design can utilize an existing DBMS or can be built as a special-purpose system. Data extraction can be used on large or small machines, or in computer networks.

Data Extraction Design

There are alternative configurations which would be functionally equivalent to that depicted in Figure 8-6. For example, there might be several source data base management systems and data bases. The extracted data base, its directory, and associated extracted data base management functions could be on a different computing system than the one supporting the large data base.

The source data base is large with respect to the data used by the DSS, where "large" may mean millions or billions of bytes. The source data base will cover several logical files often with different formats, and possibly stored on different media or separate computer systems. For example, a source data base might include files for inventory, accounts receivable, personnel, and parts and suppliers. The files may be maintained as part of the normal operations of the organizations, or they may result from special collections such as market surveys.

The DBMS for the source data base and its associated directory and indices are the first components of the data extraction design. These components may be the same as those used to create and maintain the source data base. Because DBMS often require large amounts of space and time overhead, many organizations use a set of special-purpose software instead. Thus the source data base is maintained with one or more DBMS. For extremely large data bases, such as national statistics, the combination of data management and file management proposed by Sibley and Rabenseifer [17] may be required to provide a single interface to on-line and off-line files.

Four sets of data extraction operations directly interface with the user: (1) data description, (2) subsetting, (3) aggregation, and (4) presentation. *Data description* operations are used to describe files in the source data base. Obviously, the data description operations should be sufficient to describe all file organizations supported in the large data base. Examples of data description languages are given in [4] and may use the data dictionary functions of a DBMS. Different descriptions may be needed for the same file in order to provide different views of the file. The same description may be used for separate files; for example, grandfather, father, son files in a batch transaction processing system would have the same description. Because

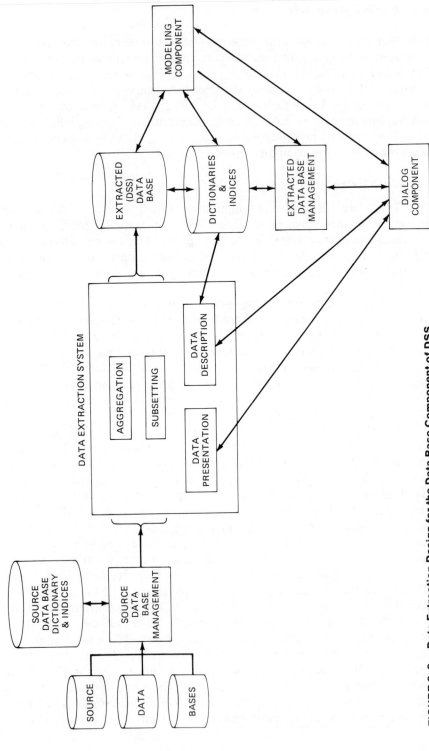

FIGURE 8-6   Data Extraction Design for the Data Base Component of DSS

data descriptions will be used frequently and because not all users will want to do data descriptions, the descriptions need to be retainable in the source data base dictionary. If descriptions can be saved and displayed, they will provide a user's directory to the source data base.

For the user, the data subsetting and aggregation operations will be most important. With these operations, users can select subsets of the source data base, compute new data items using the subsets, and store subsets or new data in an extracted data base. The *subsetting* operations should permit any arithmetic and logical criteria to be used to select fields or records from the source data base. The *aggregation* operations should permit fields or records to be summed, counted, joined, or combined in any arithmetic manner. The basis for aggregation may be common data attributes (e.g., count all items sold in the toy department) or functions of one or more attributes (e.g., count all persons who live within 5 miles of a proposed shopping center site). The aggregation operations may become laborious. For example, aggregating crimes by police districts will require a function that maps addresses into reporting districts. Aggregation may require user or system decisions about compatibility of data. For example, if two divisions have different personnel classification schemes, how does one compute total female employees by level in the corporation? Finally, aggregation may lead to the need for the inverse operation, dissaggregation.

Because of the variety of files and formats likely to be found in source data bases, conversion is an essential part of both aggregating and subsetting operations. Conversion includes both format conversions as well as data-type conversions. Usually, data from the source data base will need to be converted to match the limited set of data types and formats provided by the aggregating and subsetting languages. A second set of conversions often is required to store the data in the extracted data base, or to display selected subsets or aggregations on a display screen. Thus the efficiency of extraction depends heavily on the efficiency of the conversion operations. Extending the semantics of the aggregation and subsetting languages to handle operations on many data types may reduce the number of conversions, but will increase the size of the extraction system code. Restricting the data model of the DSS will also reduce the number of conversions, but will make the extraction system less general.

The aggregation and subsetting operations are used to produce an extracted data base for use by the DSS. Because aggregation and subsetting requests are likely to be repeated with few or no modifications, a library of aggregation and subsetting operations is useful. Users often will want to view the results of aggregation and subsetting operations without forming an extracted data base. Thus *data presentation* operations are a valuable part of data extraction. The dialog component of the DSS should be used to provide the data presentation operations for data extraction.

The extracted data base, and its associated indices and data management system, support the DSS. Many existing DSS operate with some sort of extracted data base [2]. The data structures for the extracted data base are tailored to the requirements of the DSS. If separate indices and data management are provided, they are used to improve performance and to increase the flexibility of the extracted data base. For example, direct access to the data by name may be provided. On the other hand, in many DSS the data management operations may be very limited and will not be programmed as a separate module. The exact requirements for performance and flexibility will depend on the DSS. It is possible that a subset or well-designed configuration of the large data base management system can be used for extracted data base management.

Advantages

With data extraction, the files in the source data base can be organized for efficient data entry, update, processing, output, or protection, without additional indices or data to support the DSS. Thus the source DBMS is used for those functions for which it is best suited. The additional indices and data required for the DSS are built during extraction and stored with the extracted data base, and thus do not degrade performance of the source data base management functions. Similarly, the data structures for the DSS can be designed to support efficient data analysis and presentation.

Data extraction reduces the major performance constraints of DSS—I/O times and reprogramming delays. As shown in Figure 8-7, for a fixed access time ratio between the source and extracted data bases, the smaller the number of accesses to the large data base, the better the average overall I/O time. Remember that the access time ratios depend not only on the properties of the storage devices, but also on the efficiencies of the data base management systems. Because the extracted data base will be smaller than the source data base with better indices and more efficient data management, and possibly stored in faster memory, access time ratios on the order of 1000:1 are realistic. By subsetting and aggregating the data relevant to problem solving, extraction reduces the fraction of the accesses to the source data base. Data extraction will also reduce reprogamming delays because there is less programming and faster turnaround each time a user wants different data or different levels of detail. In most organizations these savings in I/O and reprogramming times will result in reduced costs of operating the DSS, and in reduced personnel costs in using and maintaining the DSS.

The computation times of the DSS may also be reduced. If no extracted data base is used, every aggregation and subsetting will have to be done dynamically. With extraction, an aggregation or subsetting operation need be done only once. An extracted data base can be tailored for the DSS, and this may also reduce processing costs.

Let

$$t_S \quad = \quad \text{average access time to source data base}$$
$$t_E \quad = \quad \text{average access time to extracted data base}$$
$$f_S \quad = \quad \text{fraction of accesses to source data base}$$
$$f_E \quad = \quad \text{fraction of accesses to extracted data base}$$
$$\quad = \quad 1 - f_S$$
$$r \quad = \quad t_S / t_E$$
$$t_A \quad = \quad \text{average access time using source and extracted data base}$$
$$t_A \quad = \quad f_E t_E + f_S t_S$$
$$\quad = \quad (1 - f_S) t_E + f_S r t_E$$
$$\quad = \quad t_E (1 + f_S r - f_S)$$

if $\quad r \quad = \quad 1000 \left[\text{e.g.} \quad \dfrac{10^{-2}\text{secs}}{10^{-5}\text{secs}} \right]$

then if

$$f_S \quad = \quad 1/1000$$
$$t_A \quad = \quad 2t_E$$

if $\quad f_S \quad = \quad 1/10000$
$$t_A \quad = \quad 1.1t_E$$

if $\quad f_S \quad = \quad 1$
$$t_A \quad = \quad t_S$$

if $\quad f_S \quad = \quad 0$
$$t_A \quad = \quad t_E$$

FIGURE 8-7   Extracted Data Base Access Time Analysis

Data extraction combines the power of a DBMS (e.g., query, protection, backup) with the performance of the tailored, extracted data base. More important, it reflects the following data management requirements of DSS: data reduction, varying levels of detail, varying amounts of data, multiple sources, catalog of sources, public and private data, performance, interface to other DSS components, and end-user interface.

DSS using data extraction can be implemented on a variety of computing configurations. On a small computer, data definition, aggregation, and subsetting can be a separate system which produces the extracted data base for the DSS. Source data base maintenance, extracted data base creation, and the DSS would operate separately, possibly on a scheduled basis. On large or virtual memory machines, the components of data extraction would time-share the resources. In distributed computing systems the extracted data base would be stored in a local system, and the source data base would reside in the host or "shared-file" system.

If data extraction operations can produce multiple extracted data bases, with different structures, a single data extraction interface can support multiple DSS. In addition, existing DSS can be supported and enhanced by data extraction without major program or data structure revisions.

Disadvantages

If one disagrees with the data base requirements for DSS stated previously, one can identify several disadvantages of the data extraction design. For example, if varying levels of detail and data from several files are not required, data extraction may result in unnecessary file processing and data storage. If one accepts the design criteria, there are at least three possible disadvantages of data extraction. First, it may result in duplicating data from the source data base in the extracted data base, which leads to a problem of consistency between the two copies. Second, there may be some duplication of functions in the two data management components. Third, the extracted data will be current but not real time.

Given the decreasing costs of storage and the increasing costs of programmer and user time, the duplication disadvantages seem outweighed by the operational and functional advantages. Duplicate data management functions often can be avoided by using a single, reentrant program module. Few DSS have a requirement for real time data. In fact, some DSS users prefer not to use real time data in order to keep the problem description (i.e., the extracted data base) focused on a static time frame.

DATA BASE QUERY AND DSS

With the data extraction design for DSS, there is a dual role for data base query. Both of these roles are different from the usual role of query in DBMS. The first role is in the extraction system. In this role, the query functions are used not to produce reports or displays on a terminal, but to produce the extracted data base. The second role of query is as part of the DSS. In this role, the query operations are invoked by the dialog component to produce reports or on-line displays. However, the query is only part of any dialog and it must be integrated with the other operations invoked via the dialog. This integration can be accomplished by using the input-in-context dialog style (Chapter 7) and by realizing that there are a variety of possible syntactic forms for query languages, many of them graphical. In this section we discuss these two expanded roles of data base query in DSS.

Data Base Query for Extraction

The users of query functions for data extraction will probably be specialists (e.g., data base administrator or the DSS Builder) or experienced DSS users. The need for trained users is because of the complexity of the extraction task and the need to understand the structure of the source data base. Because we are assuming experienced users, the emphasis in the design of the query language for use in extraction should be functionality.

A general form for extraction queries as proposed in [12] is:

EXTRACT (name) = (query) WITH RESPECT TO (reference) USING (function)

where

> 'name' is the name to be given the extracted data;
> 'query' is the selection rule—an arithmetic or boolean combination of data in the source data base—used to develop the extracted data of the given 'name';
> 'reference' is the index giving membership classes for the extracted data base (e.g., polygon map, chart of accounts, or organizational directory);
> 'function' is a predefined and stored operation which specifies an aggregation, grouping, or matching to be used in forming the extracted data. Examples of functions include: geocoding, which determines the zone or polygon containing the site of events, and table lookup in a chart of accounts to determine to which expense category an expenditure belongs.

An example of the general form is:

EXTRACT(BURGLARIES) = (SELECT FROM CRIME FILE WHERE CRIMECODE = 45) WITH RESPECT TO (SAN JOSE MAP1) USING (COUNT-IN-POLYGON)

The query operations in this general form are the standard query operations of a DBMS. The extensions are the reference and function operations, which are related in that the functions are used to compute data with respect to a reference. The references and functions are likely to be DSS dependent. Two function operations of general use are COUNT and SUM.

The results of extraction operations are stored in the extracted data base and the names of extracted data are added to the dictionary for the extracted data base. Because the source data base may be large, extraction can be an expensive process. To help reduce the costs, the query language for extraction should contain the following additional operations:

1. *A sampling operation*: provides various sampling alternatives (e.g., random, blocked, sequential) for selecting records from source data base

2. *A monitor operation:* allows the user to monitor the extraction process
3. *An interrupt operation:* allows the user to stop an extraction (with appropriate recovery)
4. *A preview operation:* allows the user to see a preview list of the extraction inputs and outputs before proceeding with the full extraction

If the DBMS being used provides optimization, it will be especially useful for data extraction.

Query Languages as Part of DSS

The use of query in making a decision spans all phases of the decision-making process, although it appears that query is used more heavily during intelligence and choice phases, and used least during design. Ease of use and performance (response time) are the key goals in providing query operations for use in part of a DSS. The query operations required are likely to be a subset of those provided by most DBMS. Selection of a subset will be the most used operation.

The important observation about query as part of a DSS is that queries usually arise after data are presented to a user. That is, the need to use query operations arises after the results of another function (possibly another query) are presented to the user. Thus queries should be able to be specified in the context of DSS outputs. After seeing a display of customer assets and liabilities, the user should be able to formulate queries about customer detailed financial information without having to switch contexts (e.g., without having to proceed through a long series of additional displays designed to "help" formulate a query).

Because of the importance of "query in context" and of the importance of ease of use, we suggest that the syntax for a query language as part of a DSS be as "graphical" as possible. By "graphical" we mean that the users can specify queries by pointing or drawing rather than by typing, and that the position of query symbols be meaningful. QBE [19] is an example of a stand-alone query language with a positional syntax. The user enters queries in appropriate columns of two-dimensional templates for the data tables to which the query applies. With a pointing device, such as light pen or joystick-controlled cursor, queries can be even more graphical and more positional than in QBE. For example, the user could select a set of customers for which financial detail data are desired by pointing at a customer's name in a displayed list of customers, or a user could select the data attributes to be displayed by pointing at column names in a template of the data structure containing those attributes. Contrast the simplicity of these "queries" with having to type queries such as:

SELECT ACCOUNTS RECEIVABLE, CASH ON HAND, ACCOUNTS PAYABLE, SHORT-TERM LOANS FROM CUSTOMER FINANCIAL DATA WHERE CUSTOMER = IBM, NCR, DEC, TANDEM, XEROX, APPLE.

The contrast is even greater when a conventional query is compared to specifying a selection of customers by circling a section of a scatterplot of asset/liability ratios.

SUMMARY

In this chapter we provided an overview of data models and data base management systems because data base management is both a prerequisite and an ingredient for building a DSS. We then summarized data base requirements for DSS, and described the data extraction design for the DSS data base component as an approach which matched the requirements. Finally, we showed how data base query can be used in data extraction and how query operations can be used in DSS dialog.

The data base component of DSS provides for the memory requirements in decision support. The data extraction design allows the data base component for a Specific DSS to be tailored to these requirements, while retaining the generality, power, and flexibility of a DBMS for the source data. A DSS Generator therefore must interface with at least one DBMS for managing the source data. For the DSS data base management, a special-purpose DBMS may be developed for the DSS Generator, or an existing DBMS may be modified.

QUESTIONS AND PROBLEMS

REVIEW QUESTIONS

1. Why is data base management important in building a DSS?
2. Compare the record, relational, hierarchical, network, and rule models of data.
3. What is a data base management system? How can such systems be used in building a DSS?
4. What are the data base requirements for DSS? Why are these requirements important?
5. What is a two-level data base management design? Why is it appropriate for DSS?
6. What is data extraction?
7. Describe two roles for a query language in building a DSS.

DISCUSSION QUESTION

1. Should DSS have their own data base and data base management system, or should they be integrated (embedded) within the source data base and DBMS that manages it?

EXERCISES

1. Pick a set of data with which you are familiar. Organize it using the five data models described in this chapter. Which model do you think is most appropriate for use in a DSS requiring these data? Why?
2. Pick a DBMS, obtain documentation on it, and describe the operations it provides.
3. Design a data base for a DSS of your choosing.

REFERENCES

1. BLASGEN, M. W., et al. "System/R: An Architectural Overview," *IBM Systems Journal*, Vol. 20, No. 1, 1981, pp. 41–62.
2. CARLSON, E. D. (ed.). "Proceedings of a Conference on Decision Support Systems" *Data Base*, Vol. 8, No. 3, Winter 1977.
3. CARLSON, E. D., et al. "Observations on End-User Requirements for Interactive Problem-Solving," *Management Information Systems Quarterly*, Vol. 1, No. 1, March 1977, pp. 51–63.
4. CODASYL Systems Committee. *A Survey of Generalized Data Base Management Systems*, Association for Computing Machinery, New York, 1969.
5. CODD, E. F. "A Relational Model for Large Shared Data Banks," *Communications of the ACM*, Vol. 13, No. 6, June 1970, pp. 377–387.
6. CODD, E. F. "Data Models in Data Base Management," *Proceedings of the Workshop on Data Abstraction Data Bases, and Conceptual Modeling*, ACM Order Number 474800, 1980, pp. 112–114.
7. DATE, C. J. *An Introduction to Data Base Systems*, 2nd ed., Addison-Wesley Publishing Company, Inc., Reading, Mass., 1977.
8. DAVIS, R. "A DSS for Diagnosis and Therapy," *Data Base*, Vol. 8, No. 3, Winter 1977, pp. 58–72.
9. HASEMAN, W. D. "GPLAN: An Operational DSS," *Data Base*, Vol. 8, No. 3, Winter 1977, pp. 73–78.
10. JOYCE, J. D., and N. N. Oliver. "Impacts of a Relational Information System in Industrial Decisions," *Data Base*, Vol. 8, No. 3, Winter 1977, pp. 15–21.
11. KLAAS, R. L. "A DSS for Airline Management," *Data Base*, Vol. 8, No. 3, Winter 1977, pp. 3–8.

12. MANTEY, P. E., and E. D. CARLSON. "Integrated Geographic Data Bases: The GADS Experience," *Data Base Technique for Pictorial Application*, Lecture Notes in Computer Science 81, Springer-Verlag, New York, 1980, pp. 173–198.
13. MAYO, R. B. *Corporate Planning and Modeling with SIMPLAN*, Addison-Wesley Publishing Company, Inc., Reading, Mass., 1979.
14. METHLIE, L. B. "Data Management for Decision Support Systems," *Data Base*, Vol. 12, Nos. 1-2, Fall 1980, pp. 40–46.
15. SANDBERG, G. "A Primer on Relational Data Base Concepts," *IBM Systems Journal*, Vol. 20, No. 1, 1981, pp. 23–40.
16. SHORTLIFFE, E. H. *Computer Based Medical Consultation: MYCIN*, American Elsevier Publishing Company, Inc., New York, 1976.
17. SIBLEY, E. H., and R. RABENSEIFER. "Extremely Large Data Systems for National Statistics," *Information Processing 74*, North-Holland Publishing Company, Amsterdam, 1974, pp. 1072–1074.
18. WIEDERHOLD, G. *Data Base Design*, McGraw Hill Book Company, New York, 1977.
19. ZLOOF, M. M. "Query By Example," *Proceedings of the National Computer Conference 1975*, AFIPS Press, Montvale, N.J., 1975, pp. 431–437.

CHAPTER NINE

MODEL MANAGEMENT IN DSS

OUTLINE

INTRODUCTION

This chapter explores the modeling component as one of the three major sets of capabilities needed to build DSS. After reiterating the importance of modeling in DSS, we look at the traditional use of models and the problems that have limited model usage in the past. Responding to the needs and problems, the second section summarizes the requirements for modeling in DSS. This section includes a list of what models must do for decision makers and suggests what it means to have a model base and a model base management system. An example of a DSS with a strong modeling component for commercial banks illustrates these concepts and relationships. The third section presents three techniques for storing and handling models in computer form, and the last section is a suggested design approach for providing the modeling capability in DSS.

IMPORTANCE OF MODELING IN DSS

The dialog component supports the use of the system by decision makers, and the data component provides access to the raw material for decision making. It is the modeling component that gives decision makers the ability to analyze the problem fully by developing and comparing alternative solutions. In fact, it is the integration of models into the information system that moves an MIS which is based on integrated reporting and data base/data communication approaches into a full decision support system.

To explore this point further, consider the technology of the data base approach, which seems to characterize much of the current research and development in computer science. Data base technology is primarily concerned with:

1. Managing a large amount of data in physical storage
2. Providing a variety of logical data structures which are independent from physical storage structures
3. Providing independence between data and application programs to reduce data redundance and to decrease program maintenance when system needs change
4. Providing access to data in a flexible (user-oriented) way, usually through a generalized report generator and information retrieval capabilities

Obviously, these capabilities are important to DSS as well as other types of information systems, and we spent all of Chapter 8 dealing with the technology and approaches for developing them. With only strong data capabilities, however, the decision maker is limited to browsing through the data, classifying and summarizing in various ways. These are basically descriptive operations that support primarily the intelligence phase of decision making.

In providing these capabilities the data base approach depends heavily on report generation and information query and retrieval. This dependence is based on the implicit assumption that if (1) a decision maker can gain access to the data to answer specific questions, or (2) the decision maker can define a report to suit the problem or satisfy information "needs," and (3) those answers or reports are available quickly, then the decision-making needs have been met and the decisions are obvious.

This philosophy reflects the accounting-oriented, structured reporting, information flow emphasis of much of MIS work. However, a system designed to improve management performance by supporting decision making must go further than just providing access to data in a quick and flexible way. It must provide a set of mechanisms for the use of decision/analysis models which draw on the data base and are closely integrated with it. It must also provide the dialog mechanisms for the decision maker to interact with the data *and models* in a convenient, supportive manner. In other words, we might say that the data base approach is *necessary*, but not *sufficient*, for decision support.

Traditional Use of Models

The argument for model usage may seem unnecessary in the face of strong modeling activities to support decision making in recent years. Since the development of operations research (OR) during World War II, and its subsequent application to business problems under the label "management science" (MS), modeling has indeed been a potent tool for decision-making and problem-solving assistance. Models have been applied primarily to well-structured problems, however. In fact, one of the definitions of modeling activity is the conversion of ill-structured problems into well-structured problems.

Computers have proven useful and valuable in modeling, primarily as large, fast calculators or "computational engines." In fact, the capabilities of computers have been mandatory for models that use large quantities of data or those that depend on many successive iterations (e.g., linear programming algorithms or simulation models). In spite of the use of computers as a computational aid, traditional models have generally been stand-alone analysis projects, not integrated within a larger information processing system. The view of traditional modeling efforts might be depicted as shown in Figure 9-1. The structure of the model is the center of attention. Input data are submitted to the model and output is delivered by the model to the user or model builder.

Problems with Traditional Modeling

Although modeling activities have been very useful in many areas, there is a general feeling that they have not lived up to their full potential. In

FIGURE 9-1   A Traditional View of Modeling

fact, there has been much discussion in the literature of the disuse, misuse, and nonuse of models by managers [5, 7]. Most reasons can be traced to the lack of a set of integrated models and an easy way to manage their use in the decision-making process. The lack of integration, in turn, stems in part from the common practice of separating management science and information systems activities [3, 9]. Specifically, model usage has suffered from the following problems.

- The necessary input data or parameters are often not available or are very difficult to generate. A common example is the inventory model based on the economic order quantity equation, which requires a coefficient for the cost of placing an order. Even with a good cost capture and accounting system, this number is quite difficult to ascertain.
- The output from the model is often difficult to use. The output from a model run on a computer is generally a computer printout. Even if it is in report form, it is usually static, hard to manipulate, and seldom in action-impelling form.
- For complex, multifaceted problems, large comprehensive models have proven difficult to build and maintain. The long development time and the major data gathering efforts they require make the process expensive and not responsive to changes in the situation they are designed to model. Common results are models that can only be used once, or problems that must be compromised to fit off-the-shelf models.
- Big, complex models are difficult for managers to understand, and therefore they are not trusted. Managers have resisted heavy reliance on large models for important decisions when they cannot assess the assumptions and do not understand the workings of the model.
- A growing response to some of these problems is to utilize a library of small models, such as those available on a time-sharing system. Typically, each model needs its own data in its own format, and each model helps in only one of the phases of decision making (intelligence, design, choice). It is left to the decision makers or problem solvers to integrate the modeling steps and activities as a mental or manual process.
- Generally, there is a minimum of interaction between the decision maker and the model. Even if the model is run in an interactive environment (e.g., timesharing), the interaction is usually limited to supplying the necessary data or parameter values, and selecting certain options for execution or output format.

For these and other reasons, the traditional process of building and running "stand-alone" models has had limited impact on decision making for underspecified tasks. There have, of course, been many attempts in recent years to neutralize some of the problems cited above. However, DSS make demands on the modeling component that go beyond even these enhancements to traditional modeling.

MODELING REQUIREMENTS FOR DSS

The kinds of problems DSS support, and the nature of DSS usage by decision makers, places a unique set of requirements on models and modeling activities. Our suggested design for the model component in DSS satisfies those special needs and neutralizes most of the problems discussed in the preceding section.

Task Requirements

Throughout the book we have referred to decision-making activities that DSS must support. In Chapter 2, and again in Chapter 4, we listed and described six overall objectives for DSS that derive from the nature of the tasks that decision makers face. The modeling component is the primary tool for supporting many of the activities that decision makers will perform in the process of making decisions and solving problems. The data component supports activities that are primarily in the intelligence phase. The modeling component supports activities that emphasize the design and choice phases. These activities include:

- Projection
- Deduction
- Analysis
- Creation of alternatives (suggestion)
- Comparison of alternatives
- Optimization
- Simulation

The design of the modeling component of DSS must allow users and decision makers to support these kinds of activities directly.

In general, support for the activities listed above will depend on feedback and interaction between the user and the modeling component which allows the examination of intermediate results, accommodation of subjective judgment during the problem-solving process, and modification of the "objective function" if the user's perception of the problem changes. Barbosa and Hirko [1] identify several capabilities required for use of modeling in DSS.

1. Interface
    a. The user should be able to work in the problem-solving environment without unnecessary distractions. The user should not have to interrupt

this process and laboriously supply some control parameters before continuing.

    b. The control parameters should be expressed in terms with which the user will be familiar. He or she should be able to think about only those parameters that have a direct bearing on the problem-solving process.

2. Control

    a. The user should be given a spectrum of control. If possible, the system should support manual operation as well as fully automatic operation. This permits the user to select the level of algorithmic operation that seems most suitable. It also enables the user to learn more easily by allowing him or her to proceed as slowly as desired.

    b. The control mechanism should allow the user to introduce subjective information as demanded by the problem solution process. It should not require the user to specify all constraints a priori. This direct human control of the solution process can make up for deficiencies in the algorithm and will often permit the system to contain a simpler algorithm, frequently resulting in a smaller information burden on the user.

3. Flexibility

    a. The algorithmic and manual operations should be interchangeable in the sense that the user can develop part of a solution via manual methods and then continue with the algorithm, or vice versa. This statement implies that the range of all operations should be contained in the domain of the operations; that is, the result of one operation can be used as input to any other operation. This way, operations can be cascaded in an arbitrary way. Both flexibility and control allow the user to construct a solution process that best suits the problem. This idea of interchangeability of operations is deceptively simple, but it has far-reaching implications. This is the manner by which flexibility and control are achieved. That is, an arbitrary solution process can be composed of a sequence of primitive subprocesses.

4. Feedback

    a. The system should provide sufficient feedback so that the user is fully cognizant of the state of the solution generation process at all times. This feedback is essential for supporting human control of the process.

    b. The design process itself should make use of feedback. Valuable information can be derived from introduction of the initial system or prototype to the users. Their feedback should be especially meaningful in the area of usability.

System Requirements

The design will also have to satisfy several system requirements in order to meet objectives of DSS usage. Specifically, the design will require:

- A model base and a set of software functions to manage it
- Integration of the modeling component with the dialog component
- Integration of the modeling component with the data component

Model Base. First, there will need to be a library of models which comprise a model base (analogous to a data base). The model base will consist of permanent models; ad hoc models; user-built and "canned" models; models for operational, tactical, and strategic decision support; and models to support a variety of tasks and analysis approaches. They will range in size from very small to very large, with some of the smaller ones acting as model "building blocks" to support the construction of other models.

The comprehensive set of integrated models for decision support becomes a major corporate resource, just as the data base is a resource. Like the data base, this "model base" also requires careful management. In fact, the parallels between these two resources and their management are quite pervasive. Before the advent of data base management software, data files were defined for a specific purpose and used only by one (or a few) computer programs. This approach led to data redundancy and self-contained data processing jobs. Later evolutionary developments led to broader subsystems and shared data files, but it was not until the development of Data Base Management Systems (DBMS) that the full potential of the data base could be realized. In a similar way, the model base will need to be stored, handled, and operated under control of a Model Base Management System (MBMS) analogous to a DBMS.

Model Base Management Functions. The analogy between Data Base Management Systems and Model Base Management Systems can be extended to the requisite functions that each must perform. The most important functions are those that will enable decision makers to utilize the model base fully for decision support. Four general functions that are extremely important are:

1. *Generation*: a flexible mechanism for building or generating models, perhaps through a type of model definition language.
2. *Restructure*: a way to redefine or restructure a model in response to changes in the modeled situation (e.g., a change in the basic form of the model).
3. *Update*: a procedure for updating a model in response to change in data (e.g., a revised parameter estimate without a change in structure).
4. *Report generation–inquiry*: operation of the model to obtain the decision support desired. Alternative forms may be:
   a. Periodic run of a well-established model
   b. Special results from an ad hoc model
   c. Use of data analysis models
   c. Iterative rerun of a model or set of models
   e. The sequential run of a set of interrelated models according to a predefined procedure

Integration with the Dialog Component. The model base and its management system must be integrated with the dialog directly, to give the user direct control over the operation, manipulation, and use of models. It is this link that gives the user the ability to do true interactive modeling, instead of just running a model in an interactive environment. The decision maker can interrupt the model, run model segments in a variety of sequences, change parameters, and even change objective functions in response to intermediate results if necessary. Later we present a more precise definition of interactive modeling, but it is clear that the modeling component must be closely integrated with the dialog component as well as the data component.

Integration with the Data Component.   Many of the problems with traditional modeling derive from the lack of integration between models and data. In contrast to Figure 9-1, which depicts each model as the center of attention receiving input and generating output, Figure 9-2 depicts a more modern view of models integrated with a data base. Each model draws inputs and parameter values from the data base and returns output to the data base. With this direct linkage, models can be updated as the data values are updated, and modified or restructured when the data have changed enough to require it. With model output returned to the data base, the dialog component can be used to examine and manipulate the output data (answers), using the full range of data formatting and display capabilities.

An Example

The nature of a model base and its management for use in DSS can be illustrated with an example of a DSS for a commercial bank [10].

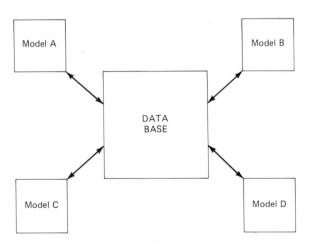

FIGURE 9-2   Integration of Models and Data

The Model Base. In our example, the commercial bank employs a strategic model for the long-range forecasting and evaluating of alternative plans of action. The model is aggregate and macro in focus, and econometric in nature. The major outputs are a 5- to 10-year forecast of demand deposits and the anticipated demand for loans. Loan demand is categorized into residential mortage loans, construction loans, installment loans, business loans, and so on. Inputs to the model are historical data on these variables from the bank's financial records, and forecasts of economic conditions in the market area in which the bank operates. The long-range planning model also includes management input for major plans and directional strategies the bank wishes to evaluate. For example, the introduction of a new major credit card service aimed at consumers is assessed in light of the model's forecast of retail consumption levels in the bank's marketing area. Figure 9-3 symbolically shows the flow of data between its sources, the decision support data base, and the strategic model.

At the tactical level, the bank utilizes a financial planning and control model to forecast the performance of the bank in terms of its balance sheet and income statement for the coming 12 months. This model is important in the month-to-month funds management decisions required of investment and loan officers, and serves as a control device by comparing actual against planned performance. The tactical model's basic variables are those found in the monthly balance sheet and income statement. It maintains a 24-month history data base in financial statement format, and projects 12 months forward using the same format. At the end of each month the new data are inserted in the data base and the oldest month's data are discarded. At that time, the model uses the updated historical data in regenerating the forecast for the coming 12 months. The model draws upon a linear programming subroutine which allocates funds across lending and investment categories

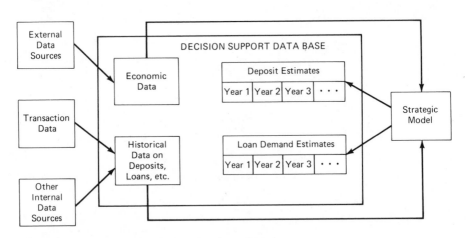

FIGURE 9-3   Data Flows for the Strategic Model

based on the tactical model's estimates of available funds. Recommendations are developed to maximize profitability within constraints on liquidity and capital adequacy set by regulatory agencies and bank management.* Figure 9-4 represents the data flows for the tactical model.

At the operational level there are many models that the bank can use to support short-range operational decisions. For example, a credit scoring model develops guidelines for the granting of consumer credit loans based on the characteristics and past records of borrowers [8]. The model analyzes past installment loans, both repaid and defaulted, and develops recommended guidelines for granting loans. When new loan applications are coded and submitted to the model, it generates recommended actions based on the guidelines.

A second example is a bond selection model that analyzes a portfolio and recommends the purchase or sale of bonds [2]. The inputs include the inventory of bonds currently held, a maturity schedule, similar data on other bonds available for inclusion in the portfolio, and other relevant data. Output is a list of recommended actions that result from the model's analysis. Figure 9-5 represents the data flow for the operational models.

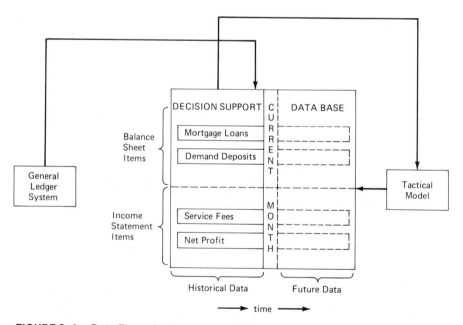

FIGURE 9-4   Data Flows for the Tactical Model

---

*For a further description of this tactical model and linear programming submodel, see [11, 12].

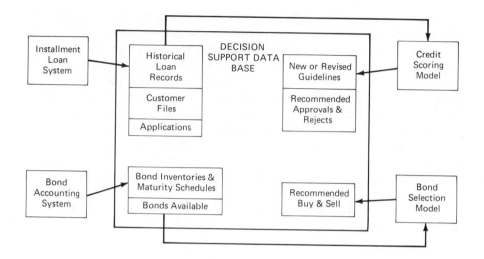

FIGURE 9-5   Data Flows for the Operational Model

Model Interfaces. These models need to be implemented in an integrated manner if the overall objectives of the bank are to be pursued effectively. If they are used autonomously or on an ad hoc basis, there is significant danger that they might actually work against each other. The result can be good decisions in narrowly defined areas, but conflicting or self-defeating decisions in a broader context.

The necessary integration and coordination of model usage is achieved largely through the data base. The importance of integration is evidenced by the need for data flow between the strategic and tactical models. For example, the strategic model's estimate of total deposit levels and loan demand levels for the coming year are necessary inputs to the tactical model. The forecast of total deposits is an annual figure that is converted to an estimate of monthly balances by a combination of time series analysis and seasonal adjustment procedures. The same basic concept holds for the loan demand estimates, which become constraints on the linear programming model for the allocation of available funds among the lending and investment alternatives.

Data may also flow from the tactical level to the strategic level if the linear programming analysis reveals an area of lending or investment that is particularly profitable. Top management can then use the strategic model to assess alternative strategies for pursuing that opportunity more aggressively.

Operational models also interface with the tactical model. In the case of the credit scoring model, the threshold level for loan approval must be based on the availability of funds for this purpose. If the tactical model is suggesting an extension of consumer lending, the credit scoring model must be adjusted to allow additional loans (and vice versa).

To avoid suboptimization, the bond selection model must also interact with the tactical model by accepting the level of available funds as an important input to the analysis. Expansion or contraction of available funds from the tactical model will significantly affect the bond analysis and selection. Moreover, the tactical model may recommend, for reasons of liquidity or capital adequacy, a shift from one type of bond to another. For example, the linear programming subroutine may suggest a shift from municipal bonds into U.S. government bonds. Data interfaces of this type significantly increase the comprehensiveness and scope of the model's use.

Data must also flow from the operational models into the tactical model. If the threshold level on the credit scoring model results in many potentially good loan customers being refused, it may signal a need to reconsider the maximum installment loan limit imposed by the tactical model. Similarly, the bond selection model might encounter bonds that are highly desirable, even though their purchase would exceed the recommended limit. This information should be available to the tactical model for reevaluation of the imposed limits.

In short, there must be a spectrum of models to serve the decision maker at the strategic, tactical, and operational levels. These models must work together to avoid suboptimization at any one level or in any one functional area. The mechanism for interfacing them is the system's design philosophy, which recognizes and plans for this interaction, and a carefully designed data base to implement it. We have discussed several examples to illustrate the concept. Figure 9-6 represents the combined system of models and data and shows the linkages between the model levels. For simplicity, only the data linkages that interface between the three levels are shown.

Model Update.   The initial definition of the model and its equations is often based on data analysis. Subsequent modification and revision of the model require reexamination of the data, particularly to include more recent data that may signal a change in the basic relationships between variables in the model.

There are three modes of periodic update for models. First, the model is rerun with new data inputs but without any changes in the structure of the equations or the values of the equation constants and coefficients. An example is the tactical model as it accepts the data for the most recent month, deletes the oldest month from the data base, and regenerates the pro forma financial statements for the coming 12 months. The new forecasts reflect the influence of the new data, but there is no change in the model itself.

Second, periodic analysis of historical data can result in a change in the equation constants and coefficients without changing the structure or the variables in the equation. For example, consider the demand deposit equation:

$$\text{DEMAND-DEPOSITS } (t) = c \times \text{TOTAL-DEPOSITS } (t)$$

Because of the changing savings pattern of customers, the value of the coefficient c is based on analysis of the relationship between demand deposits and total deposits in the past. Changing savings patterns may signal a change in c as new data are added to the data base.

Third, modifications in the basic structure of the equations in the model may be required. For example, an equation to forecast the service fees from demand deposits may be developed by performing a stepwise regression analysis. All the variables thought to be useful in forecasting service fees are included initially, and the analysis selects the best variables for predicting service fees. The initial variable set might include demand deposit balances, the number of checks processed, the ratio of special checking accounts to regular checking accounts, and average account balances. The stepwise regression might eliminate all but the first two variables, giving the following equation:

$$SF = a + bDD + cCA$$

$$SF = \text{service fees during } t$$
$$DD = \text{demand deposit level during } t$$
$$CA = \text{check activity level during } t$$

Several months later, this stepwise regression should be rerun. With an increasing number of special checking accounts, the ratio of special to regular accounts might become a more important variable, leading to a revised equation which includes this factor as a variable.

The frequency of these three types of revision to the model varies with their importance and extensiveness. The first type of update occurs monthly in conjunction with the normal planning and control cycle. The changes occur automatically unless specifically suppressed. The second type of change, revision, and reestimation of constants and coefficients occurs automatically with notification to the model users on a quarterly or semiannual basis. Major structural changes such as the third type occur only annually as a result of major analysis reruns which indicate that structural changes in the model are necessary. These changes are implemented only on specific action by the model builders. The important point is that there should be periodic use of the models and a scheduled review and "maintenance" program.

COMPUTER STORAGE
AND REPRESENTATION
OF MODELS

If models are to be more than just self-contained, stand-alone computer programs (i.e., if there is to be a model base), we must consider alternative ways of representing and storing the models in a computer. This section continues the analogy between model base and data base; it is analogous to the

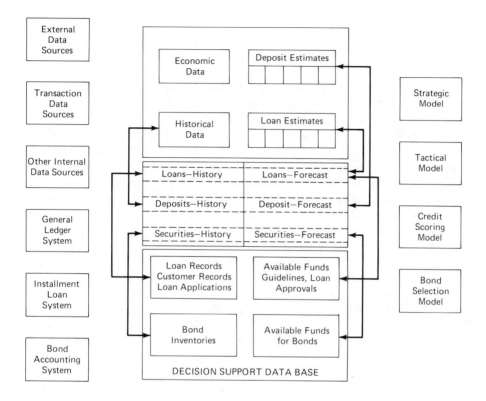

FIGURE 9-6   Models, Data, and Linkages

section on data models in Chapter 8, which described alternative ways to organize and store the data (we chose not to title this section "model models").* We discuss three storage representations for models in this section: subroutines, sets of modeling statements, and models stored as data.

Models as Subroutines

The typical form for traditional modeling is the storage of models as computer subroutines. Instead of a complete program with its own input, output, and execution stream, a model may be a subroutine which is called by a main program. Each model is a set of computer statements with an entry and return linkage mechanism to enable it to be used as an execution module in another program. Values for data and parameters that are needed

---

*Although we repeatedly use the generic word "model" without an adjective in this chapter, we are referring to models of decision processes or analysis/problem-solving approaches which are represented by computer programs or algorithms.

by both the subroutine and main program are passed through an argument list as part of the linkage, or defined by a common set of data definition statements that allow both main program and subroutine access to the same data.

The subroutine approach to modeling is hardly new. A classic example is IBM's Scientific Subroutine Package (SSP) written in FORTRAN, which provided a library of subroutines for statistical and matrix operations, all with a common CALL and RETURN structure. The programmer merely wrote a driver program and pieced together the necessary modules to perform the complete modeling or analysis tasks.

Expansion of this approach has led to current "modeling systems" which provide a set of models or programs, usually stored as subroutines, to handle a type of analysis task. The BMD system for statistical analysis and the Mathematical Programming System (MPS) for problems susceptible to linear and nonlinear programming are good examples. In fact, systems such as this can be viewed in our terms as a model base plus some model management functions, usually for a well-defined domain of problems or tasks. The subroutine form of model representation is also typical of many time-sharing sytems which provide a large number of subroutines for financial and statistical analysis that can be called from the system's command language.

For most modeling uses, the subroutine is a program segment that accomplishes an entire analysis task, but subroutines can be of any size. The model base for a DSS will consist of entities (in this case subroutines) ranging from very small to very large. The MBMS will need to handle a wide range of relationships between them, including hierarchical, association, aggregation, concatenation, and so on. The nature of these entities and the relationships between them are discussed more fully in the design section.

Models as Statements

A second form of computer representation for models is a set of modeling statements. It is possible for this set of statements to be in a general-purpose language, but modeling statements usually have some characteristics that make it easier for them to perform modeling functions. In general, modeling statements will have more limited input and output functions, stronger operators, and perhaps a prescribed framework or context such as the row–column report structure used by most financial planning languages.

If the statements can be grouped and stored as a set for repeated future use, this representation method is the same as the subroutine method. If not, the set of statements (model) must be embedded in a sequence of problem-solving activities and interpreted each time it is needed. Hence the difference between a model stored as a subroutine and a model as a set of modeling statements is the difference between compiled and interpreted sets of code.

The modeling statements may be strictly sequence dependent (procedural) or not sequence dependent (nonprocedural). The current belief is that nonprocedural languages are easier to use, especially by nontechnical users for DSS-type applications, but there is little or no firm evidence to support that belief.

Models as Data

The third method of representing models in a computer is to store the model as data. Strictly speaking, of course, each of the other two methods stores the model as data also, since computers store everything as data, including all procedures and executable program statements. Specifically, we mean here the storage of models in such a way that they can be treated like a set of data (rather than a set of executable statements) and managed with a set of data management functions. Konsynski describes a Generalized Model Management System (GMMS) which seems to be a models-as-data approach growing out of the traditional subroutine approach [6]. The GMMS treats models as a data abstraction consisting of elements, equations, and solution procedures. Figure 9-7 shows the "types" of each category and the specific instances that comprise an econometric model and a linear programming model.

Another example of the models-as-data approach is the use of the rule form of data storage presented in Chapter 8. It is this form of model storage that begins to merge decision models and data into "knowledge representation," which is an important thrust of artificial intelligence. The relative inefficiency of this storage form has limited its use in DSS, except in the

COMPONENTS	ECONOMETRIC MODEL	LINEAR PROGRAMMING MODEL
1. Elements		
• Time series	X	
• Sets		X
• Variables		X
• Parameters		X
2. Equations		
• Recursive	X	
• Simultaneous	X	
• Constraints		X
• Objective functions		X
3. Solution Procedures		
• Specific techniques and algorithms	Gauss–Seidel	Simplex

FIGURE 9-7   Models as a Data Abstraction

case of MYCIN, the Specific DSS to assist in medical diagnosis. Work in this direction is continuing and promising, so there should be some significant developments in the future [4]. The advantages of storing models as data include the following.

- It is easier to trace the operation of the model to see what it does and what it did in the past.
- It is easier to explain or depict the operation of the model to others to facilitate communication.
- It is easier to update the model.

A DESIGN FOR THE MODEL BASE COMPONENT

The design for the modeling component of DSS is an integral part of the dialog–data–models paradigm we have discussed throughout the book. Figure 9-8 is a version of that paradigm for reference. In this section we discuss the recommended structure and characteristics of the three elements labeled in the figure.

(a)   The modeling capability (the model base and its management)
(b)   Which is integrated with the data base (the data–model link)
(c)   Which is invoked using dialog (the dialog–model link)

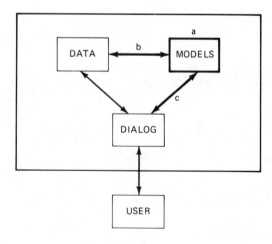

FIGURE 9-8   The Dialog–Data–Models Paradigm

Modeling Capability

To build Specific DSS, the builder must utilize capabilities in the box labeled "Models" in Figure 9-8 to build a collection of specific models (model instances) stored in one of the three ways described above. If the SDSS is large and covers a large problem domain, the set of models may be extensive, but it is still a specific and finite set. Because of the predominant use of subroutines, it is typically a set of modeling subroutines together with the calling mechanism for invoking them. It may, however, be a set of statements that can be sequenced together to create a modeling procedure or a set of rules. From the user's point of view, the model instances in the SDSS are operations (in the ROMC sense) to manipulate representations.

To give the builder this capability, the modeling component of the DSS Generator contains a "language" out of which to build and store model instances using one of the three storage representations. Specifically, it is one or more of the following:

- A mechanism for building and storing subroutines
- A model statement interpreter
- A way of building and storing models as data

This language consists of two types of entities, operators and control constructs. There is a basic set of operators, which can be combined hierarchically to form the model building blocks or entities in the model base. The control constructs can be mapped onto the hierarchy of operators; that is, different controls are available and appropriate at each level. Figure 9-9 illustrates the nature of these entities together with examples for the subroutine representation form.

The Model–Data Link

This link is what operationalizes the integration between the models and the data base. The link requires mechanisms to facilitate the following:

- Each model draws all values and input data from the data base. This provides *accuracy* because the data base values will have been subject to the validity and edit-checking procedures in the DBMS.
- All models draw on the same data base. This feature provides *consistency*. If more than one model uses the same data item, it will be the same for all uses. It also facilitates model *currency*. As data are updated, all models based on the data are updated.
- Models put all output data and values back into the data base. This feature provides *linkage* between models when any model needs input generated as output from a different model. It also permits use of the dialog–data link to display, format, and present output from a model.

- The model itself is stored as data in the data base using one of the three storage formats. This feature allows the models to be more easily managed and updated because they can be manipulated with the assistance of the functions in the DBMS.

The Model–Dialog Link

The model–dialog link is needed to facilitate the building and the operation of the model by the builder. It is this link, in the context of the entire design of course, that is the primary mechanism to support interactive modeling by which decision makers analytically explore, test, and probe the nature of a problem and its solution. Before presenting the specifics of the link, let us trace the typical steps in model usage with this design. First, the user directs the model to run. It is drawn out of the data base into working storage and execution begins. The model draws input values from the data base and requests any required parameters from the user. As execution continues, the user has the option to interrupt at any time to examine intermediate results. The results in the form of output from the model (intermediate or final) are placed in the data base. Upon notification that the model has completed its activity (or reached the end of an interrupt cycle),

MODEL OPERATORS		CONTROL MECHANISMS	
ITEM	EXAMPLE	ITEM	EXAMPLE
Basic Operator	+ - / *	Sequence, Repeat Conditional	x = A + B DOWHILE
Macro (function)	SQRT, MIN, MAX	Invocation	x = SQRT(A)
Subroutine	ANOVA (Analysis of Variance)	Transfer of Control	CALL (subname)
Modeling Program	Linear Program— Simplex	Command List	EXECUTE (procedure)
Modeling System	BMD, SPSS, MPS	Result Specification	SOLVE (problem specification)

FIGURE 9-9   Elements of a Modeling Language

the user may examine the results using the dialog–data link and all the facilities of data presentation and display.

The messages that pass over the model–dialog link can be summarized as follows:

1. Invocation of a model (message flows D ⟶ M)
2. Parameter request (message flows D ⟵ M)
3. Parameter collection (message flows D ⟶ M)
4. Interrupt (message flows D ⟶ M)
5. Notification (of completion or interrupt) (message flows D ⟵ M)

The two main differences in the model–dialog link for our DSS design from that of traditional modeling are that (1) no results are passed back from the model to the user (these results are accessed through the dialog–data link instead), and (2) sequencing of messages on the link is not always the same. The sequence of steps in traditional model execution (even if implemented on a time-sharing system) is:

1. *Invocation*: user calls and starts the model.
2. *Parameter request*: program requests data or parameters.
3. *Parameter collection*: user supplies data or parameters.
4. *Interrupt*: not usually available other than unrecoverable terminate (break) or pause.
5. Model completes run, notifies, and presents results in a predefined format or report.
6. Return to step 1 for another cycle if desired.

Some variations of this sequence are possible in some modeling systems (e.g., return to step 2 to change only some parameters for the next run), but the sequence given here is quite typical. Interactive modeling, on the other hand, permits a variety of sequencing.

A more precise definition of interactive modeling is now possible. In interactive modeling, the sequence of messages over the model–dialog link is determined by the user, not the model, and thus is not fixed for each use of the model. Recalling our general DSS objectives from Chapter 2, this capability is what makes the modeling activity process–independent and controlled directly by the user.

SUMMARY

The use of decision models and analytic procedures has proven valuable in assisting problem-solving and decision-making activities. The use of computers in recent years has increased the power and usefulness of these models. There have, however, been limitations to the traditional implementation of computer-based models in which each model uses a set of input data to provide a set of answers or reports. The integration of analysis procedures and decision models into an information system promises to avoid many of those limitations.

Our framework for DSS includes modeling and model usage as one of three basic components, completely integrated with data base and dialog capabilities. This full integration is necessary to support decision-making activities such as projection, deduction, creation, and comparison of alternatives. These activities require close interaction and rapid feedback between the decision maker and the computer, with strong and flexible control mechanisms.

To provide these capabilities, the modeling component of the DSS must have a "model base" of analytic procedures and algorithms which is subject to a comprehensive set of model base management functions. The model base and its management system must be integrated with the data base (the model–data link) and with the dialog (the model–dialog link).

Design and implementation of the modeling component may use one of three approaches to the storage and representation of models in the computer. The subroutine approach is the most common because it has evolved from the early creation of models as subroutines built from general-purpose languages. The modeling statement approach is characterized by many current systems which provide special-purpose statements to perform model functions with interpreters for execution. The models-as-data approach has been used in a few DSS and has promise for strengthening and extending the modeling functions by combining data and models into "knowledge bases."

QUESTIONS AND PROBLEMS

REVIEW QUESTIONS

1. List the key characteristics of traditional modeling approaches.
2. What are the problems and limitations of traditional modeling approaches?
3. List the key characteristics of the DSS approach to modeling.
4. Explain how the modeling component of a DSS neutralizes or counteracts each of the problems and limitations identified in Question 2.
5. What is a model base?
6. List the important model base management functions.
7. What is the difference between interactive modeling and models run in an interactive environment?
8. Identify three approaches to computer representation of models and give the differences and similarities among them.

DISCUSSION QUESTION

1. Attempts to increase the strength and role of models in DSS are inappropriate and misdirected, especially attempts to provide heuristic guidance or "intelligence." The decision maker will always need to supply the intelligence, and the DSS should be used only for computational analysis of data. Discuss.

EXERCISES

1. Select a "modeling system" available in the software market. Identify and describe:
   a. the model base
   b. model management functions
   c. model–data relationships
   d. model–dialog relationships
2. For an organization with which you are familiar, develop a macro design for the modeling component of a DSS (similar to the commerical bank example).

REFERENCES

1. BARBOSA, L. C., and R. G. HIRKO. "Integration of Algorithmic Aids into Decision Support Systems," *MIS Quarterly*, Vol. 4, No. 1, March 1980, pp. 1–12.
2. BRADLEY, S. P., and D. B. CRANE. "Management of Commercial Bank Government Security Portfolios: An Optimization Approach under Uncertainty," *Journal of Banking Research*, Vol. 4, No. 1, 1974, pp. 18–30.
3. CHERVANY, N. L., and W. C. PERKINS. "Organizational Relationships between Management Science and Management Information Systems: Some Empirical Evidence," *Proceedings, Seventh National AIDS*, Cincinnati, Ohio, November 5, 1975, pp. 216–218.
4. ELAM, J., and J. HENDERSON. "Knowledge Engineering Concepts for Decision Support System Design and Implementation," *Proceedings, Fourteenth Annual Hawaii International Conference on System Sciences*, Western Periodicals, North Hollywood, Calif., 1980.
5. HAYES, R. H., and R. L. NOLAN. "What Kind of Corporate Modeling Functions Best?" *Harvard Business Review*, May–June 1974, pp. 102–112.
6. KONSYNSKI, B. "On the Structure of a Generalized Model Management System," *Proceedings, Fourteenth Annual Hawaii International Conference on System Sciences*, Western Periodicals, North Hollywood, Calif., 1980.
7. LITTLE, J. D. C. "Models and Managers: The Concept of a Decision Calculus," *Management Science*, April 1970, pp. 466–485.
8. ORGLER, Y. E. "Evaluation of Bank Consumer Loans with Credit Scoring Models," *Journal of Banking Research*, Vol. 2, No. 1, pp. 31–37.
9. SCOTT, J. H. "The Management Science Opportunity: A Systems Development Management Viewpoint," *MIS Quarterly*, Vol. 2, No. 4, December 1978, pp. 59–61.

10. SPRAGUE, R. H., and H. WATSON. "A Decision Support System for Banks," *Omega — The International Journal of Management Science*, Vol. 4, No. 6, 1976, pp. 657–671.

11. SPRAGUE, R. H. "Conceptual Description of a Financial Planning Model for Commercial Banks," *Decision Science*, Vol. 2, No. 1, 1971, pp. 66–80.

12. SPRAGUE, R. H. "Systems Support for a Financial Planning Model," *Management Accounting*, Vol. 53, No. 6, 1972, pp. 29–34.

CHAPTER TEN

DSS ARCHITECTURE

OUTLINE

INTRODUCTION

The functions provided by every DSS can be divided logically into the three components described in Chapters 7, 8, and 9. For reasons of simplicity of development, maintenance, and reuse of software, it has generally been more effective to separate the functions of the three components in building DSS than to intermix them. If the software structure separates the functions, it must also provide mechanisms for integrating them. In this chapter we discuss four alternative DSS architectures for integrating the dialog, data base, and model management components of DSS.

Effective integration of the components is important for more than just technical elegance of the DSS software structure. In Alter's study of DSS, many of the causes of problems with a DSS were technical difficulties which can be related to ineffective integration [1]. Among the integration problems discovered by Alter were:

1. Poor integration of the DSS data base with other (internal and external) data bases
2. Poor response times
3. Inability to run large models
4. Inability to interface the dialog component with the modeling and data base components
5. Inability of maintenance programmers to understand the software structure
6. High development, operating, or maintenance costs

The importance of effective integration of the components of a DSS, and the goals for an effective DSS architecture can be summarized as (1) usability, (2) cost, (3) performance, (4) adaptability, and (5) reliability. Effective integration is necessary to meet these five "requirements," and alternative DSS architectures can be compared with respect to these five "criteria."

The four software architectures for DSS which we describe are not the only ones possible. They are architectures for which there are operational examples. They are intended primarily for DSS Generators, but could be used for Specific DSS built with or without the use of Generators. The names chosen for the four architectures are suggested by their software structures. We conclude the chapter with a comparison of the four architectures and a discussion of the architectural relationships among DSS Tools, DSS Generators, and Specific DSS.

FOUR DSS ARCHITECTURES

The DSS Network

The DSS network architecture, shown in Figure 10-1, is perhaps the most adaptive approach to component integration. The primary goals of the

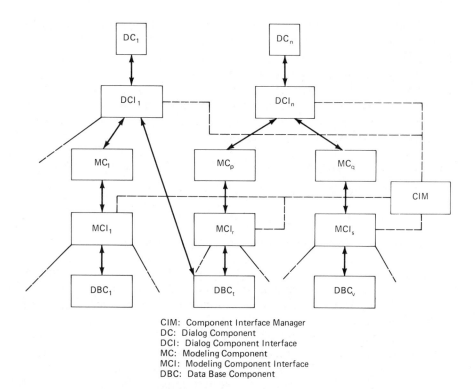

CIM: Component Interface Manager
DC: Dialog Component
DCI: Dialog Component Interface
MC: Modeling Component
MCI: Modeling Component Interface
DBC: Data Base Component

FIGURE 10-1   The DSS Network Architecture

network approach are to permit different modeling and dialog components to share data and to simplify addition of new components. The architecture permits the components to be nonhomogeneous. That is, the architecture is designed to permit intermixing of components developed by different groups, at different times, in different programming languages, and for different operating environments.

The DSS network integrates the dialog, modeling, and data base components through component interfaces. For each dialog or modeling component, there is a component interface. A component interface can be viewed as a communication portal between one component and another. The network structure of the architecture comes from the fact that a component interface is a one-to-many interface and that multiple component interfaces can communicate with the same component. Another view of a component interface is as a "back end" to a component for communicating with other components.

Component interfaces do not communicate directly with each other. This asymmetry has two consequences. First, if a component is to be shared by more than one other component (i.e., by more than one component interface), the shared component itself must provide a "multi-user" interface. That is, the shared component (such as a data base component) must provide for the scheduling and isolation of communications (such as retrieval and updates) from component interfaces. The second consequence of the asymmetry is that a component interface manager is required to establish and break connections between component interfaces and shared components. Establishing connections involves:

1. Checking authorization of the component interface to access a shared component
2. Checking to see if the shared component is active (and if not, activating the component)
3. Periodically checking to see if the connection is still active
4. Handling monitoring, logging, recovery, and supervision functions

A connection is broken when (1) a component interface sends an "end-of-session" message to a component, (2) either a shared component or component interface fails, or (3) the connection is inactive for a specified length of time (timeout).

The component interface permits flexibility in combining (integrating) components and permits independently developed components to be integrated more easily. For each dialog and modeling component to be integrated into the DSS, a component interface must be developed. For each data base component to be integrated, the component interfaces of the other components which are to use this data base component must be extended. Thus the component interfaces isolate the connections among components but do not reduce the number that have to be developed, nor do they provide automatic or standard interfaces which can accommodate arbitrary components.

Component interfaces must handle both data and control communications among components. For both types of communication, format conversion and message synchronization are required. Format conversion involves converting the data/control formats from one component into the data/control formats for another component. Synchronization involves signaling, sending, and waiting for communication among components.

For data and control communications, the component interfaces may use message passing, shared memory, shared files, or a combination of the three. However, the choice of a communication technique depends largely on the components being interfaced. New components developed for a DSS network architecture probably should use message passage and/or shared memory because these are faster and more reliable than shared files. Existing components probably will require shared file communications because this technique is the simplest. The output of one component is written to a file which becomes the input to the other component. Shared files is a particularly effective technique for interfacing components developed for a batch environment. Some existing components may be able to be interfaced using subroutine calls, which is a form of shared memory interface.

There are many variations on the network architecture. For example, modeling and dialog components are often integrated and have a single component interface. That is, one component interface serves a combined modeling and dialog component. Obviously, with this variation the modeling component cannot be used with a different dialog component. Another variation is to have a single data base component. In this case, the "network" structure becomes a "tree" structure with the data base component as its root and the dialog components as its leaves.

GMIS [4, 5] is an example of a DSS with a network architecture. GMIS was designed to provide an environment in which a variety of modeling components needed to share data stored in multiple data bases. GMIS relies heavily on IBM's Virtual Machine (VM) operating system to provide the component interfaces [8]. Experience with GMIS indicated that the component interfaces introduced about a 10 percent overhead compared to direct component-to-component communication. Shared memory communication was found to be about three times faster than shared files as a technique for component interfaces, but could not be used in all cases. If shared components were accessed on a "one at a time" basis, additional degradation occurred because of queueing for shared components. The amount of additional degradation was dependent on the degree of sharing, volume of message traffic to the shared component, and the queueing mechanism. The GMIS experience also indicated that the network architecture did permit independently developed components to be integrated without modifying the components. The developers of GMIS also felt that the costs of building the component interfaces were less than the costs of modifying components to interface to each other, although there were no reported experiments to verify this conclusion. The isolation of the integration problem to the component interfaces, however, rather than having to do pairwise modification of components that are to be integrated, probably does reduce the costs of building DSS from components developed independently.

The GMIS experience and a simple analysis of the network architecture thus indicate the following advantages:

1. Ease of integration of independently developed components
2. Localization of component interface code, which simplifies maintenance and extension
3. Flexibility for component sharing

The disadvantages of the network architecture are:

1. Multiple dialog components (which probably decrease ease of use)
2. Performance degradation due to interface overhead and queueing

3. Dependence on an operating system that supports multiple environments, inter-environment communications, and inter-environment process management

4. Reliability problems because of the multiplicity of component interfaces, the loosely coupled nature of the interfaces, and the integration of components that were not originally designed to work together

The DSS network architecture seems appropriate for prototyping, for ad hoc DSS [6] which are intended for one-time or infrequent use, and for reducing the fixed cost of developing DSS by using existing components.

The DSS Bridge

To reduce the number of component interfaces required by the DSS network architecture, but to retain the ability to integrate new components, the DSS bridge architecture provides for a unified interface component between (1) the dialog and local modeling and data base components, and (2) shared modeling and data base components. A local component is one that is not shared (i.e., single user). Figure 10-2 shows the DSS bridge architecture. The bridge provides a standard interface, or a set of standard interfaces, for integrating local and shared components. DSS components must be developed to use this interface.

The bridge performs format conversions and synchronization functions similar to those of the component interfaces in the network architecture. The difference is, of course, the centralization (standardization), which reduces the number of interfaces and incorporates the interface management functions into the bridge. The bridge architecture requires that all local components and all shared components execute in the same environment. The shared and local environments can be different. For a set of local (or shared) components to communicate with each other, they must either have special-purpose, pairwise interfaces, or they must use a common, shared component. The use of a shared component, in particular a data base component, is the simplest, easiest to maintain, and therefore the preferred technique for integrating a set of local (or shared) components.

A pioneering example of the DSS bridge architecture is IDAMS [7]. IDAMS was developed to provide an environment where application specialists with little computer experience could assess and analyze data in an unstructured and interactive manner. In IDAMS the local components all execute in an APL [11] environment and provide functions for data and function definition, user guidance, query, statistical, and data presentation (graphics). The shared components operate in a non-APL environment and provide data base and PL/1 and FORTRAN program libraries. The bridge consists of a set of APL "auxiliary processors" and an operating system extension for APL to permit an APL user to load and execute non-APL programs dynamically. The APL auxiliary processors are used for data format conversions, and the operating system extensions are used for the intercomponent control functions of the bridge.

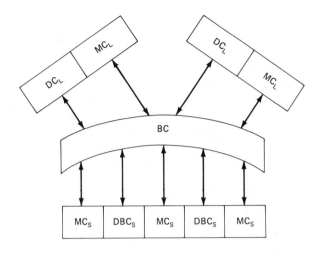

DC_L : Local Dialog Component
MC_L : Local Modeling Component
BC: Bridge Component
MC_S : Shared Modeling Component
DBC_S : Shared Data Base Component

FIGURE 10-2   The DSS Bridge Architecture

IDAMS has been used in a number of organizations, and its main advantages seem to be the integration of APL and non-APL modeling components, and the integration of a unified dialog and user guidance facility with a relational data base and a variety of modeling components. Usability and performance seem adequate for application specialists, who have been mostly analysts rather than line managers. The support for APL and the integration of APL and non-APL programs provide an adaptable environment for integrating existing modeling or data base components and for developing new components. Although no studies of reliability or performance have been published, the interpretative nature of APL suggests possible performance problems, and the simplicity of the bridge technique suggests better reliability for the bridge architecture than for the network architecture.

In IDAMS there is a unified dialog component for all the modeling components. However, the bridge architecture does permit separate dialog and modeling components and multiple dialog components.

The DSS Sandwich

Whereas the network and bridge architectures attempt to integrate multiple dialog, modeling, and data base components, the DSS sandwich architecture attempts to integrate the components by using single dialog and data base components with a variety of modeling components. Figure 10-3 illustrates how the shared dialog and data base components "sandwich" the modeling components. Each modeling component shares the same data base and dialog components. Data communication among modeling components is via the shared data base component. Communication of control information among modeling components is via the shared dialog component. Like the bridge architecture, there are thus standard data and control interfaces. In the sandwich architecture, however, the standard interfaces are provided by the single dialog and data base components rather than by a separate interface, as in the bridge architecture. In the sandwich architecture each modeling component has to be developed, or modified, to meet the two interfaces. In the network architecture, most of the modifications would be in the component interface.

REGIS is an example of a DSS which can be thought of as having a sandwich architecture [9]. REGIS combines a relational data base and a unified command language interpreter with statistical, graphics, and data access (query, definition, update) components. The dialog command interpreter handles "English-like" commands which invoke the modeling and data base components. REGIS has been in use for a number of years in the General Motors Corporation, and there have been numerous applications from several GM divisions. One of the main advantages of REGIS has been the ability to integrate a variety of previously separate decision support tools. Use of common data formats (tables) simplified data sharing and increased user understanding of the tools (modeling components). The common dialog component made it easier for users to learn to use new tools. Potential users were more willing to put their data into a common data base knowing that there was a common interface available for accessing the data. Although there are no published reports on the costs or performance of REGIS, its widespread use indicates that both costs and performance are acceptable. Where users did have problems, better performance was not thought to be a solution. Rather, the problems were thought to be in the need for an even

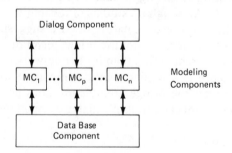

FIGURE 10-3   The DSS Sandwich Architecture

more powerful dialog component (with less typing and less rigid command syntax).

The main disadvantage of the sandwich approach appears to be the difficulty of integrating external data. Because there is a single data base component, external data must be converted or reentered. The REGIS reports indicate that users were willing to do this in order to be able to use the powerful modeling functions. However, if a substantial amount of external data is required, as indicated in the GMIS studies [4], one would expect a DSS based on the sandwich architecture to require a substantial data conversion effort. It is difficult to tell whether data integration via conversion or reentry is more difficult or expensive than data integration via software interfacing (as in the bridge or network architectures). The relative costs would probably depend on the amount of data, the variety of data formats, the number of times the conversion program can be used, and the number of modeling components. The DSS sandwich architecture would have a relative advantage when all of these factors were high (i.e., large volumes of data, many formats, repetitive usage of the conversion programs, and many modeling components). We hypothesize an advantage for the sandwich architecture in this case because the external data integration can be accomplished with a single conversion program. In the bridge and network architectures, multiple-component interfaces would need to be developed.

A second relative disadvantage of the sandwich architecture is that control interfaces among components are restricted to those provided by the dialog and data base components. These interfaces may be very general (to support multiple modeling components), and therefore their performance may be poor.

A third relative disadvantage is that all the components must execute in the same operating environment. This requirement makes it difficult to incorporate independently developed components from different environments.

The DSS Tower

The DSS tower architecture (Figure 10-4) attempts to provide component modularity and flexibility to support a variety of hardware devices and source data bases, while maintaining simple interfaces among the three major DSS components. The main difference between the tower architecture and the network architecture is that the tower architecture is designed for a single operating environment at any "level" in the tower. Like the sandwich architecture, only single dialog and data base components are present in a Specific DSS, and dialog, modeling, and data base components are layered (rather than intermixed as in the bridge and network architectures). In terms of the interface to the modeling components, the tower architecture is identical to the sandwich architecture. The main difference from the

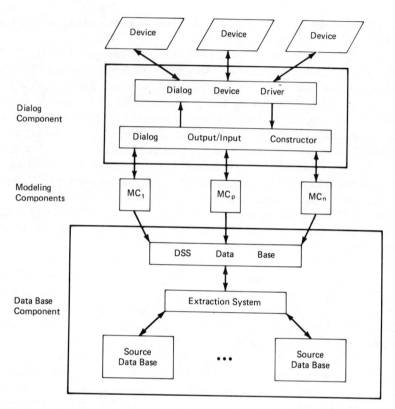

FIGURE 10-4   The DSS Tower Architecture

sandwich architecture is that to support a variety of user interface devices and variety of source data bases, the tower architecture separates the dialog and data base component into two parts each.

As shown in Figure 10-4, the tower architecture is based on a set of source data bases, possibly internal or external, operating in possibly different environments (e.g., different computers, different operating systems). The extraction component interfaces the source data bases to the DSS data base. As described in Chapter 8, data extraction is used to integrate diverse data base components, and thus is similar to the component interfaces between modeling and data base components in the network architecture. The DSS data base is used as an interface between modeling and source data base so that every modeling component need interface to only one data base component.

The dialog component consists of a device driver, which communicates with user interface devices (CRTs, keyboards, printers, etc.), and an output–input constructor, which creates the output formats and interprets the input commands. Separating the dialog component into these two parts has three advantages. First, new devices can be more easily incorporated

288

because the device-specific code is localized in the device driver. Second, additional dialog capabilities (input commands and output formats) can be easily added to the output–input constructor. Third, communication among dialog and modeling components is enhanced because the output–input constructor can control multiple "dialogs" between the user (who interfaces with the device handler) and the modeling components. The output–input constructor thus performs functions similar to the component interfaces between dialog and modeling components in the network architecture, but provides a single interface for the modeling components as in the sandwich architecture.

GADS used a version of the tower architecture. Because GADS components are described in several case examples in this book, we will not repeat the descriptions here. The reader is encouraged to review the GADS case example in Chapters 2 and 6 to compare the GADS architecture with Figure 10-4. References [2] and [10] also provide details on the GADS architecture.

Compared to the three other DSS architectures described in this chapter, the tower architecture has the following advantages and disadvantages:

ADVANTAGES:

1. The flexibility of the network architecture to incorporate external data bases with better performance through use of the extracted data base
2. Layered dialog modeling and data base management components
3. Adaptability of the dialog component for new device and output/input formats
4. A unified interface for modeling components, as in the sandwich architecture, and the flexibility for integrating independently developed models, as in the network or bridge architectures

DISADVANTAGES:

1. Difficult to integrate independently developed ᴄ alog, modeling, or data base management components which require different operating environments
2. Heavy dependence on single dialog and data base interfaces
3. Possible performance problems because of the multiple layers

THE CENTRAL ROLE OF THE DATA BASE COMPONENT

In each of the four architectures, the data base component itself is used in integrating the dialog, modeling, and data base components. From the DSS users' point of view, this integration occurs because the data base component provides the memories used in decision making (see Chapter 4). From the builder's point of view, the data base can be used to simplify implementation and maintenance of the DSS. In all four architectures, the data base is used as a vehicle for sharing data among modeling components. In the network and bridge architectures, the data base can also be used to share data among dialog components and between dialog and modeling components. The data base can be used to store parameters for the modeling component, and when the network or rule data model (Chapter 8) is used, models themselves can be stored in the data base. The data base can be used to store the output formats and response logic for inputs for the dialog component [3].

The use of the data base to support the modeling and dialog components has three advantages. By separating out parameters of models and dialogs, it makes them easier to modify. By storing the parameters in the data base, data base management functions (retrieval, update, backup) are provided and do not have to be replicated in the other components or in the tools used to build the other components. By storing parameters as data, sharing among components is simplified. For example, parameters for a model can be entered via the dialog component, stored in the data base by the dialog component, and then directly accessed from the data base by a modeling component.

In Figure 10-5 we illustrate how the data base can be used to integrate data base, modeling, and dialog components of a DSS. For simplicity we use the relational model of data and the DSS sandwich architecture, although the other data models or architectures also could be used. In the figure the arrows show the data flow among the components. The data flow among the relations and the components shown for model A would have a parallel for model N, but are not shown in the figure. The data flow and the use of the data base to integrate the DSS components are:

1. The user enters an input (via the dialog component) requesting the DSS to execute model A and provides some parameters for the model.
2. The dialog component accesses a relation (e.g., a decision table) the contents of which describe the actions to be taken in response to each allowed user input.
3. Based on the actions specified for the inputs received, the dialog component stores the parameters entered by the user in an output format relation (so that the parameters can be shown to the user).
4. Based on the actions specified in the response relation, the dialog component invokes model A for execution.
5. Model A accesses its parameters and input data from its output format relation and from a data relation. The data relation stores the data used by the model (e.g., the independent variables in a regression forecasting model). The parameters in the output format relation are user-supplied parameters used to "tune" the model (e.g., the forecasting assumptions for alternative runs of the model).
6. Model A stores its results in the output format relation and transfers control back to the dialog component.

7. The dialog component accessess the output format relation, which contains the data to be displayed to the user (the results of the model), and the formatting attributes to be used in displaying the data (e.g., position, color, symbology). For example, the results of a forecasting model might be displayed as a set of line graphs, one for each set of forecasting assumptions.

8. The dialog component uses the output format relation to create a display for the user to show the results of the model.

For each display "frame" in the DSS, there would be output format and response logic relations. Every model would have one or more data relations and would be referenced by one or more response logic relations, and possibly would access parameters in an output format relation. Thus the "scenario" of steps 1 to 8 would be repeated for every user input.

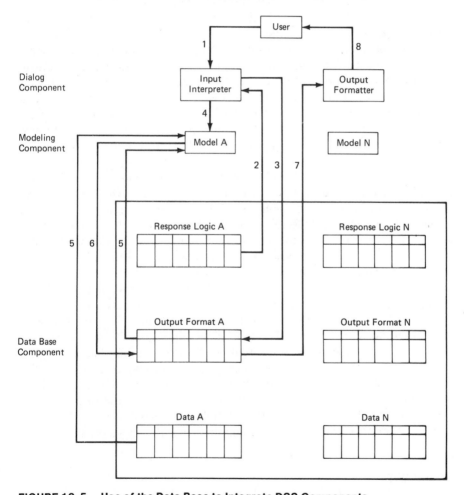

FIGURE 10-5   Use of the Data Base to Integrate DSS Components

DSS GENERATORS AND TOOLS

Using Figure 10-5, we can now describe a DSS as a set of interpreters which are "data driven." The dialog component consists of an output interpreter which creates displays and an input interpreter which interprets user inputs. Each of these interpreters is driven by data stored in the data base describing output formats and input response logic. The modeling component consists of a set of interpretive models, each of which interprets a set of data stored in the data base. Finally, the data base component is an interpreter which accesses the data for the other components (steps 2, 3, 5, 6, and 7, Figure 10-5). A Specific DSS can be defined by a specific set of data for the interpreters. A DSS Generator is a set of interpreters and data creation utilities. DSS Tools are used to build and modify the interpreters.

The four architectures and the central role of data base which we have described can be applied in building either Specific DSS or DSS Generators. A Specific DSS will contain dialog, modeling, and data base components which provide specific representations, operations, memories, and control aids. A DSS Generator will provide a starting set of representations, operations, memories, and control functions which can be used, modified, and extended for a variety of decisions. Through the use of data-driven interpreters or other techniques, the DSS Generator can be "loaded" with new representations, operations, memories, and control aids to produce a Specific DSS.

This "loading" of a DSS Generator, and modifications to the Generator code, are facilitated by software which we have called DSS Tools. These tools may include: general-purpose programming languages, such as COBOL, PL/1, and FORTRAN; general-purpose interpreters such as APL; and special-purpose editors for creating output formats [12]. Considering the dialog, modeling, and data base components of a DSS Generator as sets of interpreters which operate on data to produce data, DSS Tools are used either to create/modify the interpreters or to create/modify the data used by the interpreters. This simplified view of the relationship between DSS Generators and DSS Tools is shown in Figure 10-6, again using the sandwich architecture for convenience. The tools shown in Figure 10-6 are examples rather than a complete set. Some tools (e.g., programming languages) are used to create interpreters; some tools (e.g., the display management system) are themselves interpreters which can be used or modified for direct incorporation into the DSS generator. Some tools (e.g., the dialog editor) are used only to modify the data used by the interpreters. Some tools (e.g., a model generator) create interpreters and the tables that drive them.

SUMMARY

In this chapter we have seen that in the 1970s a great deal was learned about how to build DSS, and that at least four architectures have emerged. A com-

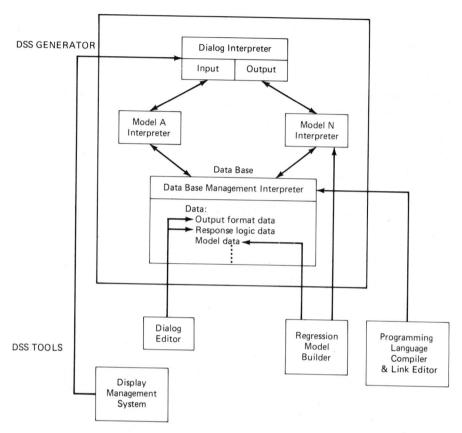

DSS GENERATOR

Dialog Interpreter

Input | Output

Model A Interpreter

Model N Interpreter

Data Base

Data Base Management Interpreter

Data:
→ Output format data
→ Response logic data
Model data ←
⋮

DSS TOOLS

Dialog Editor

Regression Model Builder

Programming Language Compiler & Link Editor

Display Management System

FIGURE 10-6   DSS Generators and Tools

parison of these four architectures for DSS depends on many variables (organizational, decision, user, economic, hardware, software). In Figure 10-7 we have listed some of the variables which we think help differentiate the architectures, and we give our ranking (1 is highest) of each architecture with respect to these variables. These rankings are subjective, and other variables (such as the fact that an organization already has several DSS based on one of architectures) could be more relevant than the variables we have selected. If these variables are the important ones, if these rankings are used, if you assume rankings can be added, and if you are interested in an overall comparison, the bridge architecture has a slight edge over the others. As mentioned in their descriptions, however, each architecture has advantages and disadvantages when compared to the others, and each has been successfully used in building one or more DSS.

Perhaps more interesting than the differences among the architectures are the similarities among the choices of components that have been made in building DSS using each of the architectures. In each example we cited, a

Variables for Comparisons:	Network	Bridge	Sandwich	Tower
Ease of Obtaining Consistent User Interface	4	3	2	1
Cost of Adding Functions	2	1	4	3
Cost of Adding External Data	2	3	4	1
Operating Costs	4	2	1	3
Performance	4	3	1	2
Reliability	4	3	1	2
Adaptability	1	2	4	3
Efficiency with Data-driven Interpreters	4	2	1	3
Availability of Tools for Construction	1	2	4	3
Independence from Operating Systems	4	3	1	2

1 : highest ranking
4 : lowest ranking

FIGURE 10-7   Comparing DSS Architectures

relational data base was used, usually because of the simplicity of the data model and of the data base management system. In each example, inter-preters were extensively used to implement the three major DSS com-ponents, and in two of the four examples (GMIS and IDAMS), the APL interpreter was a part of the modeling and dialog components. Finally, in each of the examples the underlying environment (e.g., the operating sys-tem) provided features (such as intercomponent communication and device support) which were used in integrating the three DSS components.

In summary, there are at least four architectures which have been successfully used to build DSS. These architectures can all be used for Specific DSS or for DSS Generators. When used for DSS Generators, each of the architectures becomes more flexible if the three major components are designed as data-driven interpreters, with their data stored in the data base component. DSS Tools are software used to create and modify the interpreters or their data, and may be editors, languages, generators, or prototype components.

QUESTIONS AND PROBLEMS

REVIEW QUESTIONS

1. Describe the network, the bridge, the sandwich, and the tower architectures for DSS.
2. What is the feature of the DSS network architecture that permits independently developed components to be integrated?
3. What is the function of the bridge component in the DSS bridge architecture?
4. What are the advantages and disadvantages of having single dialog and data base management components in the DSS sandwich architecture? Why are there multiple modeling components?
5. Why are the dialog and data base management components in the DSS tower architecture divided into layers?
6. List the advantages and disadvantages of each of the four DSS architectures described in this chapter.
7. How can the data base component play a central role in all four of the DSS architectures?
8. What are the relationships among DSS tools, DSS Generators, and Specific DSS for any DSS architecture?

EXERCISES

1. Obtain a detailed systems description of a Specific DSS that was developed from basic tools. Which architecture best describes the system? Do any of the four architectures suggest improvements that could be made?
2. Obtain a detailed systems description of a more general software system for DSS (an evolving DSS Generator) other than the four used as examples in this chapter. Which architecture best describes the system? Do any of the four architectures suggest improvements that could be made?

REFERENCES

1. ALTER, S. L. *Decision Support Systems: Current Practices and Continuing Challenges,* Addison-Wesley Publishing Company, Inc., Reading, Mass., 1980.
2. CARLSON, E. D., et al. "The Design and Evaluation of an Interactive Geo-Data Analysis and Display System," *Proceedings of the IFIP Congress 74,* North-Holland Publishing Company, Amsterdam, 1974, pp. 1057–1061.
3. CARLSON, E. D., and W. METZ. "Integrating Dialog Management and Data Base Management," *Information Processing 80,* North-Holland Publishing Company, 1980, pp. 463–468.
4   DONOVAN, J. J. "Database System Approach to Management Decision Support," *ACM Transactions on Database Systems,* Vol. 1, No. 4, December 1976, pp. 344–369.
5. DONOVAN, J. J., and H. D. JACOBY. "Virtual Machine Communication for the Implementation of Decision Support Systems," *IEEE Transactions on Software Engineering,* Vol. SE-3, No. 5, September 1977, pp. 333–342.
6. DONOVAN, J. J., and S. E. MADNICK. "Institutional and ad hoc DSS and Their Effective Use," *Data Base,* Vol. 8, No. 3, Winter 1977, pp. 79–88.
7. ERBE, R., et al. "Integrated Data Analysis and Management for the Problem Solving Environment," *Information Systems,* Vol. 5, 1980, pp. 273–285.
8. *IBM Virtual Machine Facility/370: Introduction,* IBM Form GC20-1819, White Plains, N.Y.
9. JOYCE, J. D., and N. N. OLIVER. "Impacts of a Relational Information System on Industrial Decisions," *Data Base,* Vol. 8, No. 3, Winter 1977, pp. 15–21.
10. SUTTON J. A. "Evaluation of a Decision Support System: A Case Study of the IBM Office Products Division," *IBM Research Report RJ2214,* IBM Research Division, San Jose, Calif., 1978.
11. *VSAPL for CMS: Terminal Users Guide,* IBM Form SH20-9067, White Plains, N.Y.
12. WELLER, D. L., and R. WILLIAMS. "Graphic and Relational Support for Problem Solving," *Computer Graphics,* Vol. 10, No. 2, Summer 1976, pp. 183–189.

PART FOUR
CONCLUSION

Part Four is a single chapter that treats three subjects. First, we summarize the key concepts, issues, and approaches discussed in the book to provide a concise overview of the framework, process, and components required to build a DSS. We wish it were possible to present a straightforward simple checklist of "things to do" to build effective DSS, but the field is not (and may never be), that well defined. In the absence of such a checklist, we feel that these principles, concepts, and definitions provide guidelines for discussing, using, and building DSS.

Second, we assess what is currently available and, in the case of DSS generators, suggest a way of developing a set of criteria against which to measure potential systems. Finally, we summarize the areas in which we see substantive potential changes in the near future.

CHAPTER ELEVEN

BUILDING EFFECTIVE DSS

OUTLINE

WHAT DOES IT TAKE?

The past decade of experience with DSS has shown that an organization that intends to develop effective DSS will need:

1. A *framework* for organizing and guiding the creation of a DSS environment (Chapters 1 and 2)
2. A *process* for developing DSS (Chapters 3 to 6)
3. A set of *components* with which to build DSS (Chapters 7 to 10)

Most DSS failures can be traced to failures in one of these three areas. Most DSS successes are based on success in these three areas. In this book we have presented specific definitions of the framework, process, and components for building effective DSS. There are, of course, other definitions, but these have proven valuable in organizing our thinking about DSS and our activities in building them.

Framework

Our framework for DSS consists of four parts. The first is a set of characteristics of an effective DSS—it specifies the goals for DSS. The second part identifies the levels of technology that can be used to provide DSS with the characteristics identified in the first part—it specifies what will need to be built. The third part of the framework identifies the roles that will be involved in building DSS—it specifies *who* will be needed. The fourth part of the framework identifies the components of DSS—it specifies what technical capabilities will be required. Overall, the framework provides a common guide and basis for communication among all those involved with DSS.

Characteristics of DSS. The key characteristics of effective DSS are:

1. Support for semistructured (underspecified) decisions
2. Support for all phases of decision making (intelligence, design, choice, implementation)
3. Combination of modeling (analytic) techniques with data base and data presentation techniques
4. Emphasis on ease of use and flexibility/adaptability (compared to execution efficiency)
5. An interaction with transaction processing (EDP) and other information systems, such as MIS and office systems

DSS tend to differ from MIS and EDP primarily in these five characteristics. Some proponents of DSS claim that DSS are intended for higher-level managers than are MIS or EDP systems. If this is true, it is primarily because of the first characteristic rather than because of a specific intent to support decisions, or decision-making behavior, characteristic only of high-level managers.

Levels of DSS Technology. In analyzing the hardware/software that has been used to develop systems with the characteristics of DSS, three levels (or classes) of technology can be identified. Specific DSS (SDSS) provide support for a specific set of the characteristics. That is, they support a specific decision, specific decision-making processes, specific combinations of modeling, data base and data presentation techniques, specific ease-of-use and adaptability features, and they interface with specific transaction processing and organizational information systems. DSS Generators (DSSG) are a second level of DSS technology, which can be thought of as packages of hardware and software that can be used to build SDSS. That is, DSSG support sets of the characteristics of DSS which facilitate the building of SDSS. The third level of technology, DSS Tools (DSST), is the most fundamental level of DSS technology. DSST are used to build SDSS or DSSG. DSST are used to develop systems that have specific or general characteristics of DSS.

Roles in Building DSS. To use DSS technology to build systems with the characteristics of DSS, three roles will be filled by people in the organization. The user role, consisting of the end users and possibly intermediaries (or DSS "chauffeurs"), is the client role. Persons in this role are concerned with using SDSS to get work done. The second role is the builder role, which is concerned with providing SDSS for the user role. Persons in this role usually see DSS as DSSG. The third role, the most technical, is that of toolsmith and technical supporter. Those in the toolsmith role are concerned with DSST. Each role is characterized by a different view of DSS. From the technology point of view, each role is associated with one of the technology levels of DSS. From a performance point of view (effectiveness or efficiency), each role also has a different perspective. The user is concerned with decision-making performance. The builder is concerned with development performance. The toolsmith is concerned with technology performance. It is these different points of view that make it essential, beneficial, and difficult for those in the different roles to work together to develop DSS.

DSS Components. Although there are different roles in developing DSS, each with different perspectives, each can describe DSS in terms of dialog, data base, and modeling capabilities. Dialog is the user-interface component. Data base is the memory component. Modeling is the analytic component. Integrating the three forms a DSS.

Process

The process of building DSS consists of an action plan and a set of steps or phases for carrying out the action plan. The goal of the process is to develop a DSS environment in which SDSS can be built from DSSG and DSST.

An Action Plan. An action plan is based on a philosophy or approach to responding to the need for DSS. A variety of approaches is possible. We have identified three approaches, each with different motivations, advantages, and disadvantages. The quick-hit approach is a short-term, meet-an-immediate-need approach, focusing on a SDSS. The staged approach is an intermediate-range, meet-a-set-of-needs approach, focusing on developing a sequence of SDSS, with a DSSG evolving from the development. The complete DSS is a long-term, fully committed, mature technology approach which focuses on DSSG and DSST as the basis for reducing the costs of developing many SDSS.

Having picked an approach, an organizational unit will be needed to develop and effect the action plan. This DSS group can be formed from individuals from many parts of an organization, and can be located in several places within an organization. In general, the best DSS organization consists of individuals who represent the major roles in developing DSS and is situated such that it does not report to an individual who has a vested interest in only one of those roles.

The action plan developed and carried out by the DSS group should consist of a study and feasibility assessment, pilot projects or baseline studies, establishing the DSS environment in which DSS can be built, and a plan for producing SDSS. Obviously, the specifics of the plan depend on the organization, the overall approach chosen, and the DSS group.

Systems Analysis. Beginning with the preliminary study/feasibility assessment part of the plan, a series of system analyses will be done to define the performance requirements of the SDSS. We recommend that systems analysis focus on what support the SDSS will provide rather than on decision makers or decision-making processes. This recommendation follows directly from the characteristics of DSS (particularly the semistructured nature of the decisions to be supported). In addition, experience indicates that the intended users cannot describe their decision-making process either before or after decision making, and that DSS which support specific processes tend to be less flexible/adaptable than those which support a variety of processes. To develop DSS which support semistructured decisions and a variety of processes, the systems analysis approach should identify the representations (R), the operations (O), the memories (M), and the control techniques (C), which are used or required. Every SDSS can be defined in terms of a specific set of ROMC, and DSSG and DSST can be defined in terms of the ROMC they can provide.

Iterative Design. In building SDSS, an iterative design process seems most appropriate because of the need for flexibility in DSS and because the decisions and decision makers require a short development cycle. The required flexibility can be defined in terms of how easy it is for the DSS to respond to changes in user decision-making processes and how easy it is for the DSS environment to develop SDSS. Iterative design compresses the traditional steps in the systems life cycle to generate repeated versions of a SDSS. Clearly, the iterative design process depends on the ROMC approach to systems analysis because compressing the system development life cycle would be difficult if new decisions and decision-making processes had to be analyzed each time a change in a SDSS was required. Iterative design is also facilitated by DSSG which reduce development time for SDSS. The key aspects of iterative design are:

1. Focus on a subproblem.
2. Focus on a small but usable SDSS.
3. Plan for refinement/modification cycles.
4. Evaluate constantly.

Implementation. Implementation is an informal or formal step which can be considered as part of the iterative design process. Implementation consists of education, installation, and evaluation; in the iterative design process each of these is repeated. Implementation is particularly important as the number of users of SDSS increases, and for DSS intended for collective use (e.g., group or organizational support). There are a variety of techniques that can be used for the three parts of implementation. These techniques are not necessarily unique to DSS, but should be understood by DSS users and builders.

Components

To provide the representations, operations, memories, and control required for effective decision support, a set of capabilities will be required from SDSS, DSSG, and DSST. These capabilities are provided by dialog, data base, and modeling components of DSS. The relationships among these three technical components, the ROMC approach to systems analysis, and the SDSS/DSSG/DSST views of DSS are shown in Figure 11-1. Dialog components provide the representation and control (R, C) capabilities. Data base components provide memory (M) capabilities. Modeling components

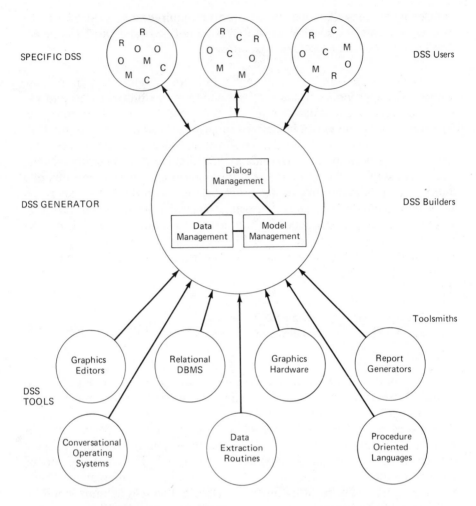

SPECIFIC DSS

DSS Users

DSS GENERATOR

DSS Builders

Toolsmiths

DSS
TOOLS

Dialog
Management

Data
Management

Model
Management

Graphics
Editors

Relational
DBMS

Graphics
Hardware

Report
Generators

Conversational
Operating
Systems

Data
Extraction
Routines

Procedure
Oriented
Languages

FIGURE 11-1   A Framework for DSS

provide the operation (O) capabilities. DSS users, builders, and toolsmiths should work together to develop capability lists for the dialog, data base, and modeling components. In the next section we suggest a set of capabilities in each of these three areas that appears to be necessary for building effective DSS.

DSS Architecture. A DSS architecture is an integrated set of capabilities for a SDSS or DSSG. The integration is defined in terms of the interfaces among the dialog, data base, and modeling components. Four architectures (which we have called the network, bridge, sandwich, and tower architectures) have been used for existing DSS. The choice among these or other architectures depends on the desired flexibility, the need to integrate with or use existing EDP or MIS systems, performance requirements, and the hardware/software environment being used.

WHAT IS AVAILABLE?

With at least a decade of DSS history, plus a myriad of MIS and EDP systems, one need not start to develop a SDSS or a DSSG from scratch. It is not our purpose here to give a survey of available hardware and software, nor to promote specific products that could be used. Rather, we attempt to summarize the state of the art of SDSS, DSSG, and DSST.

Specific DSS

From the descriptions, surveys, and studies of existing DSS [1, 2, 7] it is easy to conclude that most are SDSS. They have been designed for specific decisions and decision makers. Several general observations can be made. First, existing SDSS do not seem to cluster around specific types of decisions or decision makers. For the SDSS described in the literature just referenced:

1. Some had executive users, some had line managers for users, some had staff users.
2. Some users had intermediaries, some did not.
3. The decisions ranged from structured planning to day-to-day operations.

This variety of decisions and users is one reason we did not include intended applications or users in our list of DSS characteristics.

Existing SDSS also seem to span a variety of industries. No particular industry group seems to be leading the way for DSS the way scientific/military groups pioneered computational uses of computers, or the way that insurance and banking pioneered record-keeping uses. SDSS have been developed for local government, transportation, banking, heavy manufacturing, retailing, entertainment, and other industries. The variety of industries that seem interested in SDSS may be one reason there are not many SDSS available for purchase. Each SDSS really is *specific* to an industry or to an organization.

Another reason sometimes cited for the lack of available SDSS is that many organizations consider their SDSS to provide them with a competitive advantage and do not want other organizations, particularly within their industry, to have access to similar decision support. It is difficult to verify any competitive advantage attributable to SDSS. If such an advantage does exist, we can expect to continue to rely on high-level, fictitious-name surveys for information of SDSS. We can also expect that the SDSS in the marketplace will continue to be primarily vendor provided rather than user-organization provided.

Another general observation on existing SDSS is that they tend to emphasize one or two of the three major DSS components we have identified. Alter's classifications of DSS into model-oriented and data-oriented is an indication of this lack of balance among the components and of the emphasis on functional support (models) and data base support rather than on support for presentations or control (dialog).

DSS Generators

With the variety of SDSS that have been developed and are likely to be needed, the need for DSSG seems certain to increase. Although there are few or no data on the value of DSSG, they seem to be the only approach that can be used to develop SDSS within the time and costs constraints that users impose. The advantages of GADS as a DSSG which we have cited in this book also seem supported for DSS such as GMIS [3], IDAMS [4], and REGIS [5]. The basic advantage seems to be the flexibility of the DSSG approach to building SDSS.

Identifying DSSG Capabilities.   Perhaps realizing the value of the DSSG approach (without using the label), time-sharing and other vendors are beginning to offer DSSG-like products. There probably are more DSSG-like products than there are SDSS products available. To identify, analyze, and compare potential DSSG, we can use the capability list approach mentioned earlier.

In Chapter 3 we began the process of developing a suggested set of criteria for DSS Generators in order to provide a target for the "staged development approach" to building DSS. To review, the process is a four-level "top-down" analysis schematically represented by Figure 11-2. The upper two levels, overall objectives and general capabilities, presented in Chapter 3, are listed here for review.

Overall Objectives for a DSS Generator.   There are two basic objectives of a DSSG:

1. To permit quick and easy development of a wide variety of SDSS. As a group, SDSS built with a DSSG must satisfy performance criteria that characterize general decision-making requirements. In other words, the DSSG must permit construction of SDSS that meet criteria such as these:
    a. Emphasize support for semistructured and unstructured tasks
    b. Support managers and users at all levels and in all functional areas of the organization and assist in integration between them
    c. Support independent (personal) as well as interdependent (organizational and group) decision making

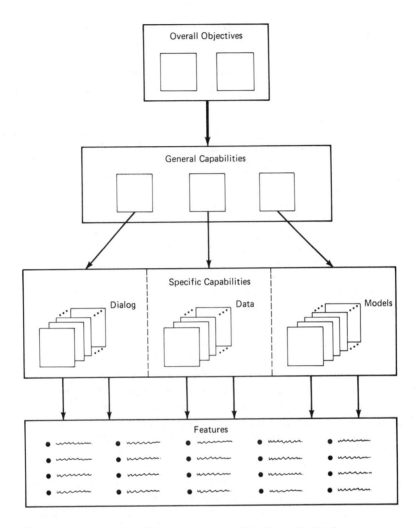

FIGURE 11-2   Criteria for DSS Generators: A Top-Down Analysis

    d.   Support all phases of the decision-making process

    e.   Support a variety of decision-making processes under primary control of nontechnical users

2. To be flexible and adaptive enough to facilitate the iterative design process by which SDSS can respond quickly to changes—in the organizational or physical environment, in the style of the user, or in the nature of the task. Specifically, the DSSG should:

    a.   Facilitate creation of an initial version of a SDSS to support decision making or problem solving for a critical subproblem

    b.   Facilitate the user's evaluation of the performance of the system and

specification for needed changes, modifications, and enhancements
    c.   Facilitate the implementation of these changes by the user or builder

General Capabilities.   In order to satisfy the overall objectives given above, the DSSG must have at least three general capabilities:

1.   It should be easy to use. Specifically:
    a.   The DSSG should create SDSS which are easy and convenient for non-technical people to use in an active and controlling way.
    b.   The DSSG should be easy and convenient for a builder to use for building and modifying SDSS.
2.   A DSSG should provide access to a wide variety of data sources, internal and external, transactional and nontransactional. These data should be available in a way that supports problem-solving and decision-making activities for a variety of users, problems, and contexts.
3.   A DSSG should produce SDSS that have analysis capability to the extent that some "suggestion" is available if requested.

Component Capabilities.   In Chapter 3 we deferred discussion of the specific capabilities in dialog, data management, and modeling pending the treatment of these technical components in Chapters 7–10. It is now appropriate to present a suggested list of these capabilities. Capabilities are organized within each of the three categories in the following general way. The first group of items deals with *entities*, both the variety (the number of types or kinds) and the extent (number of instances of each type). Next are items that relate to *function* (what can be done with the entities), followed by *relationships* among the entities, among categories, and between capabilities in the category and the user of the system. The last three items in each list deal with:

- *Documentation capability*: the SDSS's ability to depict its current status and characteristics in terms understandable to the user.
- *Tracking ability*: the SDSS's ability to keep and manage data about the use of its facilities.
- *Flexibility*: the ease with which the SDSS can be changed and modified. Flexibility is actually a part of all other items, but is listed separately for convenience and to emphasize its importance in a DSSG.

Although the items will not always fall neatly into this pattern, the list provides an overall guideline for the arrangement of items within each category.

Dialog.   The following capabilities are examples for the dialog component.

1.   The ability to present output from a SDSS in a variety of representations and output devices. The features that support this capability are the hard-

ware/software mechanisms that enable the user to visualize the problem in meaningful contexts. Examples include character printer, line printer, CRT display (with or without color and/or graphics), plotter, audio output, and so on.

2. The ability to accommodate the user actions in a variety of ways. The features that support this capability are the hardware/software elements which enable a variety of users to communicate with the system in ways that are comfortable and easy for them. Examples include standard keyboard, function keys, light pen, "mouse," joy stick, touch panel, digitizing pad, OCR wand, audio input, and so on.

3. The ability to handle a variety of dialog styles, and the ability to shift among them at the user's choice. Dialog styles can be viewed as a combination of options for display and user action, but the packaging and sequencing gives each style a form of its own. It is important enough to list as a separate capability because the ability to accommodate a variety of users' preferred styles is what gives DSS their flexibility and usability for nontechnical users. Examples include question and answer, command language, menu, fill in the blanks, modify in place, and so on. We chose to include response rate as part of dialog style, because the response rate, like the style, must be appropriate to the user, task, and organizational environment. Specifically, the response rate must be fast enough to support continuing decision-making or problem-solving activities in a SDSS. Therefore, the DSSG must permit a variety of response rates.

4. The ability to support communication between users working on the same task or problem, and between the user and the builder for the purpose of improving and modifying the system. "Communication" is used here in the broad sense, not limited to data communication. It is important for the system to promote understanding between people and provide a context for good communication and understanding.

5. The ability to support the user's "knowledge base" in a variety of ways. The knowledge base is what the user must know to communicate with the system. The variety and complexity of commands that must be remembered, any system aids that help users, diagnostic and suggestion routines—all are parts of this capability. Examples include a HELP facility, prompting at several levels, quick access to references such as a list of key commands, and so on. Taken together, these capabilities constitute the documentation capability of the system. Particularly important are built-in or self-documenting capabilities.

6. The ability to capture, store, and maintain data concerning dialog usage. This capability is important to permit:
   a. Retracing and reviewing past actions by a user
   b. Training by example
   c. Backtrack, restart, and recovery from a set of steps
   d. Analysis of usage patterns to guide development and adaptation of dialog capabilities in the future (a type of bootstrap for future potential "intelligence" capability in the dialog area)

7. The ability to produce a SDSS that is flexible, adaptive, and changeable in providing dialog support. This is meant to be an overall flexibility item for the dialog capabilities given above. For example, the system could accommodate shifting from one output device to another, or utilizing a touch panel rather than a light pen.

Data Base.   Examples of data base capabilities include the following.

1. The ability to handle interactively a variety of data structures and types. Examples include numeric/alpha, scalar/vector/matrix, qualitative/quantitative, judgmental/probabilistic, memory aids or triggers, scratch pads, workspaces, and so on. The variety is necessary to accommodate a variety of decisions. The ability to handle personal, unofficial, judgmental, and probabilistic data is necessary for the user to experiment with alternatives based on personal judgment.

2. The ability to support the extraction, capture, and integration of a wide variety of independent data sources. *Extraction* refers to tapping computerized sources of data; *capture* is the entry of noncomputer data; *integration* means they are included in the DSS data base and subject to all the available data management, modeling, and dialog functions. Update is included here because it will usually be repeated extraction from the same source over time.

3. The ability to give users access to the data using a variety of efficient, easy-to-use data-handling functions. These should include, for example:

    a. Quick and efficient data retrieval. This capability should include *specific retrieval* of designated items or records as well as *content retrieval* by attribute.

    b. Flexible data displays or reports. The variety of display mechanisms and output devices was an important item in dialog capabilities. Here the emphasis is on the specification of data and report formatting rather than on the variety of display options.

    c. User-efficient data-handling mechanisms. Examples would be ways to permit data to be aggregated at several levels of detail, and other common transformations or declarations.

4. The ability to manage the DSS data base using the basic data-handling functions of a DBMS (Data Base Management System). These functions would include:

    a. Dictionary
    b. Creation
    c. Deletion
    d. Update
    e. Query
    f. Views
    g. Protection
    h. Sharing
    i. Recovery
    j. Optimization

5. The ability to portray data in a variety of logical views to match the preference of the user and the nature of the problem. Most current DSS provide only one data model, which is usually one of the following kind:

    a. Record
    b. Relational
    c. Hierarchical
    d. Network
    e. Rule

6. The ability to tell the user what data are available and how to gain access to them. This is the documentation capability for the data component, with specific emphasis on data portrayal. This capability should allow the user to see what data are available and how they are interrelated.

7. The ability to keep statistical information on data usage patterns, access or update activity, and so on. This capability gives the system (or the builder) knowledge for improving the data-handling procedures, training new users in data-handling approaches, and so on.

8. The ability to provide flexibility and adaptability in the data capabilities listed above. This includes the ability to add and delete data items/records/sources, the ability to change logical views, and so on.

Modeling (Analysis).   Capabilities for this component might include:

1. The ability to store and manage a library of models in an integrated way. Models are defined here as named routines that perform mathematical/logical calculations. They are integrated with each other when appropriate, and all access a common data base. The strength of the library or "model base" will depend on:

   a. The variety of model *types* available in the library. "Types of models" is defined here in terms of level of aggregation. For instance,
      - Primitives, which are operators to perform basic mathematical and logical operations
      - Functions, which combine primitives to perform more complex mathematical/logical operations
      - Macros, which are similar to functions but for nonstandard operations
      - Subroutines
      - Analysis models
      - Procedures (execs or command strings)

   b. The ability of the library to maintain, catalog, and integrate:
      - Prewritten or "canned" models
      - User-built models that are permanent
      - User-built models that are temporary or ad hoc

   c. The size and extent of the canned library. Most canned models will be subroutines or analysis models but could include the other levels. There could be a variety of analysis modeling types (LP, regression, correlation, etc.) or modeling approaches (simulation, Monte Carlo, goal seeking, etc.).

2. The ability to provide support for creating and building models (of all types) quickly and easily. This is a collection of capabilities (a model definition language), which include the ability to:

   a. Specify mathematical relationships between data variables
   b. Specify mathematical relationships between model types
   c. Specify the data required for a model
   d. Integrate canned models and user-built models into new composite models

These specifications should be relatively procedure-free and self-editing (with good diagnostics).

3. The ability to support the manipulation and operation of these models. This is another collection of capabilities (a model manipulation language), which might include the ability to:

    a. Run and rerun models
    b. Perform sensitivity testing over a range of data
    c. Run a base model plus a set of "what if" questions, and compare the output from several runs
    d. Perform goal seeking
    e. Update models that are based on data in a predefined way
    f. Compile and store object code for permanent models to permit more efficient runs
    g. Play an active role in the analysis and decision-making process by supplying some guidance to the user
    h. Support heuristic search with models (requires a strong link with dialog capabilities)

4. The ability to provide basic model-handling functions in the form of a Model Base Management System (MBMS). These functions might include:

    a. Physical storage and access of models (transparent to user)
    b. Independence of models from the data that use them
    c. Limited redundance
    d. Security and backup
    e. Validation
    f. Privacy/limited access (private vs. public models, etc.)

5. The ability to show the users what models are available and to depict the relationships between them. This is the documentation item, which could include the ability to:

    a. Show the library of models of all types (a model dictionary)
    b. Show the relationships between models, including:
        • Logical relationships
        • Impact of changes
        • Similar models
    c. Show the data required by each model
    d. Give potential users or applications of each model

6. The ability to capture, store, and analyze data concerning model usage and analysis processes used by decision makers. This is the tracking item, which can lead to improvements in the capability of models and model base management systems.

7. The ability to produce a system that is flexible, adaptive, and changeable in providing modeling and analysis support. For example, the system could add and delete model types and specific instances of models, change parameter values or structure for an existing model, modify the sequence of analysis in a procedure, and so on.

The full set of criteria at the upper three levels are summarized in Figure 11-3. These criteria should be considered examples rather than a

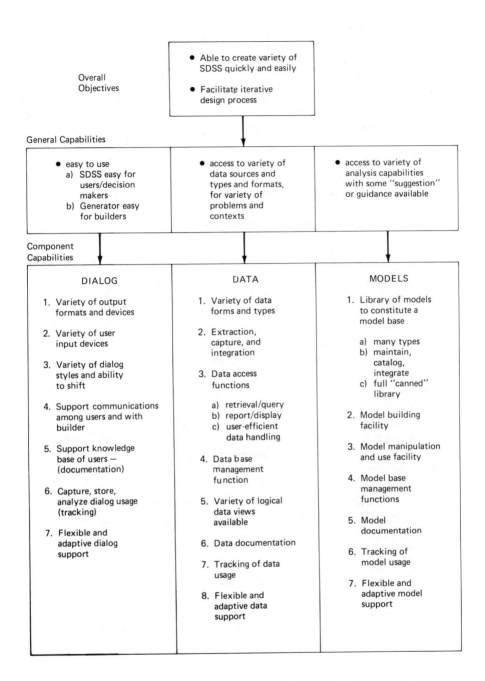

Overall Objectives
- Able to create variety of SDSS quickly and easily
- Facilitate iterative design process

General Capabilities

- easy to use
  - a) SDSS easy for users/decision makers
  - b) Generator easy for builders

- access to variety of data sources and types and formats, for variety of problems and contexts

- access to variety of analysis capabilities with some "suggestion" or guidance available

Component Capabilities

DIALOG

1. Variety of output formats and devices

2. Variety of user input devices

3. Variety of dialog styles and ability to shift

4. Support communications among users and with builder

5. Support knowledge base of users — (documentation)

6. Capture, store, analyze dialog usage (tracking)

7. Flexible and adaptive dialog support

DATA

1. Variety of data forms and types

2. Extraction, capture, and integration

3. Data access functions
   a) retrieval/query
   b) report/display
   c) user-efficient data handling

4. Data base management function

5. Variety of logical data views available

6. Data documentation

7. Tracking of data usage

8. Flexible and adaptive data support

MODELS

1. Library of models to constitute a model base
   a) many types
   b) maintain, catalog, integrate
   c) full "canned" library

2. Model building facility

3. Model manipulation and use facility

4. Model base management functions

5. Model documentation

6. Tracking of model usage

7. Flexible and adaptive model support

FIGURE 11-3   Criteria for a DSS Generator

comprehensive definition of all necessary criteria for a DSS Generator. They have, however, evolved out of an extensive examination of DSS literature and practice. Recently, a set of surrogate users and builders evaluated the criteria and rated three existing software systems against them [9]. The results of this comparison are tentative at best because the three products were not designed to be DSS Generators, and because the comparison was done by graduate students rather than by actual builders and users. However, the results of the comparison indicate that none of the three systems possessed enough capabilities to qualify as a good DSSG (defined as an average rating of 7 on a scale of 10). In addition, the comparison indicated that dialog capabilities were significantly weaker than modeling. These limited results are probably indicative of the current status of DSSG in general, not just of the three systems compared.

DSS Tools

In Chapter 10 we described DSS Tools as software that could be used to build DSSG or SDSS by facilitating the construction of the data bases or interpreters used. Existing tools can thus be classified according to whether they assist in data or interpreter creation. Tools, particularly those for interpreter construction, may be modules that can be used directly in SDSS or DSSG, as well as modules that can be used to construct SDSS or DSSG modules. Existing tools are usually oriented toward specific components (dialog, data base, modeling) of DSS. There are a variety of such tools, although dialog tools seem to be the scarcest and least used.

There are also a variety of general-purpose tools, such as general-purpose programming languages, which can be used to construct DSS. If DSS are viewed as a set of data-driven interpreters, then one would expect interpretive languages, such as APL, to be important for DSS Tools, and, indeed, this appears to be the case [6].

A third class of DSS Tools are the programming environments which are becoming available. In Chapter 10 we noted the close coupling between GMIS and the VM operating system. VM was clearly a tool that assisted in the development of GMIS [3]. Another example of a programming environment is a time-sharing system. The usefulness of time-sharing environments as DSS Tools is indicated by the widespread use of time-sharing systems for DSS.

With the introduction of personal computers and the interest in DSS for personal support, one must certainly include personal computers in general, and certain software packages for personal computers, as DSS Tools.

WHAT IS IN THE FUTURE?

At the risk of dating ourselves, and with a caveat on the difficulty of predicting developments in any field related to computer technology, we close with a discussion of trends in DSS.

Organizational Change

Almost every major development in information systems has brought organizational change, and DSS seems to be following the trend. Already DSS groups are being formed, MIS departments are being renamed, user departments are employing DSS specialists, and "knowledge of DSS" is listed in job descriptions. Data processing departments will develop increasing capabilities (via DSSG) to support DSS. DSS awareness and expectations among top management will increase.

It is likely that significant organizational changes will result from the *use* of DSS as well as from building them. Individual managers and decision makers who are able to use DSS effectively are likely to show better job performance than those who cannot use DSS. Group-support DSS seem to increase consensus decision making and simplify implementation of decisions. Although the demise of organizations that do not incorporate DSS is unlikely, there are indications that DSS provide a competitive advantage.

Technology Change

Many of the upcoming improvements in computing technology will affect DSS more than other applications. They will make other applications cheaper or faster, but they will make DSS *feasible*. Along with office automation (of clerical procedures) and design automation, decision support should be a major new business area for computing technology.

For the dialog components, better hardware (e.g., managerial workstations) appear to be a certainty. Teleconferencing (user–user dialog) will be an increasingly important improvement of DSS. Color graphics will be a requirement rather than an option. Voice and pointing will be the major input mechanisms.

On the data base front, there will be even more (external and internal) source data bases. These will be distributed (geographically) but easily accessible via computer networks. Extraction will be the key need, component, and problem. Relational, network, and rule data base systems will become efficient enough to compete with traditional record and hierarchic data bases. The data base will contain increasingly more of the dialog and modeling components (i.e., the data that control the interpreters for those components).

For the modeling component, DSS may revive a multitude of unused OR models, if they can be made interactive (see Chapter 9). The kinds of models used will expand to include heuristic and inference (artificial intelligence) models of decision making. Knowledge-based systems to support knowledge workers will be the trend.

Decision Change

Increased understanding of decision making, both descriptive (what is done) and normative (what should be done), will result from theoretical research and from the process of developing DSS. Decisions that now require DSS will become structured decisions which can be automated. Alternatives that cannot now be investigated, data that are not now accessible, will become available via DSS.

CONCLUSION

The success of DSS over the past decade, the increasing availability of organizational and technological support for DSS, and the possibilities for the future of DSS require an organizational response. We have tried to present information that can lead to an effective response. We have tried to show that an effective response consists of:

1. A framework for DSS in the organization
2. A process for developing DSS
3. Components out of which to build DSS

The specifics in each of these three areas will change over time and among organizations. However, experience indicates that framework, process, and components are required for effective DSS, and trends indicate that their importance will increase.

QUESTIONS AND PROBLEMS

REVIEW QUESTIONS

1. List and briefly describe the main elements of the framework for DSS proposed in this book.
2. What is the value and purpose of the framework?
3. What are the key elements in the process for DSS development as proposed in this book?
4. What are the technology components required to build a DSS?
5. What is the current status of Specific DSS, of DSS Generators, and of DSS Tools?

DISCUSSION QUESTIONS

1. What are alternative DSS frameworks to the one suggested in this book?
2. What are likely problems in the DSS development process?
3. What is the probable direction of DSS product development in the near future?
4. What do you think is likely to become of the "DSS movement?"

EXERCISES

1. From articles and advertisements in the periodical literature, software directories, and contacts with vendors, compile a list of DSS products available in the marketplace. Group them into the three categories we have used in the book (Specific DSS, DSS Generators, DSS Tools).

2. Examine the three levels of criteria for a DSS Generator outlined in this chapter. Refine, revise, and extend them until they form an adequate set of criteria for selecting or building a DSS Generator.

3. Choose three of the products you classified as a DSS Generator in Exercise 1. Using the criteria in this chapter, or your modified criteria from Exercise 2, rate their capabilities.

4. For each of the component capabilities in Exercise 3, identify the features that made you rate it as you did. Name some features that would increase your rating.

REFERENCES

1. ALTER, S. L. *Decision Support Systems: Current Practices and Continuing Challenges.* Addison-Wesley Publishing Company, Inc., Reading, Mass., 1980.

2. CARLSON, E. D. (ed.). Proceedings of a Conference on Decision Support Systems, *Data Base*, Vol. 8, No. 3, Winter, 1977.

3. DONOVAN, J. J., and H. D. JACOBY. "Virtual Machine Communication for the Implementation of Decision Support Systems," *IEEE Transactions on Software Engineering*, Vol. SE-3, No. 5, September 1977, pp. 333–342.

4. ERBE, R., et al. "Integrated Data Analysis and Management for the Problem Solving Environment," *Information Systems*, Vol. 5, 1980, pp. 273–285.

5. JOYCE, J. D., and N. N. OLIVER. "REGIS—A Relational Information System with Graphics and Statistics," *Proceedings of the National Computer Conference*, Vol. 45, 1976, pp. 839–844.

6. KEEN, P. G. W. "Interactive Computer Systems for Managers: A Modest Proposal," *Sloan Management Review*, Fall 1976, pp. 1–17.

7. KEEN, P. G. W., and M. S. Scott Morton. *Decision Support Systems: An Organizational Perspective.* Addison-Wesley Publishing Company, Inc., Reading, Mass., 1978.

8. ROCKART, J. F. "Chief Executives Define Their Own Data Needs," *Harvard Business Review*, Vol. 57, March–April 1979, pp. 81–93.

9. SPRAGUE, R. H., and R. R. PANKO. "Criteria for a DSS Generator," *Proceedings, 13th Annual Meeting of the American Institute for Decision Sciences,* Atlanta, Ga., 1981.

INDEX

A

B